THE DEATH OF CLASSICAL THEISM
AND THE SUBSEQUENT RISE OF
ATHEISM

The Death of Classical Theism and the Subsequent Rise of Atheism

SHANE HIMES

WIPF & STOCK · Eugene, Oregon

THE DEATH OF CLASSICAL THEISM AND THE SUBSEQUENT RISE OF ATHEISM

Copyright © 2025 Shane Himes. All rights reserved. Except for brief quotations in critical publications or reviews, no part of this book may be reproduced in any manner without prior written permission from the publisher. Write: Permissions, Wipf and Stock Publishers, 199 W. 8th Ave., Suite 3, Eugene, OR 97401.

Wipf & Stock
An Imprint of Wipf and Stock Publishers
199 W. 8th Ave., Suite 3
Eugene, OR 97401

www.wipfandstock.com

PAPERBACK ISBN: 979-8-3852-3831-6
HARDCOVER ISBN: 979-8-3852-3832-3
EBOOK ISBN: 979-8-3852-3833-0

03/14/25

To Kaitlin, for always believing in me.

And to Mom and Dad,
for teaching me the importance of hard work and perseverance.

Contents

Abbreviations | viii

Introduction | ix

CHAPTER 1   A New Theism | 1

CHAPTER 2   Classical Pushback Against Theistic Personalism | 15

CHAPTER 3   Theistic Personalism and the Existence of God | 29

CHAPTER 4   Classical Theism and the Existence of God | 67

CHAPTER 5   Theistic Personalism and the Problem of Evil | 85

CHAPTER 6   Classical Theism and the Problem of Evil | 110

CHAPTER 7   Analyzing the Differences Between the Paradigms | 123

CHAPTER 8   A Classical God in a Modern World | 145

CHAPTER 9   The Problem of Evil and Monism | 160

CHAPTER 10   Winning and Losing | 175

Closing Remarks | 182

Bibliography | 185

Index | 191

Abbreviations

CSR	Cognitive Science of Religion
DDS	Doctrine of Divine Simplicity
EAFE	Evidential Argument from Evil
ID	Intelligent Design theory
POE	Problem of Evil
PSR	Principle of Sufficient Reason
YEC	Young Earth Creationism

Introduction

"Science proves God does not exist," or so we've been told. It would be difficult to conjure up a more egregious category error, yet nonetheless this sentiment persists in the contemporary debates about God. Even theism's most ardent defenders are often sucked into this dialectic as they attempt to demonstrate the contrary: science actually proves that God does exist. One may assume it should become readily apparent that study of the physical universe cannot, in and of itself, demonstrate nor disprove the metaphysical. God is transcendent, or so Christian tradition has always claimed. Nevertheless, the confusion endures.

There is perhaps no greater example of this perplexity than Sam Harris's appearance in 2022 on the YouTube channel Triggernometry.[1] On that fateful day, Harris openly questioned why anyone believes in God anymore, considering we have telescopes that allow us to see billions of light-years away, and yet we still have not discovered heaven. If God or heaven existed, we would have noticed them by now, or so Harris argued. Again, I cannot think of a single event that could better exemplify the egregious level of discourse currently taking place concerning the question of God.

At the time, I was debating which direction to take my PhD research. I had a general idea, but this Sam Harris episode ultimately inspired me to research the intersection between Christian apologetics and metaphysics. Something seemed to be off in these modern debates, and I was eager to discover what exactly was going on. Around that same time, I had also noticed a dispute breakout among the neo-Reformed devotees surrounding the nature of God. To be honest, I had not and still do not hold Reformed theology in high regard, though growing up in the Southern Baptist Convention had made me interested in such developments, if nothing else than for nostalgic reasons. I still have friends and family in that world, after all. This debate was particularly interesting because it was taking place among

---

1. "Sam Harris." The relevant comment is around the 58-minute mark.

people whom I was accustomed to seeing agree upon most issues. And of all things, they were arguing about "biblicism" and the place Thomas Aquinas and his thought should have (or not have) in Reformed theology. Before I knew it, Owen Strachan was going on Ryan Mullins's podcast to talk about how the God of the Bible was not the God of the Greek philosophers![2] It was all happening so fast. Or maybe I was now paying closer attention to such debates than I had before. In any event, I found the proceedings to be rather humorous, as many of the neo-Reformed articulated a theology that was squarely at odds with their beloved creeds, by denying classical theism.

What is perhaps most germane to this particular book, however, is that many of these neo-Reformed who were adversaries of classical theism were also apt to apply the dreaded "heretic" label to open theists. They were fine with departing from classical depictions of God as defined by various creeds of old themselves, but for whatever reason the issue of exhaustive divine foreknowledge was too far of a departure from the classical (orthodox?) understanding of God. In thinking about this dynamic, and in reading much of the interactions between atheists and Christians in preparation for my dissertation, it became apparent to me that the classical theists and nonclassical theists were talking about two very different concepts. They almost seemed to have two completely distinct dictionaries, though they would at times use the same words.

My subsequent readings of the classical tradition confirmed this intuition. When a classical theist says that God exists, or even when they use the word "God," they mean something radically dissimilar to that of modern theism. And once that is understood, it becomes obvious when studying the question of God debates in contemporary culture. This book is an exploration into these issues; it is an examination of the intersection between metaphysics and apologetics.

The first foundational claim of this book is that a departure from classical theism has been detrimental for Christian apologetics. Such a shift in metaphysics has caused Christians to focus on the wrong discussions, and to consistently fight losing battles. What was once one of the reasons for Christianity's dominance in the intellectual sphere—that is, the fundamentality of God—has been abandoned in favor of modern models of God that would have him be simply one more being in the class of finite creatures. Hence the "you disbelieve in Zeus, I just disbelieve in one more god than you do" line of argumentation that is so common in these discussions today. My second contention is that only a return to classical theism will enable Christianity to once again become dominant in academia and the broader

2. Mullins, "Episode 109."

Western culture. Paradoxically, a consistently developed classical theism is the antidote to modern and postmodern atheism. Anything less will result in the continued ascendancy of atheism throughout our societies.

Chapters 1 and 2 provide brief historical context for the doctrine of God debates. They also establish a paradigm for viewing the current state of affairs as they will relate to arguments for God's existence. Chapters 3 and 4 survey arguments for God's existence from leading Christian scholars. I classify these scholars as adherents to various models of God for reasons that will become well defined below. Chapters 5 and 6 do something similar relating to Christian engagement with the problem of evil (POE). Chapter 7 offers further analysis of how underlying metaphysical assumptions impact a scholar's engagement with atheism. Chapters 8 through 10 make the case that a departure from classical theism has had overwhelmingly negative effects on how Christians defend God's existence. As well, they offer a positive explanation as to how reverting to a classical paradigm will enable Christians to contest atheism in ways that will prove to be far more successful than that of the last one hundred years.

This book will draw from a variety of fields. As such, the work of philosophers, theologians, and biblical scholars will be consulted. This is inevitable, given the nature of apologetics. I say this to say, though it is necessary to examine work from these distinct areas of inquiry, this is not principally a philosophical, theological, or exegetical work. This book is not a case for classical theism per se, though I do not deny my bias in favor of that position. No, this is primarily a study of Christian apologetics. Most precisely, this is a book explaining that metaphysical beliefs determine how Christian apologetics towards atheism are carried out. And this is the last point of clarification for now: this is a work about Christian apologetics as it pertains to atheism. Thus, one should not expect it to discuss apologetic work towards another religious faith, such as Islam or Judaism. The current book is a work chiefly relating to the question of God from a Christian perspective.

Chapter 1

A New Theism

I

MOST RECENTLY, THE PUBLICATION of *The Openness of God: A Biblical Challenge to the Traditional Understanding of God* in 1994 reinvigorated the debates about the nature of God within evangelical circles.[1] Roger Olson, in looking at the impact of the book's publication fifteen years after the fact, described the entire controversy surrounding open theism as "the most dismaying and disillusioning thing I have experienced in my fifty-some years of being an evangelical."[2] According to Olson and others, it would be difficult to overstate the fierceness of the debates that have come about surrounding the doctrine of God in recent decades. In 2001, at the Evangelical Theological Society, there were around thirty papers that were presented on the topic of open theism and the doctrine of God, most of which were critical of open theism.[3] Bruce Ware even presented a paper arguing that open theism was not evangelical and that it undermined inerrancy.[4] Several more notable meetings were had surrounding the topic in the following years at the Evangelical Theological Society. To this day, open theism remains a point of contention among evangelical scholars.

Yet open theism is only the beginning when it comes to debates surrounding the doctrine of God. Broadly speaking, two models of theism are of note within Christianity: classical theism and theistic personalism

---

1. Pinnock et al., *Openness of God*.
2. Olson, "Postconservative Evangelicalism," 186.
3. Rice, *Future*, 52.
4. Rice, *Future*, 52.

or mutualism.⁵ And within these two models, there are varied strands of thought, some of which significantly differ from one another. Classical theism is typically characterized by a commitment to the doctrines of divine immutability, impassibility, simplicity, and timelessness. James Dolezal adds divine aseity⁶ and the substantial unity of the persons of the Trinity to that list in his description of classical theism.⁷ Classical theists argue that God cannot derive any aspect of his being from creation, as that would make him contingent on creation to be who he is: "If the nature of God's love can be in any sense positively shaped by sin, suffering, and death, then sin, suffering, and death will always in some sense be features of who he is."⁸ Theistic personalism will typically deny one or more of the doctrine of divine simplicity (DDS), immutability, impassibility, and timelessness.⁹ Theistic personalists argue that God can, in some way, be affected by creation. Thomas Oord, a theistic personalist himself, says, "God experiences the flow of time too," and that God must be able to be affected by creation, because "a loving God is relational."¹⁰

Theistic personalism has enjoyed widespread growth in the last one hundred years in the forms of both open theism and neoclassical theism.¹¹

---

5. Dolezal, *All That Is in God*, 1.

6. Coming from the Latin *a se*, meaning "of himself" or "from himself." See Dolezal, *All That Is in God*, 11.

7. Dolezal, *All That Is in God*, 1.

8. Hart, "No Shadow of Turning," 53.

9. This term is often credited to Brian Davies, *Introduction*, 2–16. Essentially, theistic personalism is a departure from certain aspects of classical theism, such as divine simplicity and immutability, as defined by the classical tradition. Broadly speaking, theistic personalism is an umbrella term that would encompass any model of God which posits that God can be moved by creation in some way.

10. Oord, *Open and Relational Theology*, 29, 50.

11. Neoclassical theism is a term that describes one particular articulation of theistic personalism. Neoclassical theism is sometimes used to distinguish Christian theists who deny one or more aspects of classical theism from that of open theists. Yet this distinction is not always made in the same way. For example, Charles Hartshorne, a process theist, has been called a neoclassical theist. See Devenish, "Theodicy and Cosmodicy," 5–23. There was a time in the twentieth century when process theists had been termed neoclassical theists as a result of their departure from traditional conceptions of God. As time went on, however, more scholars began to openly reject both classical theism and process theism. For the purposes of this book, these scholars typically fall under the label of neoclassical theists or open theists. Ryan Mullins, a self-professed neoclassical theist, has said that for a model of God to be defined as neoclassical theism it must deny one of the four "classical" attributes of God, namely, timelessness, immutability, impassibility, or simplicity. Typically, the neoclassical theist will still affirm exhaustive divine foreknowledge, unlike open and process theists. Mullins, *God and Emotion*, 25–26.

With some notable exceptions that will be discussed in chapter 2, many modern theologians argue that God can suffer.[12] In 1986, Ronald Goetz acknowledged the growing number of theologians who advocated for divine passibility, and announced the "Rise of a New Orthodoxy."[13] This orthodoxy is in fact new, as it runs counter to what the Christian church traditionally taught before the twentieth century. And it is perhaps no surprise that theistic personalism began to see exponential growth in the twentieth century: the philosophical and cultural climates were ripe for an alternative vision of God, as Schubert Ogden argued.[14] On the philosophical front, many philosophers and theologians had begun to conclude that the classical God was too remote and indifferent to the world. The year 1929 saw the release of Alfred Whitehead's *Process and Reality*, which would prove to be the foundation for a completely new metaphysic and vision of God's relationship to the world.[15] On the cultural front, the world saw two catastrophic, global conflicts come and go in the first half of the twentieth century, and many found it difficult to believe in God, especially after World War II. For some, if they were to believe in God, he must be deeply sympathetic to suffering and even suffer along with humans.[16]

It became rather commonplace in the twentieth century for theologians to attack the idea of an impassible God and the patristic notion of *apatheia* as being the result of Greek philosophical presuppositions as opposed to apostolic teaching.[17] William Temple, for example, wrote in 1924, "We have to recognize that Aristotle's 'apathetic God' was enthroned in men's minds, and no idol has been so hard to destroy."[18] Equally as intense was the rhetoric of Evan Pollard in 1955: "Among the many Greek philosophical ideas imported into Christian theology, and into Alexandrine Jewish theology before it, is the idea of the *impassible* God (*apathes theos*), and this idea furnishes us with a particularly striking illustration of the damage done by the assumption of alien philosophical presuppositions when they

---

12. Gavrilyuk, *Suffering*, 1.

13. Gavrilyuk, *Suffering*, 1. Here he is making reference to Ronald Goetz's article "Suffering God," 385.

14. Ogden, "Reality of God," 1–20.

15. Whitehead, *Process and Reality*.

16. Feinberg, *No One Like Him*, 158.

17. As David Bentley Hart has noted, *apatheia* was not only an attribute of God, but a virtue to be pursued in patristic thought. Far from being detachment, as in the Stoic sense of the term, *apatheia* came to be seen as a condition of radical attachment. See Hart, "No Shadow of Turning," 55.

18. Temple, *Christus Veritas*, 269.

are applied to Christian theology."[19] Though less harsh in his rhetoric, John Sanders argued, in the landmark publication *The Openness of God*, that the early church fathers had synthesized Greek philosophy and biblical teaching due to their intellectual environment being dominated by Greek culture.[20] He goes on to say that this led to a theological tradition within Christianity that had caused even modern theologians to presuppose Greek philosophical ideas in their reading of the Bible.[21]

Most recently, theistic personalism has enjoyed a place even outside of the mainstream theological world. N. T. Wright wrote an article for *Time* magazine in 2020 addressing the coronavirus pandemic entitled "Christianity Offers No Answers About the Coronavirus. It's Not Supposed To."[22] In this article, Wright is presenting how he thinks Christians should make sense of the coronavirus pandemic in light of the suffering it caused around the world. Particularly relevant is what he says about God: "The mystery of the biblical story is that God also laments. Some Christians like to think of God as above all that, knowing everything, in charge of everything, calm and unaffected by the troubles in his world. That's not the picture we get in the Bible."[23] This is hardly academic writing, and it is not intended to be. It does, however, demonstrate that theistic personalism impacts how Wright does apologetics to a secular audience. He even seems to border on open theism, as he says some Christians like to act like God "knows everything," but that is not the case in the Bible. Wright has never claimed to be an open theist, but here he does articulate a theology that is firmly in the theistic personalist camp.

Though he is perhaps the most famous, Wright is not the only prominent Christian to advocate for theistic personalism in our modern times while not claiming to be an open theist. It has become quite common even for Calvinists,[24] many of whom are especially critical of open theism themselves, to depart from classical theism and embrace theistic personalism, as James Dolezal has pointed out.[25] D. A. Carson, a Calvinist, has said that even a superficial reading of Scripture reveals that God is in a kind of relationship

---

19. Pollard, "Impassibility of God," 356.
20. Sanders, "Historical Considerations," 59–60.
21. Sanders, "Historical Considerations," 60.
22. Wright, "Christianity Offers No Answers."
23. Wright, "Christianity Offers No Answers."
24. I mention Calvinists specifically here due to the fact that they have been most opposed to open theism since its resurgence in evangelicalism. For much of evangelical Calvinism, open theism represents a stark departure from the Bible's portrayal of the sovereignty of God as it concerns the history and future of human affairs.
25. Dolezal, *All That Is in God*, 23.

with creation that entails he can be affected by creation.[26] For Carson, God loves the world in such a way that results in him feeling pain.[27] Bruce Ware is another Calvinist who has been abundantly critical of open theism, and what he deems to be a departure from orthodox Christianity. Still, he has himself articulated an understanding of immutability that departs from that of classical theism: "Importantly, God is changeable in relationship with his creation, particularly with human and angelic moral creatures he has made to live in relationship with him."[28] For Ware, God does not change in essence or in nature, but he does change in relationship to creation. This causes him to have much in common with open and process theists, as Dolezal asserts: "It is crucial to understand that Ware's dispute here is an in-house disagreement with his fellow theistic mutualists. He shares common ground with process and open theists on the question of being and becoming in God."[29]

II

As the principles of the Enlightenment began to impact the church in the seventeenth and eighteenth centuries, at least in Europe, many began to question the compatibility of the Bible's teachings about God and what the philosophers were saying about God. If God is immutable and impassible, then he cannot act in history; and if he acts in history, then he cannot be the God of classical thought, or so went the argument.[30] And as a result of the observation that the Bible, when read in a grammatical-historical way, portrays God as having a kind of give-and-take relationship with the world, people began to doubt the classical depiction of God, leading to the aforementioned twentieth-century hostility to classical theism. When faced with the choice of the Bible or philosophy, theologians began to choose the Bible. This is a typical dichotomy offered in modern theology: "Everyone familiar with modern biblical studies knows that the philosophical doctrines of divine immutability and impassibility are not taught in the Bible."[31]

For many theistic personalists, a "literal" reading of the Bible is to be at the forefront of a Christian's epistemology. Of course, even that statement can be rather vague, as most Christians claim to have biblical support for their ideas about God. To be more specific, theistic personalists will typically

---

26. Carson, *Difficult Doctrine*, 55.
27. Carson, *Difficult Doctrine*, 59.
28. Ware, *God's Lesser Glory*, 73.
29. Dolezal, *All That Is in God*, 27.
30. Carter, *Contemplating God*, 26.
31. Hallman, *Descent of God*, 20.

give credence to grammatical-historical exegesis and to univocal readings of biblical descriptions of God.[32] For instance, John Frame, a scholar who is not an open theist but would nonetheless fall into the theistic personalist camp according to the definitions that have been given, asserts, "We need not be afraid of saying that some of our language about God is univocal or literal. God has given us language that literally applies to him."[33] For Frame, if the Bible's depiction of God is to be trusted, then at least some of the language needs to be understood as univocal. This intuition concerning the Bible's descriptions of God should come as no surprise, considering that modern biblical studies have trended in this direction since the Enlightenment. "The Chicago Statement on Biblical Inerrancy," for example, asserts, "We affirm that the text of Scripture is to be interpreted by grammatico-historical exegesis, taking account of its forms and devices, and that Scripture is to interpret Scripture."[34] Not all theistic personalists adhere to "The Chicago Statement on Biblical Inerrancy," but it does nonetheless demonstrate the emphasis on grammatical-historical exegesis found in modern biblical studies. For many theistic personalists, the Bible, when read in a literal way for the purpose of demonstrating truths about the nature of God, articulates God as a kind of relational person. This is especially true of their readings of the Old Testament and was a significant factor in the rise of open theism. Richard Rice utilized this epistemology in his biblical case for open theism in the aforementioned *The Openness of God*. Rice argued that Old Testament portrayals of God as entering into relationships, executing judgments, and experiencing emotion demonstrate that "God experiences the temporal world in a temporal way."[35] One may also think of Greg Boyd in this regard. Boyd tells the story of his coming across 2 Kgs 20 during his Bible reading one night. Within that chapter, Hezekiah is told by God that he is going to die from his sickness and that he needs to prepare the kingdom for this. Hezekiah persuades God, through prayer, to change his mind and heal him.

---

32. If something is "univocal" it can only have one meaning. If something is univocal, it is unambiguous. For example, if one says, "The sky is blue," that is a univocal statement. There is no ambiguity, metaphor, or analogy of any kind to be found in the statement. But, if one says, "The sun rises in the East and sets in the West," that is not a univocal statement, as the sun does not literally move in that way; we just experience it as though it does. So, if someone describes God univocally, they are not using metaphor; they mean to say something is true by virtue of the definitions of the words that are used.

33. Frame, *Doctrine of God*, 209.

34. International Council on Biblical Inerrancy, "Chicago Statement," Article XVIII, p. 6.

35. Rice, "Biblical Support," 22.

Hezekiah is successful in persuading God to heal him, and Boyd cites this story as part of the reason he came to embrace open theism.[36]

T. E. Fretheim cites Jer 4:14, 13:27, and Hos 8:5 as demonstrating that God has a history and moves through space and time with us, as he too can cry out, "How long?"[37] Clark Pinnock's views on the Bible further demonstrate the point. Pinnock too regards God as temporal and cites Jer 18:11 and 29:11 as examples that demonstrate that God makes plans and carries them out, in a temporal fashion.[38] More to the point, Pinnock questions the historically Christian assumption that God is not a corporeal being: "In tradition, God is thought to function primarily as a disembodied spirit but this is scarcely a biblical idea."[39] Pinnock goes on to cite various Old Testament texts, including Exod 24:10–11 and 33:11, to exhibit that the biblical authors viewed God as eating and drinking with the elders of Israel, in addition to talking with Moses face to face.[40] The debate about God being corporeal or not isn't the primary focus here; rather, these arguments establish that Pinnock often considers the Old Testament descriptions of God to be univocal descriptions, and thus unambiguously true at some level. They are not mere anthropomorphisms or the result of human authors attempting to make sense of the unknowable essence of God.

These examples that have been cited come predominantly from open theists, but most theistic personalists are at least somewhat in agreement with these views on the Bible, though not all would say God is temporal. The aforementioned D. A. Carson said Scripture obviously teaches that God can be affected by his creation and feel pain.[41] J. I. Packer argued similarly: "God's feelings are not beyond his control, as ours often are. . . . Scriptures expressing the reality of God's emotions (joy, sorrow, anger, delight, love, hate, etc.) abound, however, and it is a great mistake to forget that God feels—though in a way of necessity that transcends a finite being's experience of emotion."[42] Rob Lister wrote an entire book defending a notion of impassibility, but Lister's definition of impassibility is similar to Packer's, as it modifies that of classical theism. For Lister, God cannot undergo any involuntary or unexpected change,[43] but this does not exclude any voluntary

---

36. Boyd, *God of the Possible*, 7–9.
37. Fretheim, *Suffering of God*, 44.
38. Pinnock, *Most Moved Mover*, 32.
39. Pinnock, *Most Moved Mover*, 33.
40. Pinnock, *Most Moved Mover*, 34.
41. Carson, *Difficult Doctrine*, 55, 59.
42. Packer, *Concise Theology*, 29.
43. Lister, *God Is Impassible*, 33.

change in God, similar to that proposed by Packer and Karl Barth.[44] Lister would go on to establish this, as he cites Bruce Ware in support of the assertion that there can be temporal transition in God.[45] Though these scholars may differ from open theists on several points, they agree that the Bible teaches that God experiences change in some way, whether that be relationally or emotionally.

Then there is process theism, another variation of theistic personalism.[46] Process theists are similar to open theists in that they believe the future is not exhaustively foreknown by God. They are like other theistic personalists as well, considering their belief that God undergoes change of some kind throughout his existence. Yet many process thinkers do not hold to inerrancy as it is defined by "The Chicago Statement on Biblical Inerrancy." John Cobb said as much: "Clearly a process thinker cannot affirm Bible inerrancy or literal historical accuracy."[47] Nonetheless, Cobb and other process Christians do value the Bible and assert that the Bible comes closer to depicting a God who changes than a God who is *actus purus*. After citing several texts to demonstrate that the Bible teaches that God changes and is affected by creation, including Gen 6:6, Amos 7, and Ps 106:43–45, Cobb argues, "Resistance on the part of fundamentalists to the idea that God changes comes from the tradition, not the Bible. The tradition was deeply affected by the Greek view that it is better not to be moved or influenced by anything external to oneself."[48] Here, Cobb is using "fundamentalists" interchangeably with those who deny process or openness theology. Though his views on the Bible may differ from many more traditional theistic personalists, the basic arguments about the Bible are the same: the Bible reveals a God who, in some way, changes.

---

44. Barth, *Church Dogmatics*, 2.1:370, cited in Dolezal, *All That Is in God*, 30.

45. Lister, *God Is Impassible*, 179.

46. Process theism, or process theology is a view of God that utilizes the process metaphysics of Alfred Whitehead. See Feinberg, *No One Like Him*, 149. Like any other model of God, process theism is not monolithic. There are a variety of intellectual traditions that would broadly fall under what is considered process thought. Typically, process theists reject Aristotelian, substance-based metaphysics and argue that process, not substance, is what is most fundamental to reality, including that of God. Process theists differ from open theists and other theistic personalists in a number of ways that will be explored later. They do, however, agree with the most basic tenet of theistic personalism: God undergoes some sort of change throughout his existence.

47. Cobb, *Process Perspective*, 66.

48. Cobb, *Process Perspective*, 78–79.

III

The DDS essentially entails that God is not a composite being; God is not made up of parts, whether they be metaphysical or physical. He is identical with his existence and essence, and all of his attributes are identical to who he is.[49] It is divine simplicity which has long been considered the ontological condition by which God can be truly absolute and transcendent.[50] Historically, Christianity as well as most of the other great theistic traditions have held to some form of divine simplicity, as it was the logical conclusion of the claim that God was not contingent on anything else for his existence.[51] The logical necessity of the classical view of God, says Hart, is not difficult to grasp; rather, the difficulty of the classical view comes in the application of the doctrine to the rest of the faith.[52] How exactly these respective religious traditions expound upon the DDS has drastically differed. Even among Christians, there has never quite been universal agreement on what exactly this doctrine entails for the faith. Nonetheless, it was agreed throughout most of Christian intellectual history that it was a logical necessity, even through the Reformation period and the respective creeds that were produced by Protestant leaders.[53] In modern times, however, the DDS is no longer assumed to be logically necessary, or even logically coherent.

There are many modern Christian theologians and philosophers who loudly oppose the DDS. As it became normal to criticize classical theism, attacking the cornerstone of classical theism became almost the expectation, especially among the more analytically inclined. Louis Berkhof noticed this trend among theologians: "In recent works on theology the simplicity of God is seldom mentioned. Many theologians positively deny it, either because it is regarded purely as a metaphysical abstraction, or because, in their estimation, it conflicts with the doctrine of the trinity."[54] The primary reasons for rejecting the DDS, as Berkhof states, are usually related to the doctrine of the Trinity or concerns about abstract/concrete distinction in God. Christopher Hughes, for example, feels that the doctrine results in God being pure existence, but nothing more: "Since there will not be anything in God but existence, and the existence of a thing does not make it anything but existent, God will be nothing more than existent. But it seems

---

49. Dolezal, *God Without Parts*, 2.
50. Dolezal, *God Without Parts*, 2.
51. See Hart, *Experience of God*, 99–142.
52. Hart, *Experience of God*, 99.
53. Dolezal, *God Without Parts*, 8.
54. Berkhof, *Systematic Theology*, 62.

clear that nothing subsistent could be just existent: a merely existent substance is too thin to be possible."[55] For Hughes, God cannot be God in the way that Christians have described him if the DDS is true. God as being is incompatible with God as personal or loving.

Thomas Morris has also recently been critical of the DDS. The concrete-abstraction distinction in God is one of his primary concerns. He claims that if God is identical to his properties, then this would entail that either the properties are concrete or God is purely abstract: "Either view seems startlingly counterintuitive, in violation of any concrete-abstract distinction."[56] Further, if all of God's attributes are identical to who God is, then it is impossible to make a distinction between what is contingently true of God, and what is necessarily true of God.[57] This line of reasoning from Morris is similar to that of Alvin Plantinga, who is arguably the most prominent critic of the DDS.

Plantinga acknowledges that the DDS has often been a historic Christian doctrine and has even been expressed by creeds as recent as the Belgic Confession.[58] Nevertheless, he finds the doctrine to be both philosophically and theologically incoherent. The reason for this discontentment with the DDS somewhat lies in Plantinga's skepticism of God's aseity, at least in the strong traditional sense of the term. He observes that if God were ontologically distinct from his properties, then he would be dependent on them in some way: "If God were distinct from such properties as wisdom, goodness, and power but nonetheless *had* these properties, then he would be dependent on them."[59] Plantinga elaborates further: "This connection between his existence and theirs, furthermore, is necessary; it is not due to his will and it is not within his power to abrogate it. That it holds is not up to him or within his control."[60] In short, if God possesses properties that are distinct from himself, then he is dependent on those properties to be who he is; God could not be eternally wise if wisdom did not exist eternally.[61] So, Plantinga accurately represents the concerns of those who hold to the traditional notion of divine simplicity: for God to exist *a se*, then he must be a simple being, not composed of metaphysical parts such as wisdom or power. Plantinga acknowledges this: "If he had properties and a nature distinct from

---

55. Hughes, *On a Complex Theory*, 21.
56. Morris, *Our Idea of God*, 117.
57. Morris, *Our Idea of God*, 117.
58. Plantinga, *Does God*, 27.
59. Plantinga, *Does God*, 32.
60. Plantinga, *Does God*, 32–33.
61. Plantinga, *Does God*, 33.

him, then he would exist and display the character he does because of a relation in which he stands to something other than himself. And this doesn't fit with his existence *a se*."[62] It is at this point that Plantinga seems to deny that God exists *a se*, in that classical sense. For Plantinga, there are realities that exist which do not depend upon God for their existence. Natural numbers, for example, were not created by God, and they do not rely upon God for their existence; God could not do away with them if he so chose.[63] Because of this metaphysic, Plantinga boldly proclaims, "there are innumerable beings whose existence and character are independent of God."[64]

Plantinga has other objections to the DDS, but these will suffice for now. There have been many evangelicals who have followed Plantinga in their criticism of the DDS. Ryan Mullins has consistently critiqued classical theism during the last decade. As an evangelical, one of his main concerns is that the doctrine is not found in the Bible, but is rather derived from Greek philosophy; statements like "God is love" or "God is spirit," for Mullins, undermine fundamental tenets of the doctrine.[65] In addition to biblical problems, Mullins argues that God cannot be truly free if he is a simple being in so far as God cannot be pure act and be free to create or not to create; Mullins sees this as a logical incoherence, for a variety of reasons.[66] John Feinberg says that the lack of biblical data, in addition to a plethora of philosophical problems that have been raised by contemporary philosophers, has led him to deny that divine simplicity is one of the divine attributes.[67] Citing the Lutheran theologian Francis Pieper, Ronald Nash says humans could never have any real knowledge of an absolutely simple essence.[68] And, citing Frederick Copleston, Nash asks, "If human beings necessarily conceive God differently than he really is, is their conception of God not therefore false?"[69] Considering these objections among others, Nash concludes that there is no good reason for Christians to affirm the doctrine.[70] Overall, it would

---

62. Plantinga, *Does God*, 33.

63. Plantinga, *Does God*, 35.

64. Plantinga, *Does God*, 35. This is something that several prominent theistic personalists have articulated. John Feinberg is one such additional example. See Feinberg, *No One Like Him*, 336–37. It should be noted that Plantinga goes on to say that this is potentially a good argument for nominalism, but ultimately rejects it.

65. Mullins, "Simply Impossible," 182, 190.

66. Mullins, "Simply Impossible," 195. This is sometimes referred to in the relevant literature as "modal collapse."

67. Feinberg, *No One Like Him*, 335.

68. Nash, *Concept of God*, 85.

69. Nash, *Concept of God*, 86.

70. Nash, *Concept of God*, 95.

seem the contemporary theological and philosophical worlds have mostly rejected the DDS, especially in the evangelical sphere.

IV

God and his relationship to time is yet another vigorously debated topic relating to the rise of theistic personalism. For much of Christian history, it was somewhat of a presupposition that God was "outside" of time, or for the more precise philosophical minds, that he transcended time. The belief in divine timelessness, however, has come under heavy scrutiny in recent decades, and this scrutiny has undoubtedly contributed to the rise in theistic personalism.[71]

These Christian philosophers who question divine timelessness will typically hold to an A-theory of time as opposed to a B-theory.[72] Though this sentiment is not universal, many philosophers think that if an A-theory of time is true, then God must be temporal, and if a B-theory of time is true, then God must be atemporal. If there is a prioritized now, then God must be present in that now, as it is the only moment that exists. And if this is true, then God must experience sequence, and thus change in some way, as he stands in relation to a changing reality.[73] If B-theory is true, and God sustains the entirety of existence, then he must be present in the past, present, and future; thus, divine timelessness is a perfect explanation for how this can be so.

Needless to say, numerous issues can be related to the issue of God and time, such as the doctrine of creation, eschatology, free will, and even God's knowledge of the future. These are just some of the subjects that come to mind. For open and process theists, God cannot know the future with

---

71. Ganssle, "Introduction," 12–13. According to Ganssle, this was articulated from at least Augustine to the High Middle Ages by most Christian thinkers. Now, however, many Christian philosophers disagree.

72. A-theory is also known as presentism. Most open and process theists will hold to this theory of time, while some neoclassical theists will hold to a modified form of this theory. Essentially, A-theory proclaims that the present moment of experience exists in a real way, whereas the past only exists in memories, and the future exists only as possibilities. B-theory, on the other hand, says that there is no prioritized "now" as it were, as the present moment exists by virtue of the psychological state of the mind. The past, present, and future all simultaneously exist, and there is no prioritized "now" moment. Additionally, B-theory can also be referred to as eternalism, so as to describe God as existing in eternity as opposed to existing "in time." The A-theory and B-theory labels are typically credited to the Cambridge philosopher J. M. E. McTagart. See Ganssle, "Introduction," 14–15.

73. Ganssle, "Introduction," 15.

certainty, as the future can only be known as a set of possibilities.[74] In addition, it would be impossible for God or man to have genuine free will if God has exhaustive foreknowledge of the future, according to openness models of God. For example, Richard Swinburne argues, "It seems to me that it is logically impossible to know (without the possibility of mistake) what someone will freely do tomorrow. If I am really free to choose tomorrow whether I will go to London or stay home, then if anyone today has some belief about what I will do tomorrow . . . I have it in my power tomorrow to make that belief false (e.g., by staying home)."[75] He goes on to clarify that "not even God" can know today with certainty what someone will do tomorrow.[76]

Biblical considerations are also a catalyst for openness theologians and philosophers concerning the relationship between God and time. Nicholas Wolterstorff, for example, in answering questions concerning God's timelessness or lack thereof, argues that Scripture gives a narrative of God that entails God be temporal: "The God of Scripture is One of whom a narrative can be told; we know that not because Scripture tells us that but because it offers such a narrative. I hold that an implication of this is that God is in time. If something has a history, then perforce that being is in time."[77] For Wolterstorff, the Bible's narrative entails that God is temporal, though the Bible does not systematically explain this. Since God appears to experience sequence in Scripture and to interact with creation in a seemingly give-and-take relationship, this logically necessitates that God is a temporal being who experiences sequence, just as humanity does. Here, though, one simply enters the debate about univocity in the biblical text, something that has already been briefly discussed in this chapter.

Questioning divine timelessness is not limited to the openness faction of the theistic personalists. Neoclassical theists, such as William Lane Craig, have offered their own critiques of divine timelessness as it has been traditionally articulated.[78] Craig in particular argues that there is good biblical evidence both for divine timelessness and divine temporality, citing texts

---

74. Boyd, *Satan*, 91.

75. Swinburne, *Is There a God?*, 9.

76. Swinburne, *Is There a God?*, 9.

77. Wolterstorff, "Unqualified Divine Temporality," 188.

78. Ryan Mullins is another neoclassical theist who has questioned an unqualified divine timelessness. Mullins follows Craig and others by arguing that a timeless God cannot know tensed facts; therefore, a timeless God cannot be omniscient. Among other arguments, Mullins also claims that timelessness is incompatible with *creatio ex nihilo*, as that would entail succession in the life of God. See Mullins, *End*, 101–26.

from both the Old and New Testaments.[79] Ultimately, Craig agrees with James Barr, in that the debate about God's relationship to time needs to be settled on philosophical grounds, given the ambiguity of the biblical data.[80] And on those philosophical grounds, Craig again finds merit in arguments for both God's atemporality and God's temporality. One of Craig's main issues with endorsing an A-theory of time seems to be that the past cannot be infinite.[81] At the same time, he sees God's timelessness as being problematic, in part because a timeless God could have no knowledge of tensed facts.[82] Thus, Craig concludes that God was timeless without creation, but that he is temporal subsequent to creation.[83] There is no before, after, or temporal passage in God's life before creation, so it is ultimately incoherent to say that God was temporal without creation; however, he enters time at the moment of creation, as he now has a real relation to a temporal, contingent universe.[84]

There are other views within the theistic personalist camp concerning God and time, but these brief comments will suffice for now, as they have simply served the purpose of demonstrating yet another area in which theistic personalists have leveled critiques of classical theism. This discussion will be especially pertinent in chapter 7 when analyzing how various models of God confront the POE.

---

79. Craig, "Timelessness and Omnitemporality," 129–32.

80. Craig, "Timelessness and Omnitemporality," 132. See also Barr, *Biblical Words for Time*, 149.

81. See Craig, "Timelessness and Omnitemporality," 153–56.

82. Craig, "Timelessness and Omnitemporality," 146–51. Here, tensed facts just refer to facts that are known in relation to the past, present, or future. A timeless God, it is argued, can only know tenseless facts that are universally true, but not true relative to a particular moment. Essentially, God cannot know tensed facts because all facts are eternally and simultaneously present to him if he is timeless.

83. Craig, "Timelessness and Omnitemporality," 159.

84. Craig, "Timelessness and Omnitemporality," 159–60.

Chapter 2

Classical Pushback Against Theistic Personalism

I

The appearance of theistic personalism has brought about numerous different kinds of reactions; in many ways, several of these reactions have come from theistic personalists who hold to "milder" versions of that alternative way of thinking about God. As has been pointed out, it isn't uncommon for a mild theistic personalist such as Bruce Ware to critique and even to declare open theists to be anathema. Yet that is not the only kind of criticism that theistic personalism has spawned. Though they are in the minority as far as the contemporary environment is concerned, there have been those who have critiqued the whole of theistic personalism, from the milder articulations to the "hard" forms, as Dolezal puts it.[1] These scholars are classical theists in the traditional sense of the term, in that they hold to divine immutability, impassibility, simplicity, and timelessness. Generally speaking, the classical theists see theistic personalism as a departure from historic Christianity, particularly that of historic Christian metaphysics. What all classical theists seem to have in common is a rejection of the idea that God can in any way experience change, whether that be due to something external to him, or due to something intrinsic to him, such as his will. It is at this point that the differences in the two theistic paradigms can be most succinctly summarized.

---

1. Dolezal, *All That Is in God*, 3.

II

One common theme among the numerous articulations of classical pushback in the contemporary setting has been the claim that theistic personalism is a departure from historic Christian doctrine in so far as classical theism, it is asserted, is the model of God that the patristic, medieval, and early Protestant theologians held to.[2] Theistic personalism is a newer approach, and thus not the apostolic doctrine of God, despite their claims to biblical authority. In appealing to historic orthodoxy, classical theists have been forced to deal with the assertion that the patristic view of God was a result of synthesizing apostolic teaching with Greek philosophy. Modern scholarship, some classical theists admit, has come to generally draw a distinction between the active, involved, passionate God of the Bible with the God of Greek philosophy who is a cold abstraction, indifferent to and uninvolved with the world.[3] In short, the verdict in contemporary thinking has been that "on the whole," patristic theology was a departure from the biblical vision of God.[4] Gavrilyuk describes this as the "theory of theology's fall into Hellenistic philosophy." On this matter, classical theists have had much to say.

David Bentley Hart, for example, has pointed out that certain tenets of classical theism, such as that of impassibility and immutability, were the grounds by which ancient heretics argued for their positions. The Arians and Eunomians "quite plausibly" argued that real generation within the Godhead would entail a change in God, and thus could not be true.[5] They maintained similarly regarding the incarnation of the Logos; the Nestorians contended that there must be two persons in Christ, precisely because the Logos of God, being fully divine, was beyond any suffering and change.[6] And yet, Hart argues, the proto-orthodox were every bit as eager to maintain that God was immutable and impassible. These ideas were not alien to the Christian faith; they were necessary to maintain its coherence. If they had been external threats to orthodoxy, then the Fathers would have happily condemned such ideas along with the early heretical groups, so the argument goes.

And, for Hart, certain "Greek" concepts were not used by the early Christian theologians in the exact same way as they were in different Greek

---

2. For example, see Dolezal, *All That Is in God*, 1.
3. Gavrilyuk, *Suffering*, 20.
4. Gavrilyuk, *Suffering*, 20.
5. Hart, "No Shadow of Turning," 47.
6. Hart, "No Shadow of Turning," 47–48.

schools of thought. For instance, though the language of *apatheia* was borrowed primarily from the Stoics, Christians used it quite differently. For the Stoics, *apatheia* was essentially indistinguishable from indifference and could be described as an inactivity of the will.[7] But for Christians the concept was understood somewhat differently. Clement of Alexandria is one such example that Hart cites. Clement said that *apatheia* was the cultivation of understanding and charity; it was something that could be ascribed to God, as he had not simply mastered his emotions, but rather was goodness as such.[8] It was even something that Christians could strive for, because to live beyond emotion was to become entirely love; *apatheia*, then, was not detachment as in Stoicism, but was rather a condition for "radical attachment."[9]

Another problem that some classical theists see with the theory of theology's fall into Hellenistic philosophy is that "Greek philosophy" was not monolithic, thus it is difficult to know exactly what it would mean to say that early Christianity was overtaken by it. Though early Christianity may have shared some language and even some ideas with several schools of Greek thought, they also differed with many of them on a variety of points, which isn't surprising since they all differed from one another themselves. There was no unified account of divine emotion and divine-human relationship that the early Christians would have been able to borrow from.[10] Christianity was a distinct religion that shared some of the same language as other religions within the Greek culture. And the Bible was for the early Christians a pillar of epistemology; that is, they argued that what they knew about God and the world came from the Bible in so far as it witnessed to the revelation of God in Christ. The early Christians viewed God as loving and involved with the world; this was simply expressed in anthropomorphic terms, especially in the Hebrew Bible,[11] and these texts needed to be interpreted properly.

III

Biblical interpretation can be argued to have been the main catalyst behind the rise of theistic personalism. There are other factors, as have been discussed, but the biblical data seem to be the driving force behind it all,

---

7. Hart, "No Shadow of Turning," 55.
8. Hart, "No Shadow of Turning," 55.
9. Hart, "No Shadow of Turning," 55.
10. Gavrilyuk, *Suffering*, 21–22.
11. Gavrilyuk, *Suffering*, 46.

especially for lay adherents to the idea. However, the classical theists have been pushing back against this trend in recent years, arguing that theistic personalist readings of the Bible do not do justice to the historical ideas that biblical interpretation was originally based on. In addition, they argue that, although the theistic personalists desire to allow the text of Scripture to determine their metaphysical presuppositions, that is impossible, as everyone approaches Scripture with metaphysical systems that they presuppose. Craig Carter asserts as much: "The truth is that *everyone* approaches the task of exegesis with a conceptual framework derived from some source greater than one's own personal knowledge. The call for 'presuppositionless exegesis' is actually a disguised call for acceptance of the majority's presuppositions."[12] It is no coincidence, Carter says, that theistic personalism has risen to prominence during the rise of metaphysical naturalism: "During the past two centuries or so, the philosophical naturalism of modernity has been presupposed, sometimes consciously and sometimes unconsciously, by scholars in the historical-critical stream of biblical interpretation."[13] Metaphysical naturalism would presuppose that there cannot have been greater forces at work in the formation of the biblical text beyond the original intentions of the human author; thus the accusation that historical-critical scholarship is dependent on naturalism as its metaphysical framework. For Carter, it is not optional whether one is going to employ a metaphysical framework through which to understand the biblical text; rather, everyone does, and the theistic personalists are typically assuming naturalism when reading the Bible. Instead of inquiring as to what the "historical reading" of a given text

---

12. Carter, *Contemplating God*, 42.

13. Carter, *Contemplating God*, 40. I must note here, there is a bit of ambiguity when it comes to the historical-critical method and its relationship with theistic personalism. It is true that the historical-critical method is largely responsible for the emphasis on grammatical-historical exegesis that is present in modern evangelicalism. As has been pointed out, "The Chicago Statement on Biblical Inerrancy" goes as far as to say that inerrancy somewhat depends on a grammatical-historical exegesis of the text. At the same time, many evangelicals, because of their devotion to the doctrine of inerrancy, are not fond of historical-critical scholarship, as it typically concludes that there are contradictions and historical errors in the Bible. So, while process theists and others on the more "liberal" side of the theistic personalist camp are comfortable with these conclusions and thus fully embrace historical-critical scholarship, it is much more complicated when it comes to more "mainstream" theistic personalists and their relationship with the historical-critical method. In his discussion on the issue, Carter seems to indirectly contend that the liberal Protestants, as well as pantheists like Spinoza, are more consistent when it comes to the issue of historical-critical scholarship. See Carter's discussion in *Contemplating God*, 39–44.

is, Christians should understand that the biblical text is revelation from God and must be understood within a Trinitarian classical theism framework.[14]

Brian Orr makes a similar argument to Carter's, though he is specifically responding to Thomas Oord, who admits to the use of a metaphysical framework when interpreting the Bible. Orr, like Carter, contends that everyone relies on at least some metaphysical assumptions when approaching the text of Scripture.[15] Oord implements a type of process metaphysic when interpreting the Bible. And, in citing David Griffin, Orr says that process philosophy is a type of naturalistic theism, which entails metaphysical naturalism when interpreting the Bible.[16] Instead of presupposing a kind of naturalism when reading the text, Orr argues that Christians should employ a "theological interpretation" that understands the triune God as the key to properly interpreting the Bible.[17] Essentially, it would seem, a Christian should presuppose a classical view of God when reading the text of the Bible, so as to properly interpret that text via "theological interpretation."

Something like this approach to the Bible was the historic Christian understanding of Scripture, many classical theists will argue. John O'Keefe and R. R. Reno are two scholars who have done this. The specialization of modern biblical scholarship, as well as its insistence upon historical-critical disciplines, has blinded modern readers "to the basic project of patristic exegesis."[18] As opposed to the key to understanding the biblical text being strictly historical context, the patristic interpreters understood it to be a knowledge of Jesus Christ: "Unified by the conviction that Jesus Christ is the cornerstone of divine truth, the exegesis of the fathers was research into the Christ-centered unity of Scripture."[19] Any proper interpretation of the Bible must be consistent with and in some way point to Jesus. This is because Scripture was not viewed as a collection of isolated data points that told us different things about God; rather, Scripture was seen as something that needed to be theologically interpreted to produce a "total reading" of sorts, a reading that would synthesize Scripture to be one coherent message about Jesus Christ.[20] This is impossible if one is restricted to grammatical-historical exegesis of the Bible, or so the early Christian theologians would have maintained. Thus, patristic exegesis of the Bible largely consisted

---

14. Carter, *Contemplating God*, 85–86.
15. Orr, *Classical Response*, 110.
16. Orr, *Classical Response*, 112. See also Griffin, "Process Philosophy," 135.
17. Orr, *Classical Response*, 113.
18. O'Keefe and Reno, *Sanctified Vision*, 24.
19. O'Keefe and Reno, *Sanctified Vision*, 25.
20. O'Keefe and Reno, *Sanctified Vision*, 46.

of typological and allegorical exegesis.[21] This way of reading the Bible necessitates that the "literal" meaning of the text is not the only or even the primary meaning that Christians should take away from it. Allegorical interpretation, for example, was often employed by early Christian theologians; this way of reading the Bible is in some way a rejection of, or at least an indifference to, the original meaning of a given passage: "Allegories are basically interpretations that claim that the plain or obvious sense of a given text is not the true meaning, or at least not the full meaning."[22] The basic contention of O'Keefe and Reno is this: modern scholarship attempts to ascertain the meaning of a given text by reconstructing the material history of that text, whereas Christian interpretation of the Bible was historically a principally theological interpretation, with God's revelation in Christ as the guide. The original or literal meaning of a text was not the primary concern of historic Christian handlings of the Bible.

Many classical theists are aware of how counterintuitive this view of the Bible may sound to modern readers. However, several church fathers are frequently cited in support of such a view. Origen, for example, said, "And therefore the exact reader must, in obedience to the Saviour's injunction to 'search the Scriptures,' carefully ascertain in how far the literal meaning is true, and in how far impossible; and so far as he can, trace out, by means of similar statements, the meaning everywhere scattered through Scripture of that which cannot be understood in a literal signification."[23] Origen says that some Scripture cannot be understood in a literal way. In addition to Origen, Gregory of Nyssa is perhaps a less controversial early father who used allegory to interpret the biblical text: "One ought not in every instance to remain with the letter (since the obvious sense of the words often does us harm when it comes to the virtuous life), but one ought to shift to an understanding that concerns the immaterial and intelligible."[24] Here, again, a warning is issued to Christians about always taking the "letter" of the text as being the primary meaning that Christians should consider to be true and godly. Gregory goes as far as to assert that perhaps the killing of the firstborn Egyptians during the exodus did not actually happen: "Do not be surprised at all if both things—the death of the firstborn and the pouring out of the blood—did not happen to the Israelites and on that account reject the contemplation which we have proposed concerning the destruction of evil

---

21. See, O'Keefe and Reno, *Sanctified Vision*, 69–113.
22. O'Keefe and Reno, *Sanctified Vision*, 89.
23. Origen, *First Principles* 4.1; text in Roberts et al., *Ante-Nicene Fathers*, 4:369.
24. Gregory of Nyssa, *Homilies on the Song of Songs*, 5.

as if it were a fabrication without any truth."[25] It is clear from these citations among others that there is a fundamental disagreement among classical theists and theistic personalists as to how the Bible should be approached, how it should interact with theology, and what place, if any, metaphysical assumptions should have when exegeting the biblical text.

IV

It could be argued that divine immutability and impassibility are the ideas in the most need of revision, from the theistic personalist perspective. A God who does not change in any way, and undergoes no change in emotion was simply too cold and abstract for many in the twentieth century, as has been documented in the earlier sections of this book. Yet as tempting as it may be to reject this view of God, classical theists insist that divine immutability and impassibility are indispensable doctrines for Christians, and have been for most of Christian history. And the consequences for denying impassibility and immutability, the classical theists assert, are metaphysically and even morally reprehensible.

Beginning with the metaphysical, God's aseity is dependent on immutability and impassibility. Aseity entails that God is exclusively from himself, eternally being, which means he is eternal being in and of itself, as opposed to eternally becoming.[26] And if God is to be *a se*, then he must be purely actual in the Thomistic sense of the term. God is not a being for the classical theist, but rather being as such. This entails that God has no potential, instead he must be *actus purus*.[27] Aquinas classically argued that the foundational cause of being must be pure act, as anything that is in motion must have been put into motion by something external to itself; something in motion has gone from potentiality to actuality with the aid of something beyond itself. Thus, God, the foundational cause of the universe and the source of all being must himself be purely actual and possess no potential, otherwise he would have needed something external to himself to reach his potential.[28] But God is purely actual, possessing no potential, and can thus exist in and of himself. Or so the argument goes. And obviously, if God is purely actual, as Aquinas asserted, then this would logically entail immutability. God has no potential for change because he has no potential: "If there is nothing in God's existence or life that is given to Him by the creature, and

25. Gregory of Nyssa, *Life of Moses* 2.100 (Malherbe and Ferguson, 76).
26. Bavinck, *Reformed Dogmatics*, 2:152.
27. Dolezal, *All That Is in God*, 15.
28. Dolezal, *All That Is in God*, 15, citing Aquinas, *Summa Theologiae* Ia.2.3.

if He is not the cause of Himself because He is pure being, then it follows that He cannot undergo change."[29]

In discussing modern commentary on being and becoming in God, Hart recognizes that the appetite for a passible God in the twentieth century was largely moral in nature. In the wake of a century of atrocities ranging from death camps to nuclear detonation, people longed for a "companion in pain."[30] The various forms of Hegelian Trinitarian thought, which would in one way or another describe God as achieving his identity through temporal suffering, whether that be anguish at the thought of his creation suffering, or most precisely in his suffering in Christ on the cross, result in God becoming dependent on suffering to be who he is: "It is an almost agonizing irony that, in our attempts to revise trinitarian doctrine in such a way as to make God comprehensible in the 'light' of Auschwitz, invariably we end describing a God who—it turns out—is actually simply the metaphysical ground for Auschwitz."[31] For Hart, God becomes the metaphysical ground for Auschwitz if he is not impassible, because if God is not impassible and thus in some way achieves his identity in the suffering of Auschwitz, then Auschwitz is eternally a part of who God is; it is in some way necessary for God to be who he is. Hart has argued this point at length elsewhere. God cannot be the source of all being, and yet become something other than what he was; in that, God cannot become the God he is through suffering: "And if God's love were in any way shaped by sin, suffering, and death, then sin, suffering, and death would always be in some sense features of who he is."[32]

Hart sees this embrace of passibility and mutability within God to be particularly egregious in the work of Jurgen Moltmann. For Moltmann, the cross is the moment when God's identity is achieved, as that is when he constitutes himself as suffering love.[33] Furthermore, it is at the cross that God "becomes the God who identifies himself with the men and women to the point of death and beyond."[34] Commenting on this view of being and becoming in God, Hart claims this conception of God is incoherent:

---

29. Dolezal, *All That Is in God*, 17.

30. Hart, *Beauty*, 160.

31. Hart, *Beauty*, 160.

32. Hart, *Doors*, 78. He goes on: "This not only means that evil would be a distinct reality over against God, and God's love something inherently deficient and reactive; it also means that evil would be somehow a part of God, and that goodness would require evil to be good." Hart, *Doors*, 78.

33. Hart, "No Shadow of Turning," 50, citing Moltmann, *Crucified God*, 244–45. See also Moltmann, *Trinity*, 82–83.

34. Moltmann, *Trinity*, 119.

"In place of the metaphysically necessary 'God' of the system, this sort of language gives us only anthropomorphic myth, a God whose will enjoys a certain indeterminate priority over his essence, in whom possibility exceeds actuality, who is therefore composite, ontic, voluntaristic . . . and obviously nonexistent."[35] Hart goes on to argue what he has in the other works cited in the above paragraphs, that the fathers of the church would have reasoned that any God who can be so determined by finite events will inevitably have his identity established via commerce with evil, and thus God would need evil to exist in order to be who he is.[36] In closing on this point, Hart argues that, if God achieves his identity through finite causes, then he may be a supreme being but he cannot be the source of all being, as he would then belong to the system of finite causes.[37] And, more to the moral point of the matter, for God to be perfect love, he must be immutable and impassible: "Only a transcendent and passionless God can be the fullness of love dwelling within our very being."[38]

Though Hart and other classical theists seem to be in the minority from the perspective of modern scholarship, they are every bit as eager to defend the immutability and impassibility of God as the theistic personalists are to argue against those ideas. It would seem that the classical theists are concerned with the collapsing of the economic and immanent Trinity, of God as an eternal reality and God as revealed in temporal history, as Hart explicitly argues.[39] The very coherence of the notion of God as being is in doubt once immutability and impassibility are abandoned or redefined according to modern sensibilities.

V

Though the DDS has fallen out of favor in recent times, it was once deemed an indispensable part of serious philosophical reflection of many of the world's great theistic traditions, including Christianity. The concept has "rarely been in serious dispute" according to Hart.[40] Despite this, the doctrine has been the subject of highly sophisticated attacks in the contemporary era, the sophistication of which has even been acknowledged by some of the doctrine's most ardent supporters. For example, Dolezal has

---

35. Hart, "No Shadow of Turning," 53.
36. Hart, "No Shadow of Turning," 53.
37. Hart, "No Shadow of Turning," 54.
38. Hart, "No Shadow of Turning," 54.
39. Hart, *Beauty*, 165.
40. Hart, *Experience of God*, 134.

described the modern attacks on the DDS as quite formidable: "Many of the current objections to the DDS, especially those issued by the analytic philosophers, are highly nuanced and demand close attention. They represent a formidable opposition to any who would appeal to simplicity as indispensable to an orthodox doctrine of God in the twenty-first century."[41] While acknowledging the challenge that various strands of modern philosophy pose for the DDS, classical theists insist that the logical consequences of denying the doctrine are difficult to overstate. Contra scholars like Alvin Plantinga, Dolezal claims that a denial of divine simplicity is unacceptable due to the fact that God would become dependent on ideal forms or universals in order to be who he is.[42] For Dolezal, God loses his absoluteness if simplicity is denied; God cannot be the ultimate explanation of existence if he is just a being among other beings. God becomes dependent on realities outside of himself to be who he is.[43]

Hart somewhat reiterates the concerns of Dolezal, saying that for God to be the unconditioned source of all that is, he must not be ontologically dependent himself, and a denial of simplicity makes him such.[44] For Hart, simplicity is necessary for humans to say that God is the end of reason's journey toward the truth of all things.[45] Without simplicity, God becomes merely a being among other beings. He may be the most powerful being in the universe, but he is a being that cannot explain the very notion of existence itself. God becomes ontologically dependent if simplicity is denied, according to Hart. For theistic personalists like Plantinga, whom Hart specifically mentions here, at most it can be said that God is a possible being, but not a necessary being. And that, for Hart, is not satisfactory: "To put the matter very simply, the great traditions would not speak of God merely as some being who might exist in some possible world, if only because that seems to make God's reality conditional on some set of prior logical possibilities, which would appear to exclude real logical necessity from his nature at the outset, as well as to contradict the essential claim that he and he alone is the source of all reality."[46] In short, Hart and Dolezal, as well as much of the classical tradition, see the DDS not as a metaphysically problematic doctrine, but rather as an indispensable idea that makes the very conception of God coherent. For the classical tradition, to understand God as the ground

---

41. Dolezal, *God Without Parts*, 11.
42. Dolezal, *God Without Parts*, 30.
43. Dolezal, *God Without Parts*, 30.
44. Hart, *Experience of God*, 134.
45. Hart, *Experience of God*, 128.
46. Hart, *Experience of God*, 121–22.

of all being is to understand him not as a being among beings, but as being as such, and the ontological ground for existence.

VI

Like other aspects of classical theism, divine timelessness has fallen out of favor with contemporary philosophers and theologians. Classical theists such as Paul Helm have admitted as much.[47] For Helm in particular, divine timelessness has been the mainstream view of Christian theologians until recently, as demonstrated by Augustine, Anselm, Aquinas, and others throughout Christian history.[48] A God who is temporal is too anthropomorphic for many classical theists; a denial of divine timelessness essentially erodes the difference between the Creator and the created. It is people who favor a more "humanlike conception of divinity" who are more inclined to embrace a temporal God as opposed to an atemporal one.[49]

Generally speaking, one of the main motivations that classical theists have for embracing divine timelessness is a belief in God's aseity. If God has a past, present, and future, then he is made up of parts, and thus to deny divine timelessness is to deny the DDS which, for the classical theist, means a denial of God's aseity. Helm, however, is quick to argue that, although the argument for divine timelessness can be made via the DDS, it need not rest on that doctrine.[50] In addition to those arguments concerning divine simplicity, Helm states that there is a basic theistic intuition that says God possesses the whole of his life together and that any notion of temporal passage within God is incompatible with other Christian doctrines, such as divine sovereignty and divine perfection.[51]

Concerning biblical studies, classical theists again argue that the Bible supports the notion of divine timelessness, just not explicitly. As Craig has

---

47. Helm, "Divine Timeless Eternity," 28.

48. Helm, "Divine Timeless Eternity," 28.

49. Helm, "Divine Timeless Eternity," 29.

50. Helm, "Divine Timeless Eternity," 30. As Helm suggests, it has been argued that divine simplicity entails divine timelessness. Dolezal lists God's eternity as one implication of divine simplicity. Dolezal, *God Without Parts*, 67. Ryan Mullins is quick to point this out in his work as well: divine timelessness, in some ways, rests on concepts such as divine simplicity and pure actuality; by disproving those doctrines, one can disprove divine timelessness. For Mullins, this is done by arguing that divine simplicity and pure actuality lead to modal collapse: "If God is free to create or not create, then He has unactualized potential. So, God must create in order to be purely actual." Mullins, *End*, 140.

51. Helm, "Divine Timeless Eternity," 30–31.

asserted, the language about God's eternity in Scripture could be interpreted as entailing timelessness or divine temporality.[52] Helm says the same, as the issues of temporalism and eternalism did not seem to be on the minds of the biblical authors when they used such language.[53] Nevertheless, the data of Scripture are compatible with eternalism, and Christians should not shy away from embracing it, according to Helm. There are certain beliefs that Christians hold that are not systematically laid out in the Bible, Helm claims. The Trinity is one such example, where dogmatic formulations were made after the creation of the New Testament, with which the data therein is compatible but not explicit.[54] Ultimately, Helm concludes that divine timelessness is essential in order for Christians to maintain the Creator and creature distinction, as well as to sustain the act of creation as a unique metaphysical action. Moreover, divine timelessness allows for the Christian to consistently believe that the entire temporal order has been brought about by God, as opposed to creation being the result of an act by a being who is itself subject to time.[55]

VII

It is somewhat startling to see the contrast between the classical tradition and more modern theology. The differences span a wide array of categories, from biblical interpretation, to philosophy, to historical considerations, and even to moral debate. It is not surprising to see that it is predominantly Protestant theological traditions that have been more comfortable moving away from more traditional understandings of theology, given that the ideas of *sola scriptura* and *semper reformanda* have resulted in a continual examination of past beliefs. Perhaps this is why one of the most compelling aspects of this discussion is the debate among the theistic personalists concerning the orthodoxy of the competing views within that camp. The process theists, open theists, and neoclassical theists will all claim that Scripture supports their views and that they have a duty to continue reforming the

---

52. Craig, "Timelessness and Omnitemporality," 129–32.
53. Helm, "Divine Timeless Eternity," 31–32.
54. Helm, "Divine Timeless Eternity," 32–33.

55. Helm, "Divine Timeless Eternity," 33. These are just some of the reasons why eternalism is necessary for the classical theist. In addition, Helm argues that this view of God's relationship to time is necessary if one is to maintain that the Son is coeternal with the Father since, if God is temporal, then the begetting of the Son is a temporal action which necessitates succession and thus the Son would not be coeternal with the Father. Some theistic personalists have recognized this and have consequently denied that the Son is eternally begotten of the Father. See Mullins, *End*, 143–44.

tradition if the tradition gets Scripture wrong. Others will declare that certain views, such as open theism, are departures from orthodoxy, while they themselves depart from what had been considered an orthodox doctrine of God for a majority of Christian history. Bruce Ware was one such example that was highlighted, as he is not a classical theist, yet he accuses open theists of departing from orthodoxy. He wrote a book about that![56] This is not necessarily to comment on the validity of such arguments; this is simply an acknowledgment of the ambiguity within the discussion, as some theistic personalists like Ware would see themselves as closer to "classical" depictions of God than they would open or process depictions.

Nevertheless, these opening chapters sufficiently demonstrate commonality among theistic personalists, as well as commonality among various classical theists. There are discrepancies that will be explored in the next few chapters; it is still important, however, to acknowledge the fundamental agreements within the broader camps for the purposes of this book. Even though the factions have differences, it is easy to see how the essential tenets of the competing paradigms demonstrate themselves when those theologians are involved in apologetic engagement with atheists or other skeptics. For example, N. T. Wright and Thomas Oord would not be considered by most to be "similar" theologians, as Wright does not even claim to be an open theist, while Oord is considered by most to be a process theist. There are differences among them, but when they are writing on the POE and suffering, they have the same starting point: God suffers with us. Wright says this, as was pointed out, in the *Time* article[57] while Oord makes essentially the same point in his book: "Second, a relational God suffers with the harmed and hurting. Rather than aloof and unconcerned, God feels our pain immediately after we do."[58] This will be explored further in chapter 5 when examining how they respond to the POE, but it is obvious even now that the apologetic that many theistic personalists use when dealing with the POE relies on a central premise of theistic personalism: God suffers with us in his nature.

Classical theists have many differences as well, but most of them will share in some basic assumptions about God. One easy example is that classical theists do not think God, in any way, finds his identity in suffering. This is one of Hart's key arguments against the passibility of God: if God suffers, then he would need suffering in order to achieve his identity.[59] Dolezal says

---

56. Ware, *God's Lesser Glory*.
57. Wright, "Christianity Offers No Answers."
58. Oord, *Open and Relational Theology*, 86.
59. Hart, *Doors*, 98.

something similar when discussing God's aseity and eternal identity, as he claims God could not exist in and of himself if he suffered in his nature: "This means that even his relation to the world as its Creator and Sustainer does not produce any new actuality in Him."[60] Of course, Dolezal is a Calvinist while Hart is an Eastern Orthodox theologian, so the two have many differences in a variety of areas. However, they both share the fundamental belief that God cannot suffer in his nature or achieve any kind of potential.

In the next few chapters, I will turn my attention to arguments for God's existence from both classical theists and theistic personalists. This will help to exhibit the practical differences that shifts in metaphysics have made. In addition, these chapters will serve as the basis for later analysis of the competing positions, and ultimately why theistic personalists are, on the whole, unable to effectively demonstrate God's existence in the same way that classical theists can.

---

60. Dolezal, *All That Is in God*, 15.

Chapter 3

Theistic Personalism and the Existence of God

I

I HAVE CHOSEN THE FOLLOWING scholars due to their ability to speak for the competing models of God. Many are well known both for their theological prowess as well as their willingness to engage with skeptics of the Christian faith. Most importantly, they have written on at least some of the issues discussed in the previous two chapters, so their work is especially relevant to our current purposes.

Neoclassical theism is likely the most popular variety of theistic personalism. As was alluded to in the previous two chapters, many find themselves in this camp both intentionally and unintentionally. Though openness theology is advancing in relevance, many still are not comfortable with the claim that God does not know with certainty some future events. At the same time, many of those same Christians are not classical theists: thus their adherence to neoclassical theism, often perceived as a much milder departure from the classical tradition.

Let me begin by summarizing some of the work that William Lane Craig has done in response to atheism. There is perhaps no more prominent neoclassical theist alive today. The book I am primarily drawing from in this section is one of his most accessible books, and therefore represents work that is read by all classes of people—Christian and atheist alike. Craig has written extensively on the existence of God and has debated atheists in a variety of venues and formats. First, some of the common arguments used to defend God's existence will be briefly explained, using Craig's summary of the arguments. After that foundation has been laid, additional work from neoclassical theists on the relevant material will be examined.

One atheist that Craig has engaged with is Richard Dawkins. Craig asserts that Dawkins has taken the arguments for God's existence seriously, and for that, he gives him credit.[1] He does not, however, believe that Dawkins has adequately addressed the arguments. He begins this particular engagement with Dawkins by introducing what is commonly referred to as the cosmological argument. In Craig's variation of this argument, he essentially says that everything has an explanation for its existence, therefore if the universe exists, then it must have an explanation for its existence and that explanation must be God. Craig calls this an argument from contingency.[2] Of course, there are two pressing issues here: one of the pertinent concerns would relate to why it is that God must be the explanation for the universe's existence, while the other is the initial question of the contingency of existence. About the latter, Craig argues along fairly traditional lines: there are two types of things in existence, things that exist necessarily and things that exist contingently. Craig claims that even the atheist acknowledges this, but that they only want to acknowledge it so far as it pertains to the contingency of the existence of everything within the universe; but the universe itself, the very notion of existence itself, does not have an explanation because the only explanation apart from the universe would be nothingness, which obviously cannot produce anything else.[3] Thus, the universe must exist inexplicably. The atheist here is begging the question as he is assuming that atheism is true, in that he is presupposing that there could be nothing beyond the universe (or multiverse) except nothingness.[4]

This leads to the question of why the explanation for the universe's existence must be God. If the universe does indeed have a cause for its existence, and the universe is all of time and space, energy, and matter, then the cause of its existence must be something that transcends time and space; the cause must be an immaterial, nonphysical being. Craig describes this being as an unembodied mind, which Christians call God.[5] If these arguments are successful, and it is more plausible than not that they are, Craig says, then

---

1. Craig, *How Do We Know*, 6. Here Craig is alluding specifically to Dawkins's book *The God Delusion*.
2. Craig, *How Do We Know*, 11.
3. Craig, *How Do We Know*, 12–14.
4. Craig, *How Do We Know*, 14.
5. Craig, *How Do We Know*, 15.

God exists. And the explanation for God's existence lies within the necessity of his nature, seeing as that he is uncaused, timeless, and spaceless.[6]

After what principally amounts to a rehashing of his cosmological argument, Craig turns his attention to the moral argument for God.[7] The argument concerns objective morality: if God exists, then objective moral value exists; if God does not exist, objective moral values do not exist either. Objective moral values do exist, though, and therefore God exists.[8] The reality of objective morality is believed by almost everyone, even in a pluralistic world, Craig argues. This can be seen in the inconsistency with which Dawkins employs moral outrage. Initially, Craig notes that Dawkins says there is no good and no evil; there is only pointless indifference, as humans are merely machines for propagating DNA.[9] Yet Dawkins is quick to morally denounce things like the abuse of homosexuals or the religious indoctrination of children, going as far as to give a revised ten commandments for guiding moral behavior.[10] Objective morality can only exist if there is a transcendent source of moral value, something atheists like Dawkins seem to acknowledge when they admit there is no objective good or evil in the world. Nevertheless, Craig contends that even those who espouse such a position live their lives as though there are objective moral values, and Dawkins is just one such example. Their inconsistency, Craig asserts, helps to demonstrate the reality of objective morality.

The penultimate argument that Craig addresses is the teleological argument, which he describes as an argument from design. Craig begins with a succinct summary of the argument. The universe is obviously fine tuned, in that there are laws of nature that seem to govern the physical universe. As well, there is a balance of matter and antimatter in the universe: "Now all

---

6. Craig, *How Do We Know*, 16.

7. Craig, *How Do We Know*, 21–29. Here Craig advances what is known as the kalam cosmological argument. The principal difference is the focus on a temporal beginning of the universe. If the universe has a temporal beginning, then it must have a cause, as everything that begins to exist has a cause. One interesting note here is that Christian philosophers have disagreed over whether or not it is necessary for the universe to have a temporal beginning, and if that affects the question of God's existence. David Bentley Hart, for example, says that the question of a temporal beginning to the universe is irrelevant to the question of God's existence. He invokes Aquinas, who argued that creation out of nothingness should not be thought of as a temporal event, since it is not a transition from one state of reality to another, seeing as that nothingness is not a kind of substance that is capable of undergoing change. For more, see Hart, *Experience of God*, 106–7.

8. Craig, *How Do We Know*, 34.

9. Craig, *How Do We Know*, 35, citing Dawkins, *River Out of Eden*, 133.

10. Craig, *How Do We Know*, 36.

of these constants and quantities fall into an extraordinarily narrow range of life-permitting values. Were these constants or quantities to be altered by less than a hair's breadth, the life-permitting balance would be destroyed, and no living organisms of any kind could exist."[11] Given the fine-tuning of the universe, there must be a reason why the universe is fine tuned. These reasons could be physical necessity, chance, or design. Craig says that the reasons cannot be physical necessity or chance, therefore the fine-tuning of the universe must be due to design.[12] Concerning why the fine-tuning of the universe is most likely not due to a kind of physical necessity, Craig points out that the constants in the universe, like the force of gravity, are not determined by the laws of nature; rather, the laws of nature are consistent with a wide array of values for existing constants.[13] In *The God Delusion*, Dawkins ultimately agrees that physical necessity likely does not explain the universe's fine-tuning.[14] Thus, Dawkins asserts that chance must be the reason for the universe's fine-tuning. Craig argues this is highly improbable; he describes the likelihood that our universe's fine-tuning could be the result of chance as "incomprehensibly great."[15]

To substantiate the chance hypothesis, Dawkins and others have appealed to an infinite multiverse in which there would inevitably lie a fine-tuned universe like ours, even if the chance is monumentally improbable.[16] Among a plethora of other arguments, Craig asserts Ockham's razor, in that postulating an infinite number of universes simply to explain the

11. Craig, *How Do We Know*, 44.
12. Craig, *How Do We Know*, 45.
13. Craig, *How Do We Know*, 43, 46. Craig explains that this essentially means the constants in the universe are independent of the laws of nature: "The first alternative, physical necessity, is extraordinarily implausible because, as we've seen, the constants and quantities are independent of the laws of nature. So, for example, the most promising candidate for a TOE [Theory of Everything] to date, super-string theory or M-Theory, fails to predict uniquely our universe. String theory allows a 'cosmic landscape' of around 10^{500} different possible universes governed by the present laws of nature, so it does nothing to render the observed values of the constants and quantities physically necessary."
14. Dawkins, *God Delusion*, 144, cited in Craig, *How Do We Know*, 46.
15. Craig, *How Do We Know*, 46.
16. Dawkins, *God Delusion*, 145, cited in Craig, *How Do We Know*, 47. Dawkins does stress that, though the number of universes may seem extravagant, if each of those universes is simple in its fundamental laws, then what he is postulating is not too highly improbable. Craig says this response is confused in a number of ways, given that each universe in this alleged multiverse is not simple, but is rather characterized by a multiplicity of independent constants and quantities. Essentially, Craig argues that, although the universes in this multiverse are all characterized by the same laws, where they differ is in the values of the constants and quantities. Craig, *How Do We Know*, 47–48.

fine-tuning of our universe via chance is "beyond necessity."[17] Craig ultimately argues that there is no independent evidence of the existence of such an infinite multiverse, much less evidence for one where all of the universes are ordered and infinite.[18] By contrast, there is independent evidence for God's existence, considering other arguments that Craig has been articulating; given that reality, he concludes that theism is the much more plausible explanation for the fine-tuning of the universe.[19]

Lastly, Craig articulates the ontological argument, which he attributes to being original to Anselm. The version of the argument he focuses on is Plantinga's, as he says Plantinga is one of the most respected and well-known proponents of the argument in modern times.[20] Plantinga's argument is centered on possible-world semantics. Craig summarizes the argument: it is possible that a maximally great being exists, so a maximally great being exists in some possible world.[21] If a maximally great being exists in some possible world, then it exists in all possible worlds and thus exists in the actual world. As to some of the more intricate details of the argument, such as why a maximally great being must exist in the actual world if it exists in any possible world, we will return shortly when examining Plantinga's own work.[22] As for Craig, the primary point of emphasis is Plantinga's initial premise: it is possible for a maximally great being to exist. The idea of a maximally great being, says Craig, is an intuitively coherent idea, so it seems plausible for such a being to exist; for the ontological argument to fail, the idea of a maximally great being must be demonstrated to be incoherent.[23] This is because if the concept is not rendered logically incoherent, then the maximally great being could exist in some possible world. The atheist must

17. Craig, *How Do We Know*, 48.
18. Craig, *How Do We Know*, 55.
19. Craig, *How Do We Know*, 56–57.
20. Craig, *How Do We Know*, 67.

21. A maximally great being is described by Plantinga as possessing properties such as omniscience, omnipotence, and moral perfection. Craig, *How Do We Know*, 69.

22. The ontological argument that is original to Anselm states that if a maximally great being, a being to which it is impossible to conceive of a greater being, exists in the understanding alone, then reality is a contradiction. This is because to exist in reality is greater than to exist in the understanding alone; therefore if this maximally great being does not exist in reality, then it is possible to conceive of a being who is greater than the being to which it is impossible to conceive a greater being. Hart articulates Anselm's argument rather precisely: "An existent reality surpasses a merely suppositious one in greatness; thus we must affirm that God exists or accept the contradiction that we can conceive of something yet greater than that reality than which none greater can be conceived." Hart, *Experience of God*, 117.

23. Craig, *How Do We Know*, 70.

maintain that God's existence is logically impossible in order to disprove the ontological argument. Dawkins attempts to do just this, but fails, according to Craig.[24]

II

This brings us to Plantinga's work concerning the ontological argument. Plantinga's approach to the argument can be described as an exercise in modal logic, seeking to ascertain God's metaphysical necessity from his metaphysical and logical possibility. Initially in his discussion of Anselm's ontological argument, he commends Anselm's argument as being clever, seeing as that it is "profoundly difficult" to articulate what is wrong with the argument.[25] Whether it be Kant's objection or Gaunilo's objection, Plantinga says the usual criticisms of Anselm's argument leave much to be desired.[26] Yet he does find some flaws in the original argument. Anselm's premise that existence in reality is greater than existence in the understanding alone is what Plantinga focuses on. A nonexistent being would be greater than it is if it existed, says Anselm. But Plantinga questions if that really makes much sense at all to say. Thus, he restates Anselm's argument in possible-world language: "(14) For any being x and world W, if x does not exist in W, then there is a world W' such that the greatness of x in W' exceeds the greatness of x in W."[27] This supposedly leads to the premise that if God does not exist in the actual world, then there is a possible world in which God's greatness exceeds the greatness of God in the actual world, which then leads to Anselm's conclusion that this is ultimately a contradiction. Plantinga finds a problem with this though, as he says that in order for this argument to be successful, then it must be presupposed that God is a being in existence. Since (16) asserts something about God and the actual world that (14) says is true of every being and world, then (16) can only follow from (14) if it is presupposed that God is a being that exists.[28] This, Plantinga says, begs the question in the first place: "And doesn't this statement—that God is a being—imply that there is or exists a being than which it's not possible that

---

24. Craig, *How Do We Know*, 71.

25. Plantinga, *God, Freedom, and Evil*, 86.

26. Plantinga, *God, Freedom, and Evil*, 98. For his discussion of Kant's objection and Gaunilo's objection, see pp. 89–98.

27. Plantinga, *God, Freedom, and Evil*, 100.

28. Premise (16) in this argument: "If God does not exist in the actual world, then there is a world W' such that the greatness of God in W' exceeds the greatness of God in the actual world." Plantinga, *God, Freedom, and Evil*, 100.

there be a greater? But if so, the argument flagrantly begs the question; for then we can accept the inference from (14) to (16) only if we already know that the conclusion is true."[29]

If the range of quantifiers in (14) is expanded to merely possible beings as opposed to actual beings, then it must be said that God is a possible being for the argument to remain coherent. Even here, Plantinga says that the notion of possible beings can be somewhat problematic.[30] Because of some of these issues with possible beings, such as the question of what properties possible beings may or may not possess, and even the question of their status as existent or not existent, he says we must speak of properties that may or may not be instantiated in various possible worlds by these possible beings. As opposed to speaking of a being than which it is not possible that there be a greater, Plantinga speaks of the property of "having a degree of greatness such that it's not possible that there exists a being having more" that may be instantiated in a given possible world by a possible being.[31] This makes the argument more plausible, but it still fails, according to Plantinga. The key question now is in which world does this possible being instantiate the property of being greater than any being in any possible world?[32] And this is the fatal flaw in Anselm's original ontological argument, according to Plantinga: if God is a possible being who must instantiate the property of being the greatest possible being in some world, that does not entail that God must instantiate that property in the actual world.[33]

This allows us to arrive at Plantinga's version of the argument, which he calls a modal version of the ontological argument. His modified version of the argument is as follows:

29. Plantinga, *God, Freedom, and Evil*, 101.
30. Plantinga, *God, Freedom, and Evil*, 102.
31. Plantinga, *God, Freedom, and Evil*, 102.
32. Plantinga, *God, Freedom, and Evil*, 102–3.

33. Plantinga, *God, Freedom, and Evil*, 103. This is the essence of the argument. For further discussion from Plantinga on the matter, see pp. 101–4. At most, Anselm's original argument, Plantinga concludes, makes God a possible being, but not necessarily an existent being. This is because premise (21) of Anselm's original argument, which said that "It's not possible that there be a being greater than the being than which it's not possible that there be a greater" must be read as either (21ʹ) or (21#). (21ʹ): "It's not possible that there be a being whose greatness surpasses that enjoyed by the unsurpassably great being in the worlds where its greatness is at a maximum." And (21#): "It's not possible that there be a being whose greatness surpasses that enjoyed by the unsurpassably great being in the actual world." If (21) is read as (21ʹ) then at most God is a possible being. If (21) is read as (21#), then there is truth there, but there is no reason for people to suppose that God actually instantiates the property of being the greatest possible being in the actual world as opposed to any other possible world.

(22) It is possible that there is a greatest possible being.

(23) Therefore, there is a possible being that in some world W′ or other has a maximum degree of greatness—a degree of greatness that is nowhere exceeded.

(24) A being B has the maximum degree of greatness in a given possible world W only if B exists in every possible world.[34]

If W′ had been actual, then B had to exist, given that necessary existence is one of B's great-making properties; it would have been logically impossible for B to not exist in W′. But, Plantinga notes, logical possibility and impossibility do not change in possible worlds: if something is impossible in one possible world, then it is impossible in all possible worlds. Thus, B's nonexistence is impossible in every possible world.[35] And though Plantinga finds this version of the argument compelling, he says there is still work to do. Ultimately, he says that this version of the argument does not prove that God has the maximal degree of greatness in the actual world, seeing as that he may exist in the actual world given his necessary existence, but that doesn't mean he has all of the other great-making properties.[36]

Plantinga gives a final version of his modal ontological argument:

(29) There is a possible world in which maximal greatness is instantiated.

(30) Necessarily, a being is maximally great only if it has maximal excellence in every world.

(31) Necessarily, a being has maximal excellence in every world only if it has omniscience, omnipotence, and moral perfection in every world.[37]

There are essentially two refinements to this version of the argument: there is no dependence on the concept of possible beings, and necessary existence is no longer presupposed, as a being could not be omnipotent if it did not exist.[38] Given (30) and (31), it is impossible that an omnipotent,

---

34. Plantinga, *God, Freedom, and Evil*, 105. Plantinga notes here that although one could differentiate between existence and necessary existence, both could be said to be great-making properties. Charles Hartshorne and Norman Malcolm, for instance, disagree as to which it is that Anselm is asserting is a great-making property. Plantinga, however, proceeds as though necessary existence is a great-making property that God possesses.

35. Plantinga, *God, Freedom, and Evil*, 105–6.
36. Plantinga, *God, Freedom, and Evil*, 106.
37. Plantinga, *God, Freedom, and Evil*, 111.
38. Plantinga, *God, Freedom, and Evil*, 108, 110.

omniscient, and morally perfect being not exist in the actual world. This is because the being must exist in at least one possible world, given (29). Concerning this argument, Plantinga claims it is sound in its premises and conclusion; the pertinent question of interest is (29), as that is essentially what the argument hinges on: the possibility that the property of maximal greatness is instantiated. Plantinga concludes that this argument itself does not prove the existence of God, but rather that the proposition of God's existence is a reasonable one given his modal, ontological argument; this argument is itself not proof of God's existence, as (29) would need to be demonstrated to be true. If one does not accept (29), then one would reject the argument as a whole.[39]

Plantinga has also written on some other arguments for God's existence, though his work on the ontological argument seems to be the most famous. He is not impressed with some of the other traditional arguments for God's existence, such as Aquinas's cosmological argument or the teleological argument as it has been articulated by a variety of philosophers. For Plantinga, Aquinas's assertion that God is a necessary being in and of himself is problematic in so far as Aquinas argues that a contingent being could not be an eternal being, as a contingent being could fail to exist; Plantinga proclaims that there is no reason to believe that a contingent being could not have always existed.[40] But even if this point is conceded, Plantinga says this does not lead to the inference that there is a time in which no contingent beings exist: "Suppose it's true that for each thing there is a time at which it does not exist; we can't properly infer that there is some one time such that everything fails to exist at that time."[41] Similar feelings have been expressed by Plantinga towards the teleological argument. In responding to the argument as articulated by eighteenth-century philosopher William Paley, he states, "The conclusion to be drawn, I think, is that the teleological argument, like the cosmological, is unsuccessful."[42] Plantinga has rejected or significantly modified many of the classical arguments for God's existence;

---

39. Plantinga, *God, Freedom, and Evil*, 112. His conclusion: "What I claim for this argument, therefore, is that it establishes, not the truth of theism, but its rational acceptability."

40. Plantinga, *God, Freedom, and Evil*, 79.

41. Plantinga, *God, Freedom, and Evil*, 80.

42. Plantinga, *God, Freedom, and Evil*, 84. His rejection of the teleological argument seems to be rooted in the idea that the argument may lend support to the notion that the universe is in some way designed, but that is only part of theistic belief. Further, just because the universe may appear to be designed, that does not entail that there was one designer. See his discussion on pp. 83–84.

his approach has been rather to demonstrate that belief in God is reasonable and morally justifiable.[43]

III

John Feinberg has also written on the existence of God and commented on the value of traditional theistic arguments. For Feinberg, the only traditional argument that would prove the existence of the Christian God, with all of his attributes, would be the ontological argument, although, he is quick to assert that it is likely the least effective of the traditional theistic proofs.[44] Additionally, he says that though the traditional proofs do not confirm God's existence, they do make belief in God a rational, coherent option in so far as they simply prove that belief in God is not foolish and thus give the atheists and agnostics justification for further investigation.[45] Feinberg does not see much value in proving that God is a metaphysical principle, or the ground of all being, or being-itself; instead, he argues that God must be demonstrated to be a distinct being, who is himself distinct from creation.[46] God must be demonstrated to be a perfect, necessary, and infinite being, but this does not entail that God's being is quantitatively different than ours; rather, God possesses qualities like love, power, or wisdom in an infinite capacity, and thus is unlimited in respect to these attributes. It is this qualitative difference that makes God the unique creator, even though he is a being among other beings.[47]

---

43. Laing, "Introduction to New Atheism," 8.

44. Feinberg, *No One Like Him*, 203–4. He also says something interesting about the moral argument that will be relevant later in this chapter. Feinberg notes that many philosophers do not find the moral argument to be convincing, as they think moral norms in society simply reflect the outcomes of human evolution. Morality is essentially a social utility that helps humans survive, but there's nothing morally true in the abstract. Feinberg invokes Richard Swinburne who says that, although theists may think morality makes it more probable that God exists, it is not clear that this should be the case, as naturalists have good explanations for moral phenomena. Moral phenomena could come from societal pressure, just as it could come from God. Feinberg, *No One Like Him*, 203.

45. Feinberg, *No One Like Him*, 204.

46. Feinberg, *No One Like Him*, 207–8. Here, Feinberg is specifically arguing against the classical theist's definition of God, in this case espoused by Paul Tillich, which says that God is being itself, and not a being or one being among many other beings.

47. Feinberg, *No One Like Him*, 208, 213.

IV

Open theists often share much in common with neoclassical theists from a metaphysical standpoint, in so far as they reject divine simplicity. Their views on God's foreknowledge do significantly differentiate them from neoclassical theists, though the differences are much more noticeable when engaging with the POE. Nonetheless, there are still differentiations to be made, and they will become evident in this section.

Ryan Mullins and Lari Launonen have written a noteworthy article dealing with the relationship between the cognitive science of religion (CSR) and various models of God.[48] The specific models they identify are classical theism and open theism. This may sound counterintuitive, given that Mullins is a neoclassical theist as per chapter 1 of this book; nonetheless, "open theism" here is used very similarly to theistic personalism in this book.[49] In the introduction of this paper, it is noted that most societies throughout history have produced belief in supernatural agents or gods. For skeptics of religion, some tend to interpret this as evidence that belief in God is irrational; for many theists, this tends to be evidence that theism is natural, which is a traditional Christian claim given the doctrine of general revelation.[50] The problem with that particular theological interpretation of CSR is that, while belief in human-like gods or supernatural agents may be natural, it is far from clear whether belief in God, as properly understood in the Christian tradition, is natural.[51] The answer to this conundrum partly depends on one's model of God, Launonen and Mullins assert.

Citing Matthew Braddock and Justin Barrett, Launonen and Mullins say that it is natural for humans to believe that the universe is designed in some way by God or gods; and these gods are interested in morality, have a free will of their own, and may be invisible, but are not outside of space

---

48. Launonen and Mullins, "Why Open Theism Is Natural," 1–16.

49. Mullins at times does blur the line between neoclassical theism and open theism, as those definitions have been laid out in chapter 1. I do not know anything about Lari Launonen's views on God beyond what is presented in this article, as he has written a few academic articles but is more focused on the cognitive science of religion as opposed to metaphysics. I am including this article in the open theism section as opposed to the neoclassical theism section, but that will prove to be inconsequential for our general purpose, as the primary distinction of note in this work is between classical theism and theistic personalism.

50. Launonen and Mullins, "Why Open Theism Is Natural," 1.

51. Launonen and Mullins, "Why Open Theism Is Natural," 1. They elaborate: "Do the cognitive biases and systems point people to God—or do they only produce beliefs in finite supernatural agents, such as angels, demons, ancestor spirits, ghosts, and goblins? In other words, is natural cognition 'theism-tracking'?"

and time.[52] This has implications for CSR, as it would seem to support Paul's ideas about natural knowledge in Rom 1:18–20, as well as what other theologians such as John Calvin have echoed concerning Paul's remarks. According to T. J. Mawson and Alvin Plantinga, these findings may support the notion that God made people for himself, which is why humanity is restless until they find rest in God.[53] Others have argued that CSR is certainly not compatible with Christian theology, as high gods such as Yahweh or Allah are not present in the earliest religions that we know of; those religions lacked the concept of a supreme god and the theologically correct god concept was not available.[54]

Nonetheless, Launonen and Mullins are inclined to believe that CSR is evidence of theism, depending on the model of God. If one adheres to classical theism, they argue that model of God is incompatible with CSR, and certainly not natural. The main reason for this is that while some of the aspects of classical theism may be natural according to CSR, such as the belief that God is morally perfect, omnipotent, and perfectly free, the aspects of classical theism that distinguish it from other models of God are not in any way natural, as they are highly counterintuitive.[55] For example, CSR says that people presuppose that God experiences sequence in his life, whereas that directly contradicts divine timelessness.[56] In the same way, people tend to naturally believe that God can change in his relationship to people and that he undergoes some kind of emotional change; these beliefs are contrary to what classical theism teaches.[57] And of course, divine simplicity is difficult to grasp, Launonen and Mullins argue, in that CSR tells us people assume God has distinct attributes, actions, thoughts, and feelings; but this contradicts the classical understanding of divine simplicity.[58] Launonen and Mullins conclude that natural religion and CSR say virtually nothing about belief in the classical God.[59] If classical theism is true, they argue that our cognitive mechanisms are not designed to know God: "If classical theism is true, and yet our cognitive biases lead us to conceptualize God as a person not unlike human persons, there is something to the suggestion that we are

---

52. Launonen and Mullins, "Why Open Theism Is Natural," 3.

53. Mawson, "Cognitive Science of Religion," 164, and Plantinga, *Where the Conflict*, 140, both cited in Launonen and Mullins, "Why Open Theism Is Natural," 3.

54. Launonen and Mullins, "Why Open Theism Is Natural," 4.

55. Launonen and Mullins, "Why Open Theism Is Natural," 5.

56. Launonen and Mullins, "Why Open Theism Is Natural," 5.

57. Launonen and Mullins, "Why Open Theism Is Natural," 5.

58. Launonen and Mullins, "Why Open Theism Is Natural," 6.

59. Launonen and Mullins, "Why Open Theism Is Natural," 6.

'born idolaters' rather than 'born believers'. Our cognitive mechanisms are not theism-tracking."[60]

Conversely, Launonen and Mullins argue that CSR may be more compatible with open theism, and thus CSR may be proof that theism is true if one does not hold to classical theism. When an open theist says that God exists with things like thoughts, wants, and free will, and that he is involved in give-and-take relationships with people, those descriptions are used in a more normal, natural sense; the open theist depiction of God is more consistent with CSR for this reason.[61] Ultimately, when people naturally conceive of God, they do so in ways that are more in line with open theism than classical theism. God's desires can be affected by humans, in that humans can actually influence God through their actions and prayer.[62]

Yet Launonen and Mullins are quick to point out that even open theism may not be completely cognitively natural. On one hand, people naturally assume that humans have libertarian free will; on the other, the authors say that in their experience, many Christians also naturally assume that God has exhaustive foreknowledge of the future, something that obviously contradicts open theism. Thus, it is possible that open theism may not be completely cognitively natural either, though a re-examination of CSR is needed here.[63] Building on this inquiry, CSR says that people generally do not naturally conceive of God as transcending space, yet open theists will typically conceive of God as omnipresent and thus as transcending space, though not as transcending time.[64] In the same way, though open theists will affirm omniscience,[65] it is not abundantly clear whether omniscience is naturally intuitive, as some experiments with children and adults suggest that their implicit beliefs may include intuitions about God having false beliefs: "In other words, perfect omniscience, even about present facts, does

60. Launonen and Mullins, "Why Open Theism Is Natural," 8.

61. Launonen and Mullins, "Why Open Theism Is Natural," 9. The authors specifically note that God is temporal, mutable, passible, and unified in open theism, and all of these descriptions are more compatible with natural religion and CSR.

62. Launonen and Mullins, "Why Open Theism Is Natural," 9.

63. Launonen and Mullins, "Why Open Theism Is Natural," 10.

64. Launonen and Mullins, "Why Open Theism Is Natural," 10. Here, they are specifically citing Richard Swinburne and William Hasker as examples of prominent open theists who believe in omnipresence.

65. There is disagreement on the definition of this term. Both open theists and classical theists will claim they believe in omniscience. For the open theist, this entails God knowing all facts of reality; God must know all that is logically knowable. Whereas for the classical theist, God is omniscient because he knows all truth propositions, whether they be in the past, present, or future. Launonen and Mullins briefly discuss this in their article. See Launonen and Mullins, "Why Open Theism Is Natural," 9–10.

not seem to be perfectly intuitive."[66] Something similar can be said about the belief that God is a disembodied spirit, as it is unclear whether that is a human intuition. Ultimately, human intuitions about persons can interfere with theological conceptualizations, thus muddying the water concerning what exactly a natural intuition of God really consists of.[67]

Given these questions about CSR and open theism, Launonen and Mullins argue that CSR can be evidence for theism if certain questions are answered in certain ways. For example, though many theologians believe that God transcends space, the authors argue that one does not have to believe this in order to believe God is omnipresent: "Although it is now commonly supposed that God exists outside of space, this was not the standard conception among earlier theologians. Medieval Christian authors, despite being generally misread on this point, are in complete agreement that God is literally present, spatially, throughout the universe."[68] Consequently, God can be generally present everywhere, but more specifically present in particular locations, which would be more consistent with modern studies within CSR. Moreover, God could be thought of as embodied, given that the second person of the Trinity became incarnate, and remains embodied forever. This is another way that Christian open theism can be said to closely align with natural religion.[69] The authors eventually conclude that, given what we know about natural religion, open theism seems to be fairly close to what people naturally believe about God, whereas classical theism is completely counterintuitive; therefore, if CSR is believed to be evidence for God's existence, something like open theism must be the correct model of God.[70]

V

Richard Swinburne is perhaps the most notable defender of God's existence in contemporary philosophy of religion. He has extensively written on the subject from an open theist perspective. He begins his defense of theism by investigating its coherence, as before it can be determined if theism is true, it must be determined if theism is a plausible explanatory option for

---

66. Launonen and Mullins, "Why Open Theism Is Natural," 11.
67. Launonen and Mullins, "Why Open Theism Is Natural," 11.
68. Launonen and Mullins, "Why Open Theism Is Natural," 12.
69. Launonen and Mullins, "Why Open Theism Is Natural," 12–13.
70. Launonen and Mullins, "Why Open Theism Is Natural," 13. The authors do say that more work needs to be done as it relates to the relationship between CSR and the doctrine of general revelation.

existence.[71] The way in which a proposition is incoherent is if it is logically impossible, so in order for God to exist, his existence must first be proven to be logically possible.[72]

Swinburne defines a person as a mental substance, which he defines as a substance that has some mental property essentially.[73] These mental properties include the perceiving of objects and intentionally performing bodily actions. He also argues that humans, as well as many nonhuman animals, are mental substances.[74] However, even though there are some nonhuman animals that are mental substances, they are not persons because to be a person "someone must be capable of having, as well as sensations, propositional events of all the above kinds of some sophistication. Persons can have beliefs about datable events in the distant past or future, and beliefs about the invisible constituents of visible objects (for example, that observable things are made of particles too small to be seen)."[75] Essentially, Swinburne argues that a person is a mental substance that can subjectively experience the world in a sophisticated manner, in that they can have beliefs, make predictions, make moral judgments, and even acquire beliefs over time. They must have the capacity to perform intentional actions; they must have intentional agency. To say that God is a disembodied spirit is to claim that he does not acquire knowledge or cause effects by acting through any specific matter; and to say that he is omnipresent is to say that he can cause effects unilaterally at every place in the universe while knowing what is happening at every place without information coming to him through a kind of "causal chain."[76]

Swinburne responds to several objections to the logical plausibility that there exists an omnipresent spirit. For example, some have argued that in order for a person to have wants, fears, or hopes, they must have a body in order to publicly express those emotions or desires. Swinburne argues that there are many occasions when a person does not give a public expression

---

71. Swinburne, *Coherence of Theism*, 1. For Swinburne, theism entails "that there is a God in the sense of a being with most of the following properties: being a person without a body (that is, a spirit), present everywhere (that is, omnipresent), the creator of the universe, perfectly free, able to do anything (that is, omnipotent), knowing all things (that is, omniscient), perfectly good, a source of moral obligation, eternal, a necessary being, holy, and worthy of worship."

72. Swinburne, *Coherence of Theism*, 2.

73. Swinburne, *Coherence of Theism*, 105.

74. Swinburne, *Coherence of Theism*, 107. Swinburne elaborates: "They exist only as long as they have the capacity to have sensations."

75. Swinburne, *Coherence of Theism*, 107.

76. Swinburne, *Coherence of Theism*, 113.

of a desire or emotion.[77] More to the heart of the objection, he posits that a disembodied spirit may express mental feelings in a number of ways that do not require a body; perhaps the spirit can intervene for someone who is dying of thirst and cause there to be rain, or maybe the spirit can make markings in the sand if she fears someone may make a disastrous choice for themselves, in an attempt to persuade them to choose otherwise.[78] In traditional theism, Swinburne says that is exactly what has been taught: God can and often does express his mental states in a variety of ways, including keeping the world in existence and interceding in the affairs of men.[79] Swinburne concedes that the arguments surrounding the problem of the identity of persons are typically more substantive and difficult to rebut in so far as skeptics of disembodied personhood will typically say there must be some criterion that can be used to distinguish between disembodied spirits, as usually persons are distinguished by their bodies. One could use tests of memory and character to distinguish between the persons, but people like Terence Penelhum have contended that tests of continuity would be inadequate to distinguish between disembodied persons. One such reason is that people can have very similar character; and as for memories, a disembodied person cannot have their memories verified as there can be no witnesses, thus the memories cannot really be considered authentic or an adequate way to distinguish between disembodied persons.[80] Swinburne disagrees and responds in two ways. First, he states that being physically seen by other embodied persons is not the only way to verify a memory. For example, a spirit could have an idiosyncratic voice, which could be used to identify a memory of his, if someone had heard that voice.[81] In addition, what Penelhum and others fail to realize is that personal identity is something ultimate: "The identity of a person over time is something ultimate, not analysable in terms of bodily continuity or continuity of memory and character, which merely provide fallible evidence of personal identity."[82]

Swinburne goes on to consider a variety of questions, such as whether or not an omnipresent spirit could be the free creator of the universe, and if

77. Swinburne, *Coherence of Theism*, 115.
78. Swinburne, *Coherence of Theism*, 115.
79. Swinburne, *Coherence of Theism*, 115–16.
80. Penelhum, *Survival and Disembodied Experience*, 108, cited in Swinburne, *Coherence of Theism*, 117. The logical implication here is that if one cannot distinguish between disembodied persons, then it is impossible that they are really persons at all. Thus, there could not be a disembodied, omnipresent person that we call God since one would not be able to distinguish between God and any other disembodied person.
81. Swinburne, *Coherence of Theism*, 118.
82. Swinburne, *Coherence of Theism*, 119.

he could be omnipotent, eternal and immutable, omniscient, and a source of moral obligation. As for freedom, it is logically possible that God is a perfectly free person, in that he has the freedom to choose between actions when he does not believe there is a unique best action, and this could very well be the normal situation for God, given that he could logically have an unlimited number of actions available to him.[83]

Concerning omnipotence, Swinburne first addresses a simple but common objection: to assert that God is omnipotent is to assert that God can cause any logically possible event to occur.[84] Those who object to this understanding of omnipotence make the error of assuming that a logically impossible action is just another kind of action, equivalent in legitimacy to that of a logically possible event. Swinburne declares, however, that a logically impossible event is not an event, any more than a square circle is a type of circle.[85] This understanding is applied to "the paradox of the stone" as it were, which has been discussed since the Middle Ages in relation to God's omnipotence.[86] Essentially, Swinburne argues that God could remain omnipotent forever, should he not exercise his ability to create such a stone; in this case, there would be no logically contingent event that he cannot cause, for events involve substances, and there would be no logically problematic stone in existence should he not bring it into existence.[87] If God is necessarily everlasting and omnipotent then he could not cause the existence of the stone since he would cease to exist should such a stone exist—as he would no longer be omnipotent, which means he would cease to exist because he is essentially omnipotent. Hence, such a stone's existence is a logical impossibility, as its existence would violate the "truth conditions" of that reality, which include the existence of a necessarily omnipotent and everlasting being.[88]

---

83. Swinburne, *Coherence of Theism*, 148–49. As Swinburne discusses, it has been objected that God cannot be free because he must do whatever unique best action is available to him if he is perfectly good; there are no choices for God to make. Therefore, the idea that there may not always be the best unique action available to him is important here.

84. Swinburne, *Coherence of Theism*, 151.

85. Swinburne, *Coherence of Theism*, 151.

86. The paradox of the stone refers to the proposed logical dilemma for omnipotence, which usually goes something like this: Could God create a stone so large that he is incapable of lifting it? If not, then he is not all-powerful; if so, then he is not all-powerful, given that there is a stone so large that he cannot lift it.

87. Swinburne, *Coherence of Theism*, 168.

88. Swinburne, *Coherence of Theism*, 168. Thus, Swinburne goes on to say that if it is logically possible that God is forwardly everlasting and omnipotent, then there is no logically contingent event that God cannot cause, as a logically impossible event is not

Is it logically possible that there is a God who is omniscient? Swinburne responds to objections against the logical possibility of omniscience which essentially say that the only way a person could be omniscient at any given time is if that person was the only person in existence and that was the only moment of time in existence.[89] This would contradict the theist's understanding of omniscience, as God is not the only person in existence and he knows all truth propositions for many moments of time. One objection to omniscience is centered on tensed facts. For instance, the proposition that "it is now T_1" can only be known by someone who is only at T_1.[90] This perhaps presupposes that the essence of a particular time period is differentiated by its temporal relation to other time periods. And this is so until we reach a time period or periods in which its definition lies in its relation to temporal events that are believed to have taken place.[91] Swinburne claims this seems unlikely, since if one were discussing this tensed truth claim at a later date it would still be the same "now" even if other events had occurred in the past: "But that seems implausible, because the period to which we are referring by 'now' would still be the period it is, even if there were quite different events happening now and quite different events had happened earlier in the world's history."[92] His main point is that the essence of a period of time cannot be made up of simply its temporal relation to other periods of time. Conversely, he argues there must be something intrinsic to the period of time that makes up its essence other than the events that are happening at it.[93] So, temporal indexicals such as "2 October" are ways of picking out and distinguishing the essence of the period of time, but they are not themselves the essence. And because we distinguish between the events at a particular time and the essence of that time itself, we can understand that the moment in time would be what it is, even if something completely different was happening in the present or happened in the past. We do not lose understanding of what we referred to on 2 October as "now" when we think about it

---

really an event at all.

89. Swinburne, *Coherence of Theism*, 175.
90. Swinburne, *Coherence of Theism*, 175.
91. Swinburne, *Coherence of Theism*, 180. Swinburne gives the example of various propositions that use temporal indexicals. Initially, it could be said that it is now 2 October, and this would be true in so far as it is a day after 1 October. The essence of the time period is then defined purely by its relation to another temporal period of time. This can be the essence of a time period, until you arrive at a time that is defined by its relation to temporal events. For example: to say it is now 2015 is to define a time period in its relation to an event, in this case, the birth of Jesus Christ. To say it is 2015 is to say it is 2,015 years after the year it was believed that Christ was born.
92. Swinburne, *Coherence of Theism*, 180.
93. Swinburne, *Coherence of Theism*, 180–81.

on 3 October.⁹⁴ Thus, even though our grasp of what exactly the essence of a period of time is other than what we are currently experiencing, it is not logically impossible that a superior being, God, would be able to grasp the truth of a tensed proposition during a different time period than the one in which that proposition was made.

These are not the only objections that Swinburne deals with concerning omniscience. The next objections to the logical possibility of omniscience derive from the idea that God cannot be perfectly free and be omniscient at the same time. Swinburne concedes it is impossible that God, as an omnipotent being, would be free if he had exhaustive knowledge of his own future choices.⁹⁵ For reasons that he later explains, God must be understood as omniscient in a somewhat weaker than traditional sense, "knowing of all true propositions that they are true."⁹⁶ One reason is he understands God as a temporal being as opposed to a timeless being, something he presupposes until later in the book; another reason is the Christian doctrine that God has given humans a libertarian free will to choose a particular action independent of all causes acting upon and influencing them.⁹⁷ If humans are to be responsible for their moral actions, this necessitates a belief in libertarian free will; for Swinburne, this is why the Judeo-Christian tradition has mostly held to a belief in libertarian free will.⁹⁸ Various forms of compatibilism and Molinism do not suffice to solve the apparent incompatibility of exhaustive divine foreknowledge and human libertarian free will. If God has exhaustive foreknowledge of the choices he or a human will make, then those choices must logically come to pass, which makes them inevitable and thus incompatible with freedom in the libertarian sense. Therefore, for God to be free and omniscient, it is logically possible that God is omniscient, so long as omniscience is understood as knowing all truth propositions are true, as opposed to knowing all propositions that ever will be true.⁹⁹

94. Swinburne, *Coherence of Theism*, 181.
95. Swinburne, *Coherence of Theism*, 182–83.
96. Swinburne, *Coherence of Theism*, 183.
97. Swinburne, *Coherence of Theism*, 183.
98. Swinburne, *Coherence of Theism*, 185.
99. Swinburne, *Coherence of Theism*, 191, 194–95. For the compatibilist, a physical inability to do something relieves a person of moral responsibility when it comes to that action; however, the compatibilist claims there is a crucial difference between physical inability and an overwhelming desire. When one acts according to their overwhelming desire, they are morally responsible for an action. Swinburne asks, "Why should that difference matter?" when in both cases the individual is fully caused to act or not act in accordance with a physical inability or an overwhelming desire to carry out an action. Hence, Swinburne concludes that one must be able to resist a desire in order to be morally responsible for an action, so compatibilism cannot be an adequate theory

Next, Swinburne moves to the question of God as a perfectly moral person. For God to be perfectly good, he must always carry out the morally best action available to him, according to the evidence available to him.[100] An omnipotent and omniscient person will be able to determine the outcome of an action if that action is solely dependent upon himself; therefore, he will always determine a good outcome of an action, so long as that action solely depends upon himself.[101] He may, however, work with free agents and allow the outcome to be partially or wholly determined by free agents. When he does this, he has limited his knowledge of the future, so not every outcome of an action that he is somewhat involved in will necessarily have a good result.[102] Thus it is logically possible that there is an omniscient, omnipotent person who is perfectly good.[103]

The subsequent question for Swinburne concerns moral realism: can God be the grounds for moral realism and for moral obligation? The existence and actions of God "make a great difference to what are the contingent moral truths."[104] Swinburne argues both atheists and theists agree that people have an obligation to show gratitude to those who have given them gifts in so far as, if there is a God, he has given the gift of life and is largely responsible for the good that we experience. And, given the Christian doctrines of the incarnation and atonement, we have much reason to believe that God is our supreme benefactor; we have reason to believe we owe him gratitude.[105] Consequently, Swinburne argues that the theistic religions, including Christianity, teach God has claimed our obedience by virtue of his

---

of free will. As for Molinism, counterfactuals cannot be true in any meaningful sense, given that true propositions must be grounded in a state of affairs that makes them true. Regardless, Swinburne concludes that Molinism is still subject to earlier criticisms he leveled against the incompatibility of exhaustive divine foreknowledge and libertarian free will. See Swinburne, *Coherence of Theism*, 183–84.

100. Swinburne, *Coherence of Theism*, 202.

101. Swinburne, *Coherence of Theism*, 202–3.

102. Swinburne, *Coherence of Theism*, 203. Swinburne appeals to Gen 6 where God regrets that he made humankind. There, on his interpretation, humankind acted in a way that God did not expect, so even though his action of creating humankind ultimately resulted in evil in some capacity, that does not make God morally bad or evil, as the action was carried out by agents with libertarian free will who acted differently than God expected.

103. Swinburne, *Coherence of Theism*, 204.

104. Swinburne, *Coherence of Theism*, 221. Here, contingent moral truths are contingent due to the fact that they involve persons and actions that could have been otherwise. Whether or not an action taken by a human is morally good is a question of contingent moral truth, given that one must take into account persons, circumstances, and intent when determining if the action is morally good or bad.

105. Swinburne, *Coherence of Theism*, 221–22.

creating us.[106] Because of this, God's commands impose on us obligations that are carried out largely through moral behavior. Even the right of God to do this is limited, though, just as a parent's right to demand obedience from their children is limited. God cannot command us to do something that we, by virtue of some other morally necessary truth, are obliged not to do. And due to his perfect goodness, God will never command us to do something that is contrary to a logically necessary moral truth.[107] In responding to the Euthyphro dilemma, Swinburne maintains that there must be at least one necessary fundamental moral principle that is independent of the will of God.[108] He goes on to cite Aquinas as agreeing with his position that there are at least some principles of morality that are independent of the will of God.[109] It follows from these arguments, according to Swinburne, that it is logically possible for God, as he has described him, to be perfectly good and the source of moral obligation.

Swinburne goes on to discuss the issue of God's everlastingness. It is logically possible to conceive that God is eternal, if by eternal we mean forwardly and backwardly everlasting; theism claims God did not begin to exist, but has rather existed at every past moment of time, and will exist in every future moment in time.[110] It is logically impossible for time to begin to exist, as that would entail that "time existed for some period of time after a period of time in which it did not exist."[111] The same can be said for time ending: it is logically impossible for there to be a time after time ends. This is to be contrasted with the ancient Greek and subsequently Christian understanding of time as being essentially synonymous with change.[112] While there may be a time scale of sorts that measures time after the creation of the universe, God still existed before that scale was created, as he has existed for all time, which is without beginning or end. Before this time scale, God's experience from one moment of time to the next may not have been able to be differentiated, as there may not have been any events occur that would distinguish between the moments in time; Swinburne recognizes this

106. Swinburne, *Coherence of Theism*, 223.

107. Swinburne, *Coherence of Theism*, 223–24. Swinburne differentiated between contingent moral truths and logically necessary moral truths on pp. 207–8. A logically necessary truth is a fundamental moral principle that is true in all possible worlds, and whose negation would entail a logical contradiction.

108. Swinburne, *Coherence of Theism*, 224.

109. Swinburne, *Coherence of Theism*, 225, citing Aquinas, *Summa Theologiae* Ia.2a.94.5.

110. Swinburne, *Coherence of Theism*, 230.

111. Swinburne, *Coherence of Theism*, 230.

112. Swinburne, *Coherence of Theism*, 230.

distinction as that of the topology of time, and the metric of time.[113] Time logically must have a topology, but it is not logically necessary that time have a metric. This is imperative for maintaining that God is backwardly everlasting. Moreover, if God is to be forwardly everlasting, there must be in God a series of distinct conscious moments or subjective experiences so long as there exists a changing universe.[114] God's thoughts, intentions, and actions are measured on this time metric; in this way, he experiences a succession of qualitatively distinct states of events precisely because he has caused and allowed them to occur. If God's everlastingness is interpreted in this manner, Swinburne argues it is logically possible that God is an eternal being.[115]

In close connection with the doctrine of God's eternality, theists have also traditionally held that God is immutable. Though some theologians have wanted to claim that God cannot change in any respect, Swinburne claims it is only logically possible that God is immutable if that is understood in terms of his essential properties: in that, God cannot change in respect to these particular necessary properties that he possesses.[116] Even if the category of a Cambridge change is employed in order to preserve immutability in the classical sense, Swinburne says it is still logically impossible that God could be immutable in such a sense. For instance, though Cambridge changes could explain a human's change in relationship to God, it could not explain change that is inevitably intrinsic in God: "So the claim that God cannot undergo real change would not rule out God not being worshiped by Augustine at one time and being worshiped by Augustine at a later time—for the real change is not in God, but in Augustine. But it would rule out God at one time believing that some event had not yet occurred and then at a later time believing that the event had occurred."[117] Yet, if God is everlasting as Swinburne has argued, then God's knowledge of and beliefs about the future will change, which would result in intrinsic change in God. This is logically incompatible with the classical notion of immutability. Further, Swinburne sees a classically immutable God as being lifeless and impersonal; yet theists have traditionally said that God is personal and

---

113. Swinburne, *Coherence of Theism*, 230. A topology of time here just refers to a succession of periods in time, even if they are identical in experience.

114. Swinburne, *Coherence of Theism*, 231.

115. Swinburne, *Coherence of Theism*, 231.

116. Swinburne, *Coherence of Theism*, 232. Swinburne is particularly concerned here with the compatibility of God's everlastingness and his immutability as defined by the classical theologians. He says immutability as classically defined is incompatible with his everlastingness.

117. Swinburne, *Coherence of Theism*, 233.

that we can have a relationship with him. Also, this picture of God is incompatible with God as depicted in the Hebrew Bible, which is what Judaism, Christianity, and Islam are somewhat based on.[118] Conversely, God must be understood to be immutable, in that he, like any other substance, cannot change in relation to his essential properties.

Lastly, Swinburne moves to the question of God's necessity. Is it logically possible that God is a necessary being, and that he possesses certain properties necessarily? God cannot be metaphysically necessary, according to Swinburne. In fact, he argues that it is not logically possible that God's or any substance's existence is metaphysically or logically necessary.[119] God is a necessary being in that he does not derive his necessity from anyone or anything else; he has aseity.[120] Rather than being metaphysically necessary, God is said to be ontologically necessary, in that the cause of God's existence must be within himself. This intrinsic causal necessity is not an act of the will but is rather a part of God's nature; it is an essential property that God possesses which causes him to inevitably exist.[121] And given the existence of the universe, as well as the previous arguments that Swinburne has discussed, he claims it is thus logically possible that there exists an ontologically necessary substance we call God.[122]

After elucidating the internal coherence of theism and arguing for its logical possibility, Swinburne turns toward arguing for the probability of God's existence. Concerning cosmological arguments, Swinburne says the arguments that are typically linked to Aquinas are not successful; that is, the first four of Aquinas's five ways are "his least successful pieces of philosophy."[123] The two most successful cosmological arguments come from Leibniz and Samuel Clarke.[124] Though Swinburne appreciates those arguments, he also notes that it is difficult to see how a deductive argument that starts with evident facets of experience may lead to proving the existence of God. If a deductive argument could successfully do this, it would prove to

---

118. Swinburne, *Coherence of Theism*, 233. Swinburne goes on here to claim that Greek philosophy and especially Neoplatonism was the driving force behind Christians largely adopting such a definition of immutability in the third and fourth centuries AD. I could expand here on Swinburne's rejection of divine timelessness, but there's no need as he gives objections similar to those that have already been discussed in the first chapter of this book.

119. Swinburne, *Coherence of Theism*, 265.

120. Swinburne, *Coherence of Theism*, 272.

121. Swinburne, *Coherence of Theism*, 274.

122. Swinburne, *Coherence of Theism*, 276.

123. Swinburne, *Existence of God*, 136.

124. Swinburne, *Existence of God*, 136.

be logically impossible that a complex physical universe exists and that God does not exist; but, Swinburne asserts, "the only way to prove a proposition to be incoherent is to deduce from it an obviously incoherent proposition (for example, a self-contradictory proposition), but notoriously, attempts to derive obviously incoherent propositions from such co-assertions have failed through the commission of some elementary logical error."[125] Though he does not think atheism is likely to be true, Swinburne does say that atheism is a logically possible proposition, as a complex universe could exist without God existing. Therefore, since the nonexistence of God is logically possible, the cosmological argument is not a valid deductive argument.[126] Given this argument, he aims to ascertain if the cosmological argument can be a successful C-inductive or P-inductive argument.[127]

Swinburne does agree with Leibniz that if only scientific explanation is allowed, the existence of the universe, whether it has existed for a finite or an infinite amount of time, becomes an inexplicable, brute fact.[128] If the universe is to have an explanation, a personal force that isn't part of the universe must be the explanation. The universe cannot exist as a brute fact for Leibniz, due to the Principle of Sufficient Reason (PSR), which he deems a metaphysically necessary principle.[129] If God is metaphysically necessary for Leibniz, then Swinburne disagrees with his argument; if God is a metaphysically necessary being, which for Leibniz would entail that God could not fail to exist, then he is a logically necessary being. Swinburne is clear that God's existence cannot be logically necessary, as per his arguments earlier in the chapter.[130] If, however, Leibniz's argument can be interpreted in such a way that his metaphysically necessary being is not also logically necessary, then his argument could be valid in so far as God could be necessary in a different sense than that of logical necessity; God could derive his necessity from the fact that he does not depend on anyone or anything else for his

---

125. Swinburne, *Existence of God*, 136.

126. Swinburne, *Existence of God*, 137.

127. Swinburne, *Existence of God*, 137. A P-inductive argument is defined as an argument in which the premises make the conclusion probable. A C-inductive argument is defined as an argument in which the premises add to the probability of a conclusion. See Swinburne, *Existence of God*, 6–7.

128. Swinburne, *Existence of God*, 143.

129. Swinburne, *Existence of God*, 148.

130. Swinburne, *Existence of God*, 148. It is for this reason that Swinburne says the traditional ontological arguments fail as well, seeing as that they assert God's existence is logically necessary. God necessarily exists, in that he does not derive his existence from anyone or anything else. See Swinburne, *Existence of God*, 148n19.

Theistic Personalism and the Existence of God

existence. He is the supreme brute fact. And this could ultimately point to the probability of God's existence.[131]

Swinburne does not see much reason to believe in the PSR: "Whether it is rational to suppose that phenomena have complete explanations is a matter of whether we have potential explanations for them of great simplicity and explanatory power."[132] It may be true that the universe needs explanation since it is not metaphysically necessary, as Leibniz argues, but Swinburne does not see how his argument can be correct unless it is argued on the basis of greater simplicity and explanatory power when compared to a competing hypothesis. Thus, if a cosmological argument is to have merit, it must be said that the universe has a kind of complexity and particularity to it that "cries out" for further explanation, while God does not have such a problem.[133] God is an extremely simple supposition: to propose that God has infinite power, knowledge, and freedom is to postulate the most simple person there could be. Further, God is an "unextended" object, his divine properties fit well together, and they are infinite in degree, which makes them simpler than any property could be if it were instantiated to a finite degree.[134] The existence of a complex universe is less simple and therefore less likely a priori than the existence of God; therefore, if God does not exist, then the existence of a complex physical universe is highly improbable.[135] Given this argument and the existence of a complex physical universe that we inhabit, it is more likely than not that God exists. This understanding of the cosmological argument is a good C-inductive argument.[136]

Swinburne understands a teleological argument to be an argument from design that claims the intelligibility of the universe points toward the probability of God's existence.[137] He is focusing on general patterns of design or intelligibility as opposed to more particular instances of such observation. Again, Swinburne is adamant that no argument from temporal order, including Aquinas's fifth way, can be a good deductive argument; this is because, although the premise is correct, the step from the premise to the conclusion is not adequately deductive.[138] For Swinburne, the vast, general

---

131. Swinburne, *Existence of God*, 149.

132. Swinburne, *Existence of God*, 149. Swinburne had argued earlier that, all things being equal, the simplest explanation is the most probable explanation. See Swinburne, *Existence of God*, 145.

133. Swinburne, *Existence of God*, 150.

134. Swinburne, *Existence of God*, 151.

135. Swinburne, *Existence of God*, 151.

136. Swinburne, *Existence of God*, 152.

137. Swinburne, *Existence of God*, 153.

138. Swinburne, *Existence of God*, 155. The premise being the idea that the universe

intelligibility of the universe certainly points to a creator. But it is not logically impossible that the universe could exist with such order apart from God; in that, it is not a logically necessary truth that all order is brought about by a person.[139] Given that, one must investigate whether the teleological argument is a good inductive argument.

There are two basic objections that Swinburne responds to. First, there is the objection that temporal order in the universe is not an objective reality, but rather is merely a human invention. We impose order on the cosmos, and that is the order we see. Yet humans did not invent the laws of nature, we simply observed them. And these laws of nature dictate how the cosmos behaves, which points to objective intelligibility and order.[140] Second, it has been argued that the order of the universe doesn't explain anything, as it would be impossible to find anything else. If the universe were not orderly, then it would be impossible for us to be here to observe it. To this, Swinburne says that the theist's starting point is not that we perceive order rather than disorder, but that order rather than disorder is objectively present. The order that is present is extraordinary and cries out for explanation.[141] Intellectual inquiry demands that we advance the smallest number of brute facts.[142] Thus, Swinburne concludes that God's existence is a much more likely explanation for the existence of the universe than atheism.

Lastly, Swinburne's evaluation and implementation of the moral argument for God's existence will be discussed. He distinguishes between the argument from the fact that there are moral truths and the argument from human awareness of these moral truths.[143] As for the former, he again holds to the idea that fundamental moral principles must be logically necessary, and therefore cannot provide evidence for the existence of God since they are independent of the will of God.[144] Only contingent moral truths can point to God, as such truths are true because they are obligatory for us in certain contingent circumstances due to God's existence. If something is a contingent moral truth, it would not be obligatory unless God had made it so, seeing as it is not a fundamental moral truth. Therefore, if there are contingent moral truths, they point to the probability of God's existence, as they are true precisely because God has made them obligatory for humans.

---

is characterized by a vast, pervasive order or intelligibility.

139. Swinburne, *Existence of God*, 155.
140. Swinburne, *Existence of God*, 156.
141. Swinburne, *Existence of God*, 157.
142. Swinburne, *Is There a God?*, 44–45.
143. Swinburne, *Existence of God*, 212.
144. Swinburne, *Existence of God*, 214.

Theistic Personalism and the Existence of God

If God had not made them obligatory, then they would not be moral truths at all.[145] Though Swinburne thinks the argument is valid, he does not see it as having much force because he sees two of the premises as being highly questionable. One premise is that certain actions are always obligatory, like promise-keeping; some will not accept this premise. Another premise is that the very act of something like promise-keeping contributes to the highest good in the universe, and all other consequences from the action are irrelevant; some will deny this premise.[146] Unless someone is first persuaded of God's existence by another argument, Swinburne does not think that one who holds to one of these premises but not the other will be convinced by rational argument to hold the other. Therefore, he does not see the argument from the existence of morality to the existence of God as being very effective.[147]

Swinburne sees more merit in the second type of moral argument: the argument from human awareness of moral truths to God's existence. Can naturalistic Darwinism explain human awareness of moral truths? It is logically possible that it could at least explain altruistic and unselfish behavior, as people who work together are more likely to survive external threats than people who do not behave altruistically.[148] However, "having the understanding of these actions as morally good (even when we do not desire to do them) is something beyond mere altruistic behavior."[149] There is no natural reason why a purely material interaction between the mind and the body would produce moral beliefs as opposed to just beliefs, as the beliefs are just present for the purpose of survival, not for the purpose of conforming to moral truth. God would likely give moral creatures, like humans, moral intuitions and beliefs, but without invoking God there seems to be no reason to think that human beliefs are moral beliefs as opposed to simply adaptive beliefs produced by the material body-mind relationship for the purpose of survival.[150] Moral beliefs can move creatures to altruistic behavior even when they may lack the natural inclinations to do so; in that,

---

145. Swinburne, *Existence of God*, 214–15.

146. Swinburne, *Existence of God*, 215. Teleological ethicists will deny the first premise while deontological ethicists will deny the second, says Swinburne.

147. Swinburne, *Existence of God*, 215.

148. Swinburne, *Existence of God*, 216.

149. Swinburne, *Existence of God*, 216.

150. Swinburne, *Existence of God*, 216–17. Swinburne says this is further demonstrated by the fact that other animals seem to have beliefs and instincts, in that they think they should help other members of their own species and groups, but there is no reason to believe that whatever natural process gave them those beliefs could also produce in them moral beliefs.

humans can have and develop moral beliefs that may not even help them or their particular group survive. Thus, Swinburne concludes that it is highly improbable that humans would possess moral beliefs in a Godless world. This probability becomes increasingly unlikely whenever one considers all of the phenomena that would have to occur in a Godless universe: that the universe will be intelligible, governed by natural laws, contain conscious human beings who have moral beliefs, etc.[151]

VI

We now briefly move to Timothy O'Connor, who has written in defense of God's existence from an open theist perspective. Being a philosopher who specializes in metaphysics and modal logic, O'Connor wrote *Theism and Ultimate Explanation: The Necessary Shape of Contingency*, in part, to defend a version of what he calls a Leibnizian cosmological argument.[152] In this work, he is attempting to answer the question of why anything exists at all; to be more specific, he asks, "Why do the particular contingent objects there are exist and undergo the events they do?"[153] Contemporary philosophers are not as concerned with a general, comprehensive metaphysic, as they are with more specific metaphysical issues. For O'Connor, these philosophers too often assume something like naturalism or theism in order to justify an approach to another more localized issue.[154] The existence question, as it were, is thought to be unanswerable by many contemporary philosophers.[155] He disagrees, of course. If the existence question is pursued with enough diligence, we are forced to posit a relationship between contingent reality and a necessary being, something they find problematic for a number of reasons. Conversely, O'Connor thinks it worthwhile to pursue this question and to conclude that a necessary being exists.[156]

Like others, O'Connor argues that human intuition tells us the universe's existence demands an explanation. The scope and beauty of the universe that we can now examine has simply reaffirmed this long-held human intuition. The "overexuberant theoretical physicists" may give various

---

151. Swinburne, *Existence of God*, 218.
152. O'Connor, *Theism and Ultimate Explanation*, ix.
153. O'Connor, *Theism and Ultimate Explanation*, 65.
154. O'Connor, *Theism and Ultimate Explanation*, 65.
155. O'Connor, *Theism and Ultimate Explanation*, 66.
156. O'Connor, *Theism and Ultimate Explanation*, 66. God is a necessary being, but he cannot be necessary in the sense of formal logic; there is no contradiction in the denial that such a being exists, therefore his necessity cannot be logical necessity.

Theistic Personalism and the Existence of God

highly speculative cosmological models, but they invite further questions themselves and clearly do not answer the question of existence since they do not explain why the universe operates according to certain fundamental laws of nature.[157] Further, in the case of now-popular cosmological models that posit that this universe came into existence via quantum fluctuation in a quantum tunnel, why should there have been such conditions in the first place?[158] A naturalist is simply unable to give an ultimate explanation for the existence of a contingent reality, argues O'Connor. In contrast, the theist has an answer: "The reason that any contingent thing exists at all (and, in particular, the world in which we are part) is that it is a contingent causal consequence of an absolutely necessary being, a being which itself could not have failed to exist, since *that* it is inseparable from *what* it is."[159] In other words, this necessary being would exist in any possible world, since its nature would entail existence.

O'Connor is quick to point out here that he is not arguing for the ontological argument in so far as he is not arguing from the possibility that there may be a nature that includes the property of existence and so must exist; rather, he is saying that only if there is such a being can there be an ultimate explanation for existence.[160] The existence of such a being has never been proven to be incoherent, and the explanatory power of such a being has never been disproven.[161] If our universe is contingent, empirical theory will not allow for the obtaining of "fundamental facts" or higher reality ultimately responsible for our existence.[162] As was alluded to earlier, an infinite regress of contingent realities will not help in this regard. If there is an ultimate explanation for the universe's existence, that is, if the universe is ultimately intelligible, then even the most fundamental laws of nature (which are themselves contingent) need to be grounded in a necessary being whose existence is explained within its own nature.[163] O'Connor notes that this being would not compete with empirical explanations but would rather ground their intelligibility.[164]

---

157. O'Connor, *Theism and Ultimate Explanation*, 69.
158. O'Connor, *Theism and Ultimate Explanation*, 69.
159. O'Connor, *Theism and Ultimate Explanation*, 70.
160. O'Connor, *Theism and Ultimate Explanation*, 70–71.
161. O'Connor, *Theism and Ultimate Explanation*, 71.
162. O'Connor, *Theism and Ultimate Explanation*, 76.
163. O'Connor, *Theism and Ultimate Explanation*, 76.
164. O'Connor, *Theism and Ultimate Explanation*, 76. This is my interpretation of O'Connor's argument. He may not himself like to use the language of intelligibility. Here is the language he uses: "It bears emphasis that such an unconditional explanation need not in any way compete with conditional, empirical explanations. Indeed, it

Next, the transcendent, personal-creator model of a necessary being is defended against an alternative answer to the existence question. Some, following the pantheism of Spinoza, have argued that there is perhaps no such thing as contingent existence; the universe, in its totality, is a necessary being.[165] The problem with this broadly Spinozian metaphysic is that the universe is a complex entity, and a necessary being must have a kind of unity that is incompatible with the complexity of our universe.[166] Could the property of necessary existence be something that results from the rest of its essential nature, or from some part of its nature? No, says O'Connor, because if a complex set of properties gave rise to the necessary being's necessary existence, then that property itself would be conditional and dependent on more fundamental aspects of the being's nature. Thus, we are forced to conclude that necessary existence is not a derivative property of the necessary being, but a fundamental property.[167] Necessary existence cannot be simply contingently connected to other aspects of the necessary being's essential nature. If this were the case, there would be no explanation for the fact that necessary existence is connected to the nature of the necessary being.[168] Consequently, this necessary being would not have ultimate explanatory power concerning the existence question.

So, there must be an internal, necessary connection between necessary existence and the being's fundamental nature. Necessary existence cannot be a derivative property of the necessary being. Due to this realization, some classical philosopher-theologians like Aquinas posited the internal connection among properties within the nature must be that of identity; in that, all of the necessary being's properties are identical to its essence.[169] O'Connor finds this problematic, as the classical doctrine of what he calls "absolute simplicity" has a variety of conceptual problems that make it untenable.[170] It is possible, it is argued, to stop short of asserting the classical DDS and instead conceive of an intimate, internal connection between the property of necessary existence and that of the rest of the necessary being's essential nature.[171] Given this argument, is it possible that the physical universe,

---

is natural to suppose that empirical explanations will be subsumed within the larger structure of the complete explanation."

165. O'Connor, *Theism and Ultimate Explanation*, 86–87.
166. O'Connor, *Theism and Ultimate Explanation*, 87.
167. O'Connor, *Theism and Ultimate Explanation*, 87.
168. O'Connor, *Theism and Ultimate Explanation*, 87.
169. O'Connor, *Theism and Ultimate Explanation*, 88. Here, necessary existence just is omnipotence, which just is omniscience, which just is the necessary being itself.
170. O'Connor, *Theism and Ultimate Explanation*, 87.
171. O'Connor, *Theism and Ultimate Explanation*, 88. The argument he gives on pp.

being synonymous with the necessary being of pantheism, has necessary existence as a basic, fundamental property? No, argues O'Connor, as its basic properties are related to its parts, "the elementary particles and fields" and not to its nature in totality.[172]

The next remaining question, now that it has been established in O'Connor's argument that there must be a necessary being that is transcendent, unique, and highly unified, is the question of the very nature of this being. Must this necessary being be the God that Christians speak of? As O'Connor puts it, this necessary being could be either a personal agent or a mechanistic, impersonal force of sorts.[173] In referencing Peter van Inwagen, the transcendent necessary being's nature could be that of *Logos* and it could be that of *Chaos*.[174] The *Logos* model is preferable to the *Chaos* models, in part, due to the fine-tuning argument. Ultimately, given the need for a transcendent necessary being, the fine-tuning data we have seems to tip the scales in favor of the *Logos* model.[175] Things like intelligent life and consistent laws of nature are things we would more expect to see from a personal, intelligent creator than from an impersonal force of random chaos.

O'Connor concludes by explicating the model of God which he has advanced throughout the argument. He notes that many Christian theologians and biblical scholars do not like the kind of natural theology, as it typically

---

88–89 is that the necessary being's fundamental properties necessitate the existence of one another in so far as, in the example of God's perfect power, freedom, and knowledge, God cannot be all-powerful unless he is also all-knowing, cannot be perfectly free unless he is all-powerful and all-knowing, and cannot be perfectly powerful unless he is perfectly free, etc. In this way, there is an intimate interconnectedness to the fundamental properties of God's nature, and therefore none of these is contingent. He goes on to argue how necessary existence is a fundamental property of God's nature in the final chapter of the book.

172. O'Connor, *Theism and Ultimate Explanation*, 90.

173. O'Connor, *Theism and Ultimate Explanation*, 93.

174. O'Connor, *Theism and Ultimate Explanation*, 93, citing van Inwagen, *Metaphysics*, 146. The three varieties of the Chaos model mentioned by O'Connor are *Immutable Chaos*, which produces the actual dependent order out of necessity of its own nature; *Abundant Chaos*, which produces a wide range of discrete worlds, including our own; and *Random Chaos*, which is an indeterministic mechanism that can produce a wide array of worlds, none of which is necessary.

175. O'Connor, *Theism and Ultimate Explanation*, 97. When referencing the fine-tuning argument, he is similar to others who have argued for design. This argument is not, in and of itself, a great proof for theism, but it is a good supplemental argument and is especially effective when attempting to conceptualize the necessary being as the traditional God of Christian theism. In his own words: "Given that the existence of our contingent universe has its ultimate explanation in the activity of a transcendent being, the fine-tuning data provide reason to prefer the identification of the latter [necessary being] as *Logos* to that of *Random Chaos*."

depicts God as immutable, simple, timeless, and utterly transcendent.[176] These conclusions are perceived to contradict the biblical portrayal of God, as has been discussed above. One must not completely do away with any notion of natural theology, warns O'Connor, as even biblical theology requires metaphysics: "Specifically, the concept of God implicit in certain claims at the heart of Biblical revelation themselves require articulation in the metaphysical terms of necessary being."[177] Indeed, some concepts such as divine simplicity, divine immutability, and divine timelessness are problematic, either logically or because of their incompatibility with the biblical data. But the argument that O'Connor advances does not require that one believe in such things, as he makes clear in this section of the book.[178] Given this realization, it is still necessary to retain some of the conclusions of natural theology, not least of which is the idea that God is a necessary being.[179]

VII

Process theists have typically not been concerned with defending the existence of God from a metaphysical standpoint like neoclassical theists or open theists. Primarily, process theists have focused more on the POE, which will be discussed in chapters 5 and 6. There is, however, a process theist who dealt rather extensively with some of the metaphysical arguments for God's existence, specifically with the ontological argument.[180] His

---

176. O'Connor, *Theism and Ultimate Explanation*, 130.

177. O'Connor, *Theism and Ultimate Explanation*, 132.

178. O'Connor, *Theism and Ultimate Explanation*, 132–40. In fact, his argument sometimes entails his theistic personalism. For example, he mentioned on p. 89 that God must be perfectly free to choose from numerous options in order to be all-powerful. This seems to be at odds with the belief in classical theism that God is pure act and has no potential, although this point could be potentially debated. One may also think back to O'Connor's statement that people like Aquinas and Scotus pressed too hard into the notion of divine simplicity and left themselves susceptible to objections that their metaphysic left no room for any contingency at all, whether in God or in the universe. See p. 68.

179. O'Connor, *Theism and Ultimate Explanation*, xiii, 140–43.

180. Whitehead saw God as being necessary for his broader metaphysical system. God was not to be an exception to the metaphysical principles, but rather their chief exemplification. The process metaphysics that Whitehead conceptualized apparently led to a wide array of possibilities and ambiguity in the universe. God was needed to realize the "absolute wealth of potentiality." He is called the "principle of concretion—the principle whereby there is initiated a definite outcome from a situation otherwise riddled with ambiguity." Further: "He is the presupposed actuality of conceptual operation, in unison of becoming with every other creative act." And finally: "Thus, by reason of the relativity of all things, there is a reaction of the world on God." God is not independent

name is Charles Hartshorne, and he was one of the successors of Alfred Whitehead who took Whitehead's process philosophy and created a kind of process theology. Hartshorne represents the rationalist tradition within process theism, in part evidenced by his reworking of Anselm's ontological argument; the rationalist tradition focused more on a priori reasoning than empirical observation.[181]

Hartshorne believes the question of God is largely to be answered in the realm of logic. Concerning Anselm's argument, which he consistently refers to as "the Proof," he claims that no question of contingent or empirical fact is at stake in so far as the Proof refutes both empirical atheism as well as empirical theism.[182] Again, the question of theism is not to be answered in empirical observation, so things like the fine-tuning argument for God's existence or the atheist's demand for empirical evidence for God's existence are irrelevant.[183] They are logical blunders, as it were. So what Anselm did, in Hartshorne's estimation, is to disprove both empirical atheism and empirical theism, and thus forced people to say that either theism or what he calls "positivism," the belief that theism is logically impossible, is logically necessary or analytically true.[184] Theism must be necessarily true or necessarily false, and the decision between necessary truth and necessary falsity is logical, not empirical or factual.[185] One application of this realization is that the classical argument against theism which comes from the observed facts of evil becomes irrelevant, at least in so far as one is speaking of ontology.[186]

In *The Logic of Perfection*,[187] Hartshorne offers modal and ontological proofs for God's existence and responds to some objections. In doing so, he

---

of the world, and the world is not independent of God. So, God is seen as an integral part of the broader metaphysical scheme. I say this to say, process theists see God as a vital part of their worldview. In a sense, their defense of God's existence is their entire metaphysical system. For this reason, among others, they have not been as concerned with engaging in the more traditional arguments about God's existence. See Whitehead, *Process and Reality*, 343–45.

181. Feinberg, *No One Like Him*, 150. The rationalist tradition within process theism is to be contrasted with the empiricist tradition, represented by those like Henry Wieman. The empiricist tradition was more influenced by advances in science which they saw as being more conducive to process metaphysics. Some of these new realizations in the sciences were related to quantum mechanics, the theory of relativity, and evolution. See Feinberg, *No One Like Him*, 149.

182. Hartshorne, *Anselm's Discovery*, 3–4.

183. Hartshorne, *Anselm's Discovery*, 4.

184. Hartshorne, *Anselm's Discovery*, 5.

185. Hartshorne, *Anselm's Discovery*, 6–7.

186. Hartshorne, *Anselm's Discovery*, 6–7.

187. Hartshorne, *Logic of Perfection*.

tells us what kind of God he wishes to defend. Greek philosophy of being has often presided over the interpretation of various biblical texts, and this has led to theologians and philosophers defending God's existence in ways that are untenable. For example, though a few biblical passages may claim that Yahweh is unchanging, the context of those passages reveals that the changelessness is in reference to moral aims and constancy of purpose; they do not, in any way, teach a metaphysical immutability, as if the authors of the text were even aware of such a notion.[188] Further, these texts should be taken to imply a succession of acts or decisions based on a single intention. And, perhaps more importantly, whenever followers of Christ are instructed to be perfect just as the Heavenly Father is perfect, this has nothing to do with immutability; rather, this is clearly a reference to the Father's impartiality concerning conflicting claims of ourselves and of our neighbors. Yet when God is spoken of by theologians and philosophers of a classical persuasion, it is in reference to an unchanging, wholly immutable reality.[189]

This leads to an incoherent metaphysics, as the traditional religions have metaphysical systems that are infected with ambiguity, at least in their popular forms. For instance, if one takes the concept of providence seriously, what are the implications? Does it mean that everything that happens is God's will and that nothing can truly go wrong in the world? Hartshorne asserts that the classical conception of providence gives people no reason to take seriously the potential dangers that confront humanity.[190] Neither the conclusions nor the metaphysical premises make much sense, and thus the doctrine leads to much confusion. Because of this realization, some may turn to new religions or quasi-religions, such as Humanism or Communism. Even then, Hartshorne says that something like Marxian metaphysics is too vague: "No clear reason is given for supposing that reality as a whole will have gained any increment of value from the episode."[191] Thus, what is needed in a metaphysical system is a sufficient answer to tragedy in the world, as well as a ground for hope, love, and faith.[192] The kind of metaphysical system that Hartshorne wishes to defend, and consequently the kind of God he wants to defend, will seek to fulfill both of these conditions.

As we have already seen, Hartshorne is sympathetic to Anselm's original ontological argument, or what he calls the Proof or the Argument. But he does rework aspects of the argument due to his disagreement on the

---

188. Hartshorne, *Logic of Perfection*, 8.
189. Hartshorne, *Logic of Perfection*, 8.
190. Hartshorne, *Logic of Perfection*, 12.
191. Hartshorne, *Logic of Perfection*, 14.
192. Hartshorne, *Logic of Perfection*, 14.

nature of God. Hence, Hartshorne declares his argument to be the Modal Proof in order to distinguish it from the Proof.[193] For Hartshorne, perfection cannot be thought of like any other ordinary predicates, for it is of a separate logical type. Its existence cannot be a purely contingent question but rather must involve either a positive necessity or a negative one.[194] In that, perfection must either necessarily exist, or be a logical contradiction. Now, if perfection or divinity is to be defined as people like Anselm or Descartes defined it, then the Proof is said to be a cogent argument against theism, as it would force one to defend necessary existence in such a way that does violate logical principles.[195] The fate of theism, Hartshorne argues, depends upon an alternative definition of perfection and divinity.[196]

So what is this alternative conception of divinity? What this alternative has in common with the classical conception is that it connotes an excellence to God that is definable a priori, which cannot be given to any other individual entity, whether it be possible or actual.[197] From there, differences abound. Whereas God was classically conceived as *actus purus*, Hartshorne argues that we should rather be able to differentiate between a divine individual and divine states.[198] Individuals often do not actualize all of their potential, and that should not be regarded as an imperfection. This can apply to God, as even the classical tradition said of God that he could have created, or he could have not created; he could have created this world, or he could have created another world.[199] Moreover, "this divorce between being and doing is a strange notion which nothing in our experience illustrates, even by analogy, except where the analogy implies the reverse of what the theist intends."[200] For instance, Plato could have had a different impact on his readers than he actually did, without him being different than he actually was in his lifetime. His readers could have interpreted his works differently than they did, so the potential lies with them, and not with Plato himself. Yet this would make Plato's influence on his readers unconscious and involuntary. So, even in this analogy, God could actualize all of his potential, but his influence and involvement in the world would not be loving. It is incomprehensible to say that God remains in an unchanged state while

193. Hartshorne, *Logic of Perfection*, 32.
194. Hartshorne, *Logic of Perfection*, 33.
195. Hartshorne, *Logic of Perfection*, 33.
196. Hartshorne, *Logic of Perfection*, 34.
197. Hartshorne, *Logic of Perfection*, 34.
198. Hartshorne, *Logic of Perfection*, 35.
199. Hartshorne, *Logic of Perfection*, 36.
200. Hartshorne, *Logic of Perfection*, 36.

at the same time arguing that he is loving by definition. To be loving is to care about differences and respond to them differentially.[201] Anselm did not identify divine potential with divine perfection, but we should, Hartshorne argues.[202]

Earlier, Hartshorne had made it clear that Anselm not only argued that for a being to exist is better than for a being to exist only in the understanding, but he had also argued that it is greater for a being to exist when its nonexistence is inconceivable than to exist with its nonexistence being a logical possibility.[203] For Anselm, to even be able to conceive of the nonexistence of the supreme being is a defect. This is relevant when dealing with Gaunilo's famous island objection.[204] In that, this shows that nonexistence is demonstrated to be a defect solely in comparison to what is inconceivable as nonexistent.[205] And because islands are always conceivable as nonexistent, there is no logical implication that existing islands are better than nonexistent islands.[206] What is even meant by a "perfect island"? Perfect for what purpose, and by what criterion?[207] It would seem that only the divine consistently transcends such relativities, and it is that transcendence that justifies Anselm on this point.[208] Because of this, Hartshorne argues that this entire line of reasoning is really an exercise in missing the point.

There is a difficulty for the Proof as traditionally used, according to Hartshorne. Concerning contingency, a predicate may be contingent and yet nonexistent, as this modality does not entail actual existence. In other words, if a property is contingent, then it is logically possible that it either exists or does not exist. Yet necessary existence entails actual existence. So the problem then for the Proof is that the necessity of perfection must be of a higher or more abstract type than its real existence.[209] This reasoning is drawn from Anselm's claim that you must not even be able to conceive that perfection could not exist; again, the necessity of perfection must be differentiated from its actual existence. If it cannot be, then the Proof fails.

201. Hartshorne, *Logic of Perfection*, 36.
202. Hartshorne, *Logic of Perfection*, 41.
203. Hartshorne, *Logic of Perfection*, 28.
204. Hartshorne, *Logic of Perfection*, 45. This objection to Anselm's argument is summarized by Hartshorne as such: "If 'perfect' or 'greatest conceivable' guarantees existence, why not greatest conceivable, hence necessarily-existing island, mermaid, or what you will."
205. Hartshorne, *Logic of Perfection*, 58.
206. Hartshorne, *Logic of Perfection*, 58–59.
207. Hartshorne, *Logic of Perfection*, 62.
208. Hartshorne, *Logic of Perfection*, 62.
209. Hartshorne, *Logic of Perfection*, 63.

The solution to this dilemma requires that there be a concrete form of divine actuality that is extrinsic to the property of perfection.[210] In addition, this divine actuality must be perfection's contingent instantiation. And there must be another form of divine actuality that is necessary and thus not outside the property of perfection, but is itself abstract, like perfection.[211] This will enable us to distinguish between two kinds of existence, thus differentiating between the abstract existence of perfection and its concrete existence. Furthermore, one must find a basis for distinguishing between two forms of existence, so as to avoid being without rational standing in the claim.[212] In order to provide this basis, Hartshorne uses the example of humanity. Humankind exists, but that is a less concrete existence than the existence of particular persons: "There are thus at least three levels of existence: the occurrence of certain actual states of individuals; the existence of certain individuals; the existence of certain kinds of individuals or of certain class-properties."[213] The existence of particular individuals or the particular states in which they exist is, of course, contingent. Therefore, to conceive of existence as necessary, we do not need to deny all distinctions between the abstract and the concrete, nor distinctions between property and instantiation. The necessity of existence in this example need not be for a particular individual or another; rather, what is necessary is that there exists "some instance or another."[214]

Hartshorne thus argues that the Proof as classically defined stands or falls on the possibility of applying the property-instance distinction to perfection. Obviously, so long as perfection is classically defined, it is impossible to apply the property-instance distinction to it. God is said to be identical to his properties, and not to exist in states of contingency. He is said to be pure actuality and possess no potential at all. There is no distinction between his essence and his existence.[215] However, if divine perfection can be conceived as contingent, then all of the necessary criteria of the Proof can be met. That is, if divine perfection can include God as being open to various embodiments and states of being, then the property-instance distinction can be applied to perfection, so long as there is a "logical exclusion

---

210. Hartshorne, *Logic of Perfection*, 63.
211. Hartshorne, *Logic of Perfection*, 63.
212. Hartshorne, *Logic of Perfection*, 63.
213. Hartshorne, *Logic of Perfection*, 63–64.
214. Hartshorne, *Logic of Perfection*, 64.

215. Hartshorne, *Logic of Perfection*, 64–65. For a modern articulation of these ideas, one may think of James Dolezal's explicit formulation of God in exactly these terms. See Dolezal, *All That Is in God*, 42.

of no-embodiment."[216] Admitting potentiality in God strengthens the case for his necessary existence. Limited potentiality is entirely contingent in its realization, but God is not limited in his potential states; rather, God is coextensive, and necessarily so, with all actuality in his individual concrete states and with all potentiality in his possible states of being. This gives him a "non-selective, and therefore non-arbitrary, *a priori* definable, relation to actuality and potentiality."[217] Perfection therefore has two aspects: the absolute aspect and the aspect of transcendent relativity.[218] This is a key element of Hartshorne's Modal Proof: by distinguishing between the property of perfection and its particular instantiation in the divine, Anselm's argument can stand. One can only speak of the possibility of the nonexistence of perfection, or the necessity of perfection, if one applies the property-instance distinction, Hartshorne argues. By defining perfection in this manner, this modified version of Anselm's Proof is plausible.

Much more could be said concerning Hartshorne's reworking of Anselm's Ontological Argument. But, for the purposes of this section, this will suffice for now. Much of what he said will also be relevant in the coming chapters when exploring how process theists engage with the POE.

---

216. Hartshorne, *Logic of Perfection*, 65.
217. Hartshorne, *Logic of Perfection*, 65.
218. Hartshorne, *Logic of Perfection*, 67.

Chapter 4

Classical Theism and the Existence of God

I

IN THIS CHAPTER, ARGUMENTS for God's existence from several contemporary classical theists will be surveyed. Classical theists, the reader will quickly ascertain, are not as concerned with demonstrating why this particular physical universe exists. Rather, they are focused on the existence question—that is, why does anything at all exist in the first place? The starting point for exploring classical engagement with atheism will be Edward Feser's *Five Proofs of the Existence of God*.[1] That material will be supplemented with work from David Bentley Hart and Ron Highfield.

Feser introduces five classical proofs of God's existence: the Aristotelian Proof, the Neo-Platonic Proof, the Augustinian Proof, the Thomistic Proof, and the Rationalist Proof. All of these arguments in some way or another combine empirical observation with a priori reasoning, in contrast to something like the Ontological Argument given by Anselm. The Aristotelian Proof is essentially an argument based on the observed reality of change. Change occurs; no one would dispute this.[2] Coffee goes from hot to cold and leaves fall off of trees. Feser identifies four different kinds of change: qualitative, location, quantitative, and substantial.[3] For Aristotle, change is ultimately the actualization of potential. Coffee has the potential

---

1. Feser, *Five Proofs*.
2. Feser, *Five Proofs*, 17.
3. Feser, *Five Proofs*, 17.

to become cold, even if it has not yet done so. The same can be said about the leaf on the tree; it has the potential to fall to the ground, even though it has not yet done so. Everyday experience demonstrates that change occurs, and some philosophical reflection reinforces this observation.[4]

The next key tenet of the argument is that change requires a changer. For example, cool air in a given area brings down the temperature of the once-hot coffee.[5] Mere potentiality cannot bring about change. Only something that is actual can cause potentiality to become actuality. Potential coldness cannot make something cold. Actual cold air must be what makes the coffee cooler. In this way, change requires a cause.[6] However, this is not to say that everything which causes a change must itself be undergoing change. Only that which has potential must have a cause beyond itself.

Now what Feser has described so far are linear series of changes in so far as they extend backward in time. But, he says, let us suppose that there was a linear series of changes that did not have a first temporal cause as the events extend infinitely backward in time. In that case, the material world would not have a first temporal cause and would thus have been undergoing change for all time. This is precisely what Aristotle believed.[7] Some may say that Big Bang cosmology has disproven this notion. Others, however, have speculated that the Big Bang was itself caused by an earlier universe imploding; some have said the Big Bang is the result of our universe branching off from another parallel universe.[8] It is difficult to suggest that the Big Bang is the absolute beginning of existence, as that would still beg the question of where that matter came from, and what caused that explosion in the first place. Thus, theories of something like an infinite multiverse abound.

Even if this is the case, it is conducive to Aristotle's argument, as there is another kind of series of changes, something Feser describes as hierarchical.[9] What makes a series of changes hierarchical is the instrumental or derivative character of the latest members of the series.[10] The coffee, at any given moment, may be three feet above the ground on a desk. The floor holds the desk up, while the floor is sustained by the foundation of the house or office building. This building is held up ultimately by the ground outside. The coffee is cooled by the air, which is cooled by the air conditioner, and so

4. Feser, *Five Proofs*, 19.
5. Feser, *Five Proofs*, 19.
6. Feser, *Five Proofs*, 19.
7. Feser, *Five Proofs*, 20.
8. Feser, *Five Proofs*, 21.
9. Feser, *Five Proofs*, 21.
10. Feser, *Five Proofs*, 22.

on. At any particular moment, some causes are dependent upon others to bring about the actualization they now experience. So what is relevant in a hierarchical series of changes is not simultaneity, but rather the dependence of later entities within the series upon earlier members.[11] A first member in a hierarchical series is first because it is most metaphysically fundamental: "We mean it is the first cause in the sense that it has *inherent* or *built-in* causal power while the others have only *derived* causal power. It is their having only derivative causal power that makes the other members secondary rather than first or primary."[12]

When one extends the scope of this observation to the totality of existence, it can be seen that for there to exist a contingent reality where change occurs, there must be a principle that does not itself have potential. If there is no such principle, then we are left with an infinite metaphysical regress concerning change. Everything which has potential requires something actual to cause that potential to be realized. Therefore, Aristotle concludes that there must be an Unmoved Mover. This principle must be purely actual; it does not simply happen to not have potential, it could not in principle have any potential or need of a cause beyond itself.[13] Christians call this principle God, as God is the ultimate cause of all things. God, being purely actual, transcends time, because to exist within time is to undergo change. And whatever undergoes change has potential.[14] Furthermore, God is immaterial and incorporeal, seeing as that to exist materially is to exist within time. God is maximally perfect since he is devoid of unrealized potentiality. And there can only be one God, due to the fact that there can only be one purely actual principle. In order to differentiate two or more of a kind, something must in one instance have what the others would lack, but there could be no such differentiation since God does not lack anything as a purely actual being.[15] In short, Feser says we can conclude that God is one, immutable, eternal, immaterial, incorporeal, perfect, omnipotent, and fully good.[16]

The next argument is the Neo-Platonic Proof. This argument is an argument that is derived from the observation of the composition of the material universe. Our entire experience is made up of parts. A book, for instance, is made up of the cover, the pages, the glue that secures the pages to the cover, and the ink on the pages. People are made up of parts; individuals

---

11. Feser, *Five Proofs*, 22.
12. Feser, *Five Proofs*, 24.
13. Feser, *Five Proofs*, 27.
14. Feser, *Five Proofs*, 29.
15. Feser, *Five Proofs*, 30.
16. Feser, *Five Proofs*, 31.

are composed of arms, legs, eyeballs, bones, muscles, etc.[17] In one sense, the parts are less fundamental than the whole. We understand what a leg is, for example, by reference to what it does for the whole of the organism: it helps a person move around. A book cover protects the pages of the book and indicates what the book is about, as well as who wrote the book.[18] At the same time, there is another sense in which the whole is less fundamental than the parts that make it up in so far as the whole is dependent upon the parts to be what it is. A book cannot exist as a book without the cover, pages, ink, glue, and the rest; it also could not exist if its various parts were scattered about, so it is also dependent on its parts being constructed together properly.[19]

Thus, the things of our experience are composite and less fundamental than their parts, in that they depend on their parts to exist. This oftentimes is related to temporal succession, given that for many things there is a given time when its parts have not been assembled into the whole, and then are later assembled. But this principle is not limited to composite entities as they relate to temporal succession. Rather, even if something had somehow always existed, it would still be true that the whole is dependent on the parts to be what it is. Even if a book had eternally existed, it would still be a composite entity.[20] A composite depends on its parts not just in a temporal sense, but also in an atemporal sense. A composite being's existence always presupposes the existence of its parts. And it is not just that the composite depends on the existence of its parts, but also the proper arrangement of the parts. Something must be the cause of the arrangement of the parts into the whole, so Feser argues that composite things always have causes, whether those be temporal or more metaphysically fundamental.[21]

It is important to note that Feser's argument extends beyond physical parts; the same argument applies to metaphysical parts as well. Anything that is composite is also a combination of form and matter.[22] And anything that is a composite of form and matter would still need a cause for those parts to be combined in a proper manner. For Feser and other Aristotelian

---

17. Feser, *Five Proofs*, 69.
18. Feser, *Five Proofs*, 69.
19. Feser, *Five Proofs*, 69–70.
20. Feser, *Five Proofs*, 70.
21. Feser, *Five Proofs*, 70–71. Feser calls this second kind of cause a "hierarchical" cause, citing its usage in the Aristotelian Proof's argument. On p. 72, he says that a chair, for example, could depend on its parts in a linear or temporal sense, but also in a hierarchical sense as well. The chair exists only because its parts exist and are combined in the right way. And these parts can exist and themselves be combined in the right way only in so far as certain other factors exist and are combined in the right way, and so on.
22. Feser, *Five Proofs*, 73.

philosophers, form without matter is a mere abstraction, while matter without form is mere potentiality.[23] There are of course other metaphysical parts that can be identified, such as existence and essence. The implication of all of this is that contingent reality is composite, and in order to avoid an "explanatory vicious cycle" there must be a noncomposite and completely simple ultimate first principle that is the cause of all existence. This simple cause would not need a cause exterior to itself, seeing as that it is not a composite; Plotinus, the Neoplatonic philosopher, called this simple cause the One.[24]

In addition to being completely simple, the One must be immutable, as to change is to gain or lose some feature, which would entail that the One is a composite.[25] The One must also be timeless, so as to avoid experiencing sequence, which would entail a change. In addition, the One must not be abstract, as abstract entities are causally inert; but it must also not be a physical entity, as then it would be a composite.[26] In essence, the One must be something like a mind or more like a mind than anything else. Yes, the Neoplatonists located intellect within a second realm of divinity, but Feser argues that one need not agree with every specific detail in order to agree with the general Neoplatonic approach to the existence of God.[27] Ultimately, the One must be perfect, omnipotent, fully good, and omniscient. He really is identical to the Unmoved Mover.[28] One may object that these things must be understood as metaphysical parts, and so the One must be a composite. But Feser argues that along with the classical tradition, and especially that of Aquinas, we must understand that we use such terms in the manner of analogical predication. The Bible's descriptions of God, from the Christian point of view, must be understood as analogical predication in so far as if we say God is all-powerful, we should mean that there is something in God that is analogous to power as we understand it.[29]

The third argument for God's existence is what Feser terms the Augustinian Proof. This argument essentially amounts to an argument from the existence of abstract objects, such as universals, propositions, numbers,

23. Feser, *Five Proofs*, 73.
24. Feser, *Five Proofs*, 74.
25. Feser, *Five Proofs*, 75.
26. Feser, *Five Proofs*, 75–76.
27. Feser, *Five Proofs*, 76n4.
28. Feser, *Five Proofs*, 76.
29. Feser, *Five Proofs*, 77–79. Feser concludes, "In particular, what we call God's power, intellect, and goodness (as well as the other divine attributes) are all ultimately one and the same thing looked at from different points of view, whereas what we call power, intellect, and goodness in us are not the same thing."

other mathematical objects, and possible worlds. Feser argues for realism as opposed to conceptualism or nominalism; in that, abstract objects exist independently of the constructs of the human mind. They also cannot be reduced to the strictly material.[30]

Ten arguments are then given to substantiate realism and refute conceptualism and nominalism. Some of these include arguments like the "one over many" argument, which states that universals are not reducible to any one particular concrete entity. Triangularity and redness, Feser claims, can be instantiated in any number of concrete objects; and yet, if those objects went out of existence, redness and triangularity would still exist. In addition, these universals can be exemplified even when no human mind perceives them.[31] Therefore, these universals cannot be said to be a collection of material things, nor can they be dependent on the human mind for their existence. Another example of an argument Feser employs is the "argument from mathematics in general." Mathematical truths are necessarily true and cannot be changed. Something like $2 + 2 = 4$ was true long before anyone realized it was and would still be true even if there were no humans on earth. Moreover, numbers are infinite, but the actual number of concrete entities and ideas within human minds is finite, so numbers cannot depend on human minds nor on the material universe for their existence.[32] And finally, the last argument from Feser that will be mentioned is "the argument from the incoherence of psychologism."[33] The result of psychologism is often a form of radical relativism, seeing as that atheists see our minds as being formed by contingent and ever-changing biological, social, historical, and cultural circumstances, which have no necessary connection to objective reality. If when our minds perceive of logic or mathematics, we see not objective reality but strictly our own conception of reality, then our perception of logic or mathematics does not necessarily reflect objective truth; on this view, it is difficult to avoid the conclusion that it is impossible to ascertain objective truth, if it exists at all.[34] Psychologism, which Feser says is basically just a form of conceptualism, is then rendered incoherent; to defend such a

---

30. Feser, *Five Proofs*, 90. Feser describes nominalism as denying that abstract objects are real in any sense, while conceptualism grants that they are real, but are only constructs of the human mind.

31. Feser, *Five Proofs*, 90.

32. Feser, *Five Proofs*, 91.

33. Feser, *Five Proofs*, 95. Psychologism, Feser says, reduces the laws of logic and mathematics to "mere psychological principles governing the operation of the human mind." This view would argue that logic and mathematics do not describe objective reality, but rather the way in which our minds think about reality.

34. Feser, *Five Proofs*, 95–96.

view, one would have to appeal to universals like Darwinian selection pressures, class interests, and scientific and mathematical principles governing the evolutionary process in order to explain which biological and cultural forces were responsible for our particular collective conception of logic and mathematics.[35]

Due to these arguments and others, Feser asserts that some form of realism must be correct. He settles on Scholastic realism, as he finds insurmountable difficulties in Platonic and Aristotelian realism.[36] Scholastic realism agrees with Aristotelian realism in denying that there is a Platonic third realm in which eternal forms exist. Universals either exist in concrete instantiations or in the intellects which entertain them. At the same time, it agrees with Platonic realism in the assertion that there must be a realm that is distinct from the material universe and finite intellects. Universals cannot have their grounding in the finite, as Aristotelian realism seems to lead one to assume. Scholastic realism is distinct from the two other variations of realism that Feser has described, in that it grounds the existence of universals and other abstract objects in an infinite, eternal, and divine intellect; this is

---

35. Feser, *Five Proofs*, 96.

36. Feser, *Five Proofs*, 97–102. Platonic realism is problematic for Feser due to the causal inertness of the Platonic forms in the third realm. If these eternal forms are indeed inert, then they would lack the causal powers that things like material objects or minds have; in that, they would be unable to act on the material world. If triangularity, for example, exists in and of itself and not in a mind or in a concrete object, then how could it cause something? Further, Feser argues that the famous "Third Man" objection has some weight, as Plato himself considered. If a form is both something universal and also exists as a particular object in its own right, then doesn't this entail that the form of something must also participate in yet another higher form? And wouldn't that higher form need to participate in an even higher form? Platonic realism seems to be left with an infinite regress problem, argues Feser. As for Aristotelian realism, it denies the existence of this third realm, which Feser sees as a positive. Universals and other abstract objects exist independent of human thought, but they do not exist there as abstract objects. Rather, universals exist either in concrete objects or in the mind. This differs from conceptualism because, although Aristotelians do hold that universals considered in abstraction only exist in the mind, the universals are abstracted from particular things, as opposed to being free creations of the mind. Though considered to be more plausible than Platonic realism, where Aristotelian realism falls short is in the grounding of the existence of universals. If universals and other abstract objects exist only in either concrete objects or the human mind, then how can we account for certain necessary truths, like that of the logic of mathematics? The equation $2 + 2 = 4$ would still be true even if there were no material universe or human minds, yet Aristotelian realism does not have any grounding for such a reality as the existence of numbers and mathematical formulas seem to be grounded in the material universe or human minds, which could or could not exist. In other words, Aristotelian realism seems to ground the logically necessary in the logically contingent.

a thesis that is famously associated with Augustine.[37] And if abstract objects have their grounding in an infinite, eternal, and divine intellect, then their existence must be grounded in the existence of God. Thus, the existence of abstract objects is proof of the existence of God.

The fourth proof of God's existence is termed the Thomistic Proof. This is an argument that starts with the premise that there is a distinction between the essence and existence of any particular thing. We know *that* something is, and we know *what* something is. For example, we know what a human being is, and we know that human beings exist.[38] For the essence and existence distinction to be a real distinction, it cannot be merely verbal or conceptual but must be reflective of mind-independent reality itself, and Feser argues that there are good reasons for us to make such a distinction. One such reason is that we differentiate between particulars on the basis of the essence/existence distinction. If one is describing various types of creatures, Feser says, one must make such a distinction if one wishes to differentiate between the particular creatures; we differentiate between lions and unicorns not just based on their essences but based on their existence. Lions exist and unicorns do not, and we know this not just by examining the essence of *what* they are, but by examining *that* they are.[39] For Feser, examining the essence of the lion and the unicorn is not enough to differentiate them: "So, if the essence and existence of a thing were not distinct features of reality, then knowing the former should suffice for knowing the latter, yet it doesn't."[40] In other words, we cannot know whether or not lions or unicorns exist simply by studying their essence; if we could, then the essence/existence distinction would not be real.

Another reason to posit a real essence/existence distinction is the contingency of a given object's existence. Lions exist, but they do not have to exist; the history of life could have gone differently and led to a reality in which we have no lions, much like how we have no unicorns. And if the existence of lions was not distinct from their essence, then they would exist simply by virtue of their essence. The lions would exist by their very nature, making their existence logically necessary. It would be logically incoherent for a number of reasons already discussed in this book for composite beings

---

37. Feser, *Five Proofs*, 102, 104. Obviously, the intellect must be infinite, eternal, and divine if it is to coherently be considered the grounding for logically necessary truths. This intellect must be an intellect "which *could not possibly* have not existed."

38. Feser, *Five Proofs*, 117.

39. Feser, *Five Proofs*, 118.

40. Feser, *Five Proofs*, 118.

like lions to exist necessarily; the lions exist contingently. This demonstrates a real distinction between their essence and their existence.[41]

Further, if there is such a thing whose essence and existence are one and the same, then there cannot be in principle more than one such entity. If a thing's essence were not distinct from its existence, then its essence would be identical to its existence; consequently, its essence would be just existence itself.[42] On analysis, Feser claims, there would be no way to differentiate between two entities that were existence as such. Regardless of how one attempts to distinguish between two entities that are existence as such, one will always come to the conclusion that they are existence as such plus some other feature, which would not make them existence as such. And this is incoherent, given the prior premise that if there is no essence/existence distinction regarding some particular object, then that particular object just is existence itself. Its essence would be its existence, and this is incompatible with some entity or another being a composite of existence as such plus some other feature.[43] Hence, one must hold to a real distinction between the essence and existence of something in order to differentiate between particulars.

Given this essence/existence distinction, the question then arises: how are these two aspects of a given object combined into a whole? It cannot be that something's essence gives itself existence. Feser has already argued that one cannot know whether or not a lion exists simply by examining its essence. Moreover, something whose essence is contingent cannot give itself existence, as then we would have the logical incoherence of something contingent existing necessarily. Something whose essence just is existence itself, that entity's existence would naturally flow from its essence, seeing as that they are identical; but, as has been argued, there can only be one such thing in principle.[44] Neither could it be that the things of our experience impart existence to themselves. A given object cannot do something to itself, or anything at all until it first exists. Therefore, an object whose essence is distinct from its existence cannot exist unless something external to it imparts existence to its essence. Nothing to which the essence/existence distinction applies can be the cause of its own existence.[45] This is not just true for one moment of a given object's existence but at every moment of its existence. Consider a particular dog, Fido. Fido's essence is distinct from

---

41. Feser, *Five Proofs*, 119.
42. Feser, *Five Proofs*, 120.
43. Feser, *Five Proofs*, 120–22.
44. Feser, *Five Proofs*, 124.
45. Feser, *Five Proofs*, 124–25.

his existence at all times, not just when he was conceived. And since Fido's essence cannot add existence to itself, it must have a cause that continuously imparts existence to his essence, otherwise, he would not exist.[46]

Therefore, all ontologically contingent reality must have a continuous cause for its existence, whether that be in the past, present, or future. Since nothing whose existence is distinct from its essence needs existence to be imparted to itself from something external, nothing of this sort could be the ultimate cause of the existence of contingent reality. This ultimate cause must be something in which existence and essence are not distinct. Thomas Aquinas termed this cause "subsistent existence itself" meaning the cause exists in and of itself; and this cause Christians refer to as God, the one who is wholly unique, divinely simple, eternal, immutable, incorporeal, etc.[47]

The fifth and final proof of God's existence which Feser provides is deemed the Rationalist Proof. This is an argument from the PSR, which is most often associated with the rationalist philosopher G. W. Leibniz, though the principle itself has been formulated in a variety of ways since Leibniz. Feser, a Thomistic philosopher, says that one way in which Thomists have formulated the PSR is that "everything is intelligible."[48] Some arguments for the PSR are empirical in nature. Meaning, when we look for explanations in various events that take place, or in the existence of a given object, we tend to find them; and when we do not, we tend to have reason to believe that there is an explanation that we do not have access to yet.[49] An additional empirical observation is that the world does not behave in the way we would expect if the PSR were false. The world would not be intelligible, which would render science impossible; we would expect to see events occurring frequently that have no explanation.[50] Empirical observations are just the beginning of the justification for the PSR, however. In citing Alexander Pruss, Feser asserts that to deny the PSR would entail a radical skepticism concerning perception, as there may be no reason behind our having the perceptual experiences that we do have.[51] If the PSR is false, then events may occur in ways that have nothing to do with objective tendencies of things. In short, if the PSR is false, then one cannot trust in the evidence of sensory perception, nor in the empirical sciences or logic.[52] A rejection of the PSR

---

46. Feser, *Five Proofs*, 125.
47. Feser, *Five Proofs*, 126–28.
48. Feser, *Five Proofs*, 148, citing Garrigou-Lagrange, *God*, 181.
49. Feser, *Five Proofs*, 148.
50. Feser, *Five Proofs*, 148–49.
51. Feser, *Five Proofs*, 149, citing Pruss, "Leibnizian Cosmological Argument," 28.
52. Feser, *Five Proofs*, 149.

Classical Theism and the Existence of God

is self-refuting, as this undermines the possibility of any rational inquiry, including the supposed rational conclusion to reject the PSR.[53]

In embracing the PSR, we understand that the explanation of anything is going to be either in and of itself, or something external to its nature.[54] If something's explanation is to be found externally, then that thing is contingent, as it depends on circumstances outside of itself for its existence. Conversely, if something's explanation is found in its own nature, then that thing is necessary, in that its nature would necessitate that it cannot fail to exist. These are the only two possibilities, since everything has to have an explanation, according to the PSR; there can be nothing without an explanation for its existence.[55] The question then arises: can everything in existence be contingent? One may imagine that even if the most speculative cosmologies postulate a kind of infinite multiverse, everything in existence would still be contingent. If a Big Bang is caused by a previous universe collapsing in on itself, then obviously the Big Bang would be contingent on circumstances external to itself. If our universe were a branch of another universe that was itself a branch of yet another universe, and so on, we are still left with contingency after contingency. Now, Feser says, one might suppose that we have satisfied the PSR here, as we have an explanation for everything in existence, as that very explanation is the infinite multiverse. All of the explanations are contingent, yes, but there are explanations, nonetheless. David Hume famously came to this conclusion, stating that there was no need to posit anything that exists in a necessary way.[56] Even in this scenario, however, not everything that requires an explanation has one, according to Feser. In citing considerations made by rationalist philosophers Leibniz and Samuel Clarke, it is said that even if there were such an infinite series of contingent causes, the infinite series itself would have need of explanation. The series as a whole is still contingent, so it could have failed to exist. This begs the question: why didn't it fail to exist?[57]

Given the PSR, rationalist philosophers Leibniz and Clarke concluded there is no way to avoid the conclusion that there must be a necessary cause that is external to even an infinite series of contingent causes. Nothing less than a necessary being will be sufficient here. In addition, Feser notes that this is not simply a matter of temporal causation, as there would be nothing logically incoherent in the notion that this infinite series of contingent

---

53. Feser, *Five Proofs*, 150.
54. Feser, *Five Proofs*, 154.
55. Feser, *Five Proofs*, 154.
56. Feser, *Five Proofs*, 155.
57. Feser, *Five Proofs*, 155.

causes—be that an infinite multiverse or whatever else speculative cosmology asserts—could very well extend backward in time to infinity. Even so, given that there is nothing within the nature of this infinite series of contingent causes that would explain why it exists in the here and now, why does it exist presently? How does it exist? How are its essence and its existence held together? Again, given the PSR, these are vital questions. The answer, for Feser and the rationalist philosophers, is the existence of a necessary being, namely, the existence of God.[58]

II

David Bentley Hart has written considerably on the subject of God's existence and is not all too pleased with the current state of public discourse on the topic: "Not that, at the moment, there is any real public debate about belief in God worth speaking of. There is scarcely even a public conversation in any meaningful sense."[59] For Hart, there is blame to be had for the current state of public discourse on the topic by both Christians and atheists. When modern atheists speak of God, they are mostly referring to a type of demiurge, or cosmic craftsman of sorts. This God is not the transcendent source of all being but is rather an intelligent designer, another being among beings in the universe.[60] To speak of God as classically understood by all the great faiths, including Christianity, one must speak of the infinite source of all being; one must speak of the one who is eternal, omniscient, omnipresent, divinely simple, etc. In other words, God is not another being within the continuum of nature, God is "being itself," he is the ontological ground for the existence of nature.[61] This is to be contrasted with a demiurge, or gods which may be very powerful beings, and perhaps even belong to a higher or more splendid dimension of immanent reality. But these gods do not transcend reality and they are not the source of all being. They are not being itself.[62] Hence, when modern atheists say something like, "All people are atheists in regard to Zeus, or Wotan, and most other gods; I simply disbelieve one god more," then they do not understand what has been meant by "God" in Christian history.[63] The gods of mythology are

---

58. Feser, *Five Proofs*, 158–59.
59. Hart, *Experience of God*, 23.
60. Hart, *Experience of God*, 35.
61. Hart, *Experience of God*, 30.
62. Hart, *Experience of God*, 31–32.
63. Hart, *Experience of God*, 33.

composite, temporal, and filled with potential. They cannot be compared to God, as properly understood, in any meaningful sense.

Hart uses a couple of examples to demonstrate this point. Victor Stenger published, *God: The Failed Hypothesis; How Science Shows That God Does Not Exist*.[64] The book title itself, Hart argues, demonstrates a complete misunderstanding of not only the word God but science as well.[65] God is not something to be proved by the observation of the physical universe; he is not something you can locate with a telescope or a microscope. God's existence is to be settled in the realm of metaphysics, or debates surrounding consciousness or ethics. To reiterate, God is not a being among beings for Hart; rather, he is the transcendent source of all being. Thus, Stenger's book ends up being a long non sequitur based in conceptual confusion.[66] Richard Dawkins did not fare much better. In *The God Delusion*, Dawkins discusses Thomas's "Five Ways" but simply does not understand them. Dawkins mistook the Five Ways for being a comprehensive statement about why one should believe in God, while also misunderstanding the logic of the Five Ways at a most basic level.[67] For instance, Dawkins apparently did not understand the scholastic distinction between primary and secondary causation, so Thomas's discussion of a first cause is taken to mean a temporal cause in a series of other temporal causes. This is strange, says Hart, given that Thomas continuously makes it clear that his logic does not require for the universe to have a temporal beginning. In addition, Dawkins misunderstood Thomas's discussion concerning motion as pertaining to movement in space, as opposed to ontological movement from potency to act, and so forth.[68]

As was previously alluded to, Hart does not lay all the blame for the current state of public discourse on God at the feet of the new atheists. Some Christians in the West have abandoned the classical tradition and opted for things like fundamentalism, which has helped to erode the quality of public discourse. The young earth creationists, for instance, who attempt to read two contradictory creation accounts in Genesis as a single narrative that unfolded just over six thousand years ago have given the new atheists well-matched opponents.[69] This is to be contrasted with the patristic understanding of creation. Some fathers, such as Origen, John Chrysostom,

---

64. Stenger, *God*.
65. Hart, *Experience of God*, 21.
66. Hart, *Experience of God*, 21.
67. Hart, *Experience of God*, 22.
68. Hart, *Experience of God*, 22.
69. Hart, *Experience of God*, 24.

and Augustine, took the "beginning" in Genesis as a reference to the eternal principle of the *Logos*. Gregory of Nyssa and Augustine speculated that the act of creation is timeless, yet the universe unfolded progressively in a temporal sense, out of its own intrinsic potencies and principles, while nature was itself the craftsman.[70] Christian thinker John Henry Newman was a contemporary of Darwin's; he was a patristics scholar, and could find nothing in the concept of evolution itself that would be problematic for the doctrine of creation.[71] Despite this, there were both atheists and Christians who were contemporaries of Darwin who saw a logical contradiction between the idea that God created the world and that life had evolved over time. This is nonsense, says Hart, given that creation has traditionally been thought of by Christian thinkers as a timeless act. Furthermore, Christians do not normally place such an antithesis between the work of nature and the work of God when it comes to other aspects of their faith. For instance, Christians believe that God is the creator of every person, yet they do not deny that the person is also a result of spermatozoon and ovum; here, they intuitively understand that God's act of creating the person is to be understood as the whole event of nature and existence, rather than somehow being a distinct causal agency that contradicts or opposes the natural process of conception.[72]

In speaking of God as classically understood, one should be able to properly differentiate between natural theology and Intelligent Design (ID) theories. Though it may be tempting for believers in God to do so, Hart warns against perpetuating ID arguments for God's existence. ID theory is deeply problematic and a "massive distraction."[73] The literature's early emphasis was mainly concerned with "irreducible complexity" found in the biological world, which provided a foundation for the argument that there must have been some sort of intelligent agency at work in the process of evolution. Hart's primary difficulty with such a proposal is that this could only be an argument from probability, given that no one could ever prove that an organism, no matter how intricate, could not have been produced by an unguided phylogenic history.[74] And probability is an undoubtedly difficult thing to measure given the immense complexity of the systems that depend on one another within biology, as well as the huge amounts of time in which they take to develop. Additionally, the entire foundation of ID

---

70. Hart, *Experience of God*, 26.
71. Hart, *Experience of God*, 26.
72. Hart, *Experience of God*, 28.
73. Hart, *Experience of God*, 37.
74. Hart, *Experience of God*, 37–38.

theory arguments from irreducible complexity presupposes that there exist in nature discontinuities wherein natural causality proves inept. But this is deeply problematic, because if demonstrating God's existence depends on an unexplained causal gap in the natural order, then what happens when science eventually explains that gap? It would seem that the ID advocates have unwittingly painted a picture of God that could actually be disproven one day by science.[75] This is where modern ID theory departs from classical thought: the classical arguments assume the opposite of modern ID, in that God's creative power is seen in the rational coherence of the whole of nature. God was thought to have infused nature with the power of moving itself to determinate ends. Universal rational order, and not particular instances of irreducible complexity, was seen as evidence of the divine mind. Frankly, Hart says, "The total absence of a single instance of irreducible complexity would be a far more forceful argument in favor of God's rational action in creation."[76]

Similar concerns are given regarding theistic claims that are derived from the seemingly improbable cosmic conditions that hold our universe together. Though the universe seems like it is fine tuned by an intelligent designer, even these arguments remain probabilistic. Yes, the exactitudes and exquisitely fine calibrations of the universe, as Hart puts it, may be enough to make an unbeliever wonder about supernatural explanations; but in the end, people who are inclined to explain them away with Godless explanations will do so.[77] A vast or even infinite multiverse is seen by many modern atheists as doing just that. Stephen Hawking is a perfect example of this, says Hart. Hawking thought that quantum fluctuations generated many different universes and that this did away with the need for God to explain the origin of the universe. Of course, this has nothing to do with God as properly understood. Hawking apparently thought that talk of God creating was talk of a temporal action by God at some point in the past wherein he would use the cosmic conditions to erect our current universe. Thus, God would be unnecessary if there were some set of prior laws just floating around in a quantum vacuum that could spontaneously spawn our universe. The problem is that Hawking does not seem to understand, again in some part due to the departure from classical theology by most Christians and the rise of things like the ID movement, that the question of creation concerns the very possibility of existence as such.[78] In addition, Hawking thinks of God

75. Hart, *Experience of God*, 41.
76. Hart, *Experience of God*, 39.
77. Hart, *Experience of God*, 39.
78. Hart, *Experience of God*, 40.

as needing to be temporally prior to the world, while classical thought said he was logically and necessarily prior to anything existing at all. God would be just as necessary if the only things that existed were a collection of physical laws and quantum states, for those things would still require explanation for their existence. The question of God concerns the logical possibility of existence itself, not the question of the physical probability of our particular universe.[79]

Much more could be said about Hart's engagement with the new atheists, but what has been written will suffice for the purposes of this section. For Hart, the new atheists are usually not debating God, but rather are debating the demiurge, or the existence of lesser gods. When speaking of God, all of their arguments fall apart, as they are left with a philosophical naturalism that cannot begin to coherently give an answer to why anything at all exists. At the same time, modern Christian arguments for God lack the logical coherence that classical metaphysics exemplifies.

III

Ron Highfield represents classical theism while being associated with the Churches of Christ. He has written on God's existence and the traditional proofs as they relate to modern atheism. Following Hans Kung, he identifies three types of modern atheism: humanistic, political, and scientific.[80] Humanistic atheism asserts that belief in God is antithetical to human freedom and happiness. God, in this scheme, is seen as impeding human flourishing. Nietzsche is perhaps the most well-known proponent of this view, having once said, "But that I may reveal myself entirely unto you, my friends: if there were gods, how could I endure it to be no God! *Therefore* there are no gods."[81] Political atheism is related to humanistic atheism, in that it sees God as curtailing human progress, only this time specifically in the realm of politics. Karl Marx, for instance, famously saw God and religion as the opium of the masses which robbed them of their political energy by reassuring them of heavenly rewards despite their earthly oppression.[82] Then there is scientific atheism, which argues that reason demonstrates God does not exist. These atheists are materialists or naturalists. They believe that everything

---

79. Hart, *Experience of God*, 41.
80. Highfield, *Great Is the Lord*, 74.
81. Nietzsche, *Thus Spake Zarathustra*, 91, cited in Highfield, *Great Is the Lord*, 74–75.
82. Highfield, *Great Is the Lord*, 75.

within existence can be explained via natural laws; there is no need for God, as nature is its own explanation.

In citing Plantinga, Highfield identifies two types of arguments that atheists tend to make for nonbelief: *de facto* arguments and *de jure* arguments.[83] *De facto* arguments propose that the statement "God exists" is factually untrue, while *de jure* arguments contend that belief in God is unwarranted or irrational, even if true. Often, atheists opt for *de jure* arguments, as it has historically been difficult to advance a convincing *de facto* argument against God's existence. Thus, Karl Marx and Sigmund Freud argued that belief in God was unwarranted because it comes from disordered cognitive processes that are aimed not at the pursuit of truth, but rather at psychological well-being.[84] The problem for those like Marx and Freud is that their *de jure* arguments depend on their *de facto* atheism. For Marx, the cognitive processes which produce belief in God are faulty; but he can only know this because they are producing a belief in God, which is something he knows cannot be true due to his *de facto* atheism. And for Freud, belief in God is not the result of a pursuit of truth, but rather a pursuit of psychological well-being; but Freud only knows this because he knows God doesn't actually exist.[85]

Another weakness of atheism is that it typically does not fully appreciate the ramifications of denying belief in God. Denial of belief in a transcendent source of being leaves the universe without explanation. It leaves the universe ultimately unintelligible. The cosmos is simply the result of unexplained chaos, and there's no reason to think we can understand anything we observe in this random, meaningless, and unintelligible universe.[86] This is ultimately an impractical way to live, argues Highfield. No one can live consistently this way. If there is no transcendent source of being, then we cannot even place value statements on our experience in so far as we cannot consistently say it is good to marry and have a family, or to pursue world peace. We are unable to condemn even the most unspeakable evils we see in the world. On what basis would we do so? Because they impede human flourishing? We cannot even say that human flourishing is a positive goal, as there is no objective meaning in the universe if naturalism is true.[87] The ones we love have no meaning or purpose. The matter which makes up

---

83. Highfield, *Great Is the Lord*, 75, citing broadly from Plantinga, *Warranted Christian Belief*.
84. Highfield, *Great Is the Lord*, 75–76.
85. Highfield, *Great Is the Lord*, 76.
86. Highfield, *Great Is the Lord*, 77.
87. Highfield, *Great Is the Lord*, 78.

their bodies is no different in moral value than any other kind of matter. We cannot use words like *right, wrong, good, evil, justice,* or *injustice* if we are to believe we speak coherently when using such a vocabulary. Unless we deem these intuitions irrational, we must believe there is a universal moral order; God is necessary to validate our moral experience.[88] Thankfully, says Highfield, most atheists do not actually live according to their beliefs.[89]

Belief in God gives what atheism takes away. While atheism says the universe is a brute fact of sorts, and thus evidently meaningless, God gives the universe meaning and purpose. And seeing as that God does not need the world, its purpose for existence is rooted in love and goodness.[90] The relationships we have and the value statements we use in this life are coherent and meaningful. Belief in God allows us to make sense of our everyday experiences. In addition, God makes the universe intelligible, so things like science and mathematics are possible and we can be confident in them. Even something like beauty, which we do not fully understand but intuitively know, cannot just be a result of mindless chaos; it can be understood as something transcendent and objective as opposed to an objectively nonexistent façade produced by our imaginations.[91] And lastly, because of belief in God, we can confidently say that moral values and vocabulary are rooted in an objective, universal moral order that comes from a transcendent source.[92] This realization is essential for people to live out in their lives, as it provides a framework of coherence when making moral judgments.

IV

Though this has not been an exhaustive review of the arguments for God's existence from both theistic personalists and classical theists, this suffices to demonstrate the variety of approaches that are taken by those in the various camps. Both modern and classical proofs have been surveyed, as well as some interaction between the competing views. The approaches that have been reviewed in these two chapters will be scrutinized in chapter 7, where an analysis of how the underlying metaphysical presuppositions impact apologetic engagement with atheism will be provided. First, I will examine the POE as it relates to God's existence, from both classical and modern perspectives.

88. Highfield, *Great Is the Lord*, 92–93.
89. Highfield, *Great Is the Lord*, 78.
90. Highfield, *Great Is the Lord*, 99–100.
91. Highfield, *Great Is the Lord*, 100.
92. Highfield, *Great Is the Lord*, 102.

Chapter 5

Theistic Personalism and the Problem of Evil

I

THE POE HAS BEEN DESCRIBED as both an intellectual and emotional or pastoral problem.[1] For some, it is intellectually incoherent to posit that an all-loving, all-powerful God created a universe so full of evil. Greg Boyd has characterized the problem in these terms and said that it has occupied more intellectual energy within the post-Augustine church than any other single issue.[2] David Bentley Hart has similarly depicted the POE in modern discourse with the new atheists.[3] The emotional connection to the intellectual problem is obvious as well: How can we love or believe in a God who is not good? Is God as traditionally conceived a logical contradiction? Christopher Hitchens wrote an entire book on the subject, arguing that God, as traditionally conceived, especially by Christians, cannot be good in any recognizable sense of the word.[4] Thomas Oord has said that he *cannot* believe in a God who allows or causes things like rape, murder, and genocide.[5]

The aim of this chapter and the next, then, is to briefly examine how both theistic personalists and classical theists have addressed the POE. This won't be exhaustive, of course. The goal is to give a brief overview of some

---

1. Feinberg, *No One Like Him*, 777.
2. Boyd, *God at War*, 43.
3. Hart, *Doors*, 13–15.
4. Hitchens, *God Is Not Great*.
5. Oord, *God Can't*, 13.

relevant material that will then allow for a contrast of opposing apologetic approaches to the POE as they relate to the doctrine of God. As an aside, the subject of hell will not be directly discussed, as that would go beyond the scope of this book. However, when God's final victory over evil is invoked in one answer to the POE, it will be mentioned in passing so as to add appropriate context.

As has already been alluded to, modernity brought about certain negative attitudes towards the classical understanding of God. This resulted in a fundamental change in approach to the question of God and his relationship to the world. One such result of this phenomenon has been a shift in Christian answers to the POE. This section on theistic personalism and the POE will look into some of these changes and give insight as to how God's having a real relation to the created order affects how one conceives of his relation to evil. Some of the answers given by theologians and philosophers of a modern persuasion will in some ways resemble classical responses, while others are radical departures that offer entirely new avenues for Christians to explore.

II

In dealing with the POE, Plantinga employs what he calls "the Free Will Defense."[6] Freedom is defined here essentially as the power of contra choice: an individual is able to perform an action, but he is also able not to perform the action.[7] For Plantinga, God can create free creatures, but he cannot cause or determine them to freely do what is right. To create creatures capable of moral good, they must also be capable of moral evil.[8] This is not an indictment of God's omnipotence, as omnipotence does not entail the ability to perform a logical contradiction. Neither does this detract from God's goodness, as the only way to completely thwart moral evil would be to remove humanity's capacity for moral good.[9]

In countering the Free Will Defense, it has been asserted that it is possible that God could have created a world in which perfectly free creatures do only what is right, even if they are free to do what is wrong. John Mackie

---

6. Plantinga, *God, Freedom, and Evil*, 29.

7. Plantinga, *God, Freedom, and Evil*, 29. Plantinga specifically rejects compatibilism on p. 31, which he defines as the belief that causal determinism is compatible with freedom.

8. Plantinga, *God, Freedom, and Evil*, 30.

9. Plantinga, *God, Freedom, and Evil*, 30.

offered this objection.[10] Mackie argued that since it is logically possible for there to exist a world in which everyone freely chooses to do good, then God must be able to create that world if he is omnipotent. After all, if God is omnipotent, then he can create any possible world; the only limits on his omnipotence are logical limitations. Plantinga responds by reminding readers that not every logically possible world necessarily could become actual. Some states of affairs are possible but do not actualize, and we know this from experience.[11] One could say that God is not a necessary being, but a contingent being. After all, "perhaps most" theists now agree with this sentiment.[12] Therefore, there are some possible worlds that he could not actualize, namely the ones in which he does not exist.[13]

From here, the atheist could take it one step further. He could say that God could actualize any of the possible worlds in which he exists and in which free creatures do no wrong. For this reason, Plantinga doesn't find the fact of God's contingency to be a fully adequate justification for the Free Will Defense. Instead, he must demonstrate that it could be impossible for God to actualize a possible world in which he exists, and there are free creatures who do no moral evil.[14] To do this, Plantinga theorizes that it is possible that every person who could be created suffers from something he labels *transworld depravity*.[15] To give a brief summary, Plantinga's argument is that it is

10. Mackie, "Evil and Omnipotence," 100–101, cited in Plantinga, *God, Freedom, and Evil*, 33.

11. Plantinga, *God, Freedom, and Evil*, 34–35.

12. Plantinga, *God, Freedom, and Evil*, 39.

13. Plantinga, *God, Freedom, and Evil*, 39. Here, Plantinga follows what seems to be the analytic tradition's consensus: God is not logically necessary. Therefore, he is technically a contingent being. And a contingent being does not necessarily exist in all possible worlds. God may be metaphysically necessary in the actual world, in that he does not depend on anything else for his existence. Hart describes this distinction as such: "Philosophers often distinguish between the claim that something is 'metaphysically necessary' and the claim that something is 'logically necessary.' The former would describe only something that, if it happens to exist at all, also possesses the quite wondrous attribute of being eternal and incapable of dissolution." Hart, *Experience of God*, 114–15.

14. Plantinga, *God, Freedom, and Evil*, 45.

15. Plantinga, *God, Freedom, and Evil*, 48. Here, Plantinga differentiates transworld depravity from what he deems the Calvinist doctrine of total depravity. His explicit definition is as follows:

"(33) A person P suffers from transworld depravity if and only if the following holds: for every world W such that P is significantly free in W and P does only what is right in W, then there is an action A and a maximal world segment S' such that

(1) S' includes A's being morally significant for P

(2) S' includes P's being free with respect to A

(3) S' is included in W and includes neither P's performing A nor P's refraining from

possible everyone who has free will will inevitably use it to produce moral evil at least once in their life. Thus, though it may be logically possible for a world to exist in which free people produce only moral good and no moral evil, there may be no possible worlds in which this logical possibility would actualize. It is at least logically possible that everyone who could be created suffers from transworld depravity, thus making it impossible that God could create a world with free creatures who produce no moral evil.[16]

Concerning natural evil, Plantinga invokes Augustine's theodicy which attributed much of natural evil to Satan and his cohorts.[17] Natural evil, then, exists largely due to the free activities of rational, nonhuman entities. The Free Will Defense does not assert that this is undoubtedly the case, but only that it is a possibility. Accordingly, it is possible that natural evil is the result of nonhuman persons, and it is also possible that God could not have actualized a world in which these nonhuman persons produced only moral good and no moral evil. It can be said, then, that both moral evil and natural evil can be described as "broadly moral evil," in that both are the result of free creatures and not the work of God.[18] Ultimately, Plantinga concludes that the Free Will Defense solves the main philosophical POE, both logically and probabilistically.[19]

There is one more argument that Plantinga deals with that is especially pertinent for the purposes of this book. The Free Will Defense hinges on humans and other rational agents having genuine freedom when it comes to decision-making. But the atheist may say, if God is omniscient, then it is impossible for rational creatures to possess true freedom, as a rational agent must do what God knows he will do which would eliminate any semblance of genuine freedom. What God knows will come to pass must come to pass.[20] Though this argument sounds plausible at first, it is ultimately based on confusion, argues Plantinga. There is a difference between a proposition

---

performing A and

(4) If S' were actual, P would go wrong with respect to A."

For Plantinga's complete discussion on transworld depravity and the relevant definitions and context of his use of the concept, see pp. 29–53.

16. Plantinga, *God, Freedom, and Evil*, 48–53.

17. Plantinga, *God, Freedom, and Evil*, 58.

18. Plantinga, *God, Freedom, and Evil*, 59.

19. Plantinga, *God, Freedom, and Evil*, 64. Plantinga does say that although the POE does not pose a significant threat to the theist in the realm of logic or philosophy, it could pose a religious problem in so far as it may be difficult in the face of misfortune and suffering for someone to maintain devotion to God and a proper attitude towards him. This, however, is a pastoral problem as opposed to a philosophical problem.

20. Plantinga, *God, Freedom, and Evil*, 66.

being true and it being necessarily true. Plantinga illustrates this difference with the following statements:

> (49a) Necessarily, if God knows in advance that X will do A, then indeed X will do A.
>
> (49b) If God knows in advance that X will do A, then it is necessary that X will do A.[21]

The atheist's argument demands that (49b) be true, but in reality only (49a) is true. It is necessarily true that if one knows a proposition to be true, then it is true. But it does not then follow that if one knows a proposition to be true, then that proposition is necessarily true. Yes, it is necessarily true that if one knows Henry to be a bachelor, then it is true that Henry is a bachelor; however, this does not entail that Henry is necessarily a bachelor. One could have known Henry to be a married man as opposed to a bachelor. Thus, if one knows that Henry is a bachelor, then what follows is that it is false to say Henry is a married man; it does not follow that Henry is necessarily a bachelor.[22] God knows what free creatures will do, but that does not mean the free creatures necessarily do what they do. They make their decisions freely, and therefore it can be said that God's foreknowledge is not causative and is thus compatible with human freedom.

III

N. T. Wright has dealt with the POE, but he cautions against attempting to completely solve it, as doing so can minimize the severity of evil in the world.[23] This is not a problem to be dealt with strictly by clever metaphysicians or theologians. Instead, all Christians, and all of society, must deal with the issue. The way forward for Christians in engaging the POE is to celebrate both the goodness of God while also taking seriously the reality of evil: "No: for the Christian, the problem is how to understand and celebrate the goodness and God-givenness of creation and, at the same time, understand and face up to the reality and seriousness of evil."[24] In addition, the church must tell the Christian story in such a way that doesn't attempt to solve the POE but rather addresses it so as to emphasize God's final victory

---

21. Plantinga, *God, Freedom, and Evil*, 67.
22. Plantinga, *God, Freedom, and Evil*, 67.
23. Wright, *Evil*, 40.
24. Wright, *Evil*, 40.

over sin and death.[25] For the Christian, our response to evil starts with the premise that God is passionately and compassionately involved with the world, rather than with the idea that evil can be sufficiently addressed in clever works of metaphysics.[26]

With all of this in mind, Wright proceeds to tell the Christian story in a way that engages the reality of evil in the world. Essentially, Wright argues that Christianity does not have an ultimate explanation for the existence of evil. Rather, the Bible tells us what God is doing about evil. This is not to say that no explanations for the existence of evil can be inferred from the biblical text; it is simply to say that the Bible is far more concerned with telling the story of God's conquest of evil. We are not given an exact metaphysical explanation in the pages of Scripture, regardless of how badly Western philosophical and theological tradition may desire it.[27] The Old Testament in particular is written to tell the story of what God is doing about evil, as opposed to telling us how evil can exist if God is all-good and all-powerful. And the two kinds of evil in the Old Testament that God is overcoming are human evil and evil done by "the satan."[28] God restores creation by overthrowing the forces of evil and by vindicating his faithful people.[29] So, certainly, there is a responsibility on behalf of free moral creatures regarding the existence of evil in the world. Though, for Wright, although his comments may seem similar to a kind of free will defense considering that evil results from the choices of free moral agents, ultimately he considers his argument more of a "commitment to action on God's part, coupled with the settled affirmation of creation as basically good."[30] Human responsibility, and to a lesser extent, the activity of the satan, are the sources of evil in the world. But this is as far as the Old Testament goes in so far as an explanation for evil is concerned; the solution to this POE, so to speak, is that God is acting from within creation to right what sin has wronged.[31]

As for the New Testament, the story is more of the same. The Gospels tell of political evil, as well as of corruption within Israel itself. Related to this, the Gospels also speak to the reality of a kind of supernatural evil that influences human events.[32] Jesus confronts these different varieties of

25. Wright, *Evil*, 41.
26. Wright, *Evil*, 40.
27. Wright, *Evil*, 44–45.
28. Wright, *Evil*, 45.
29. Wright, *Evil*, 67–68.
30. Wright, *Evil*, 73.
31. Wright, *Evil*, 73–74.
32. Wright, *Evil*, 80–81.

evil and overcomes them. He overcomes them through healing, through associating with those who have been ostracized from society, and through overcoming the very temptation of the satan itself. Ultimately, he defeated all of these evils in his resurrection from the dead. The early Christians then took this life, death, and resurrection of Christ as something to proclaim and to live out; God was introducing the new creation in the actions of Jesus. And in the resurrection itself, Jesus has brought about forgiveness of sins, which is the way in which God's new creation will remake the world.[33]

Wright argues, then, that the atonement of Christ is essential for Christians in dealing with the POE. The Christus Victor theory in particular is relevant here, in that Jesus has already won a victory of the powers of evil.[34] It is not enough to simply say that God will one day make a new world in which there is no more pain or suffering. Even if the final generation experiences a perfect world, how would that do justice to all the evil that had persisted before? We cannot fully solve the POE merely through progress. Rather, atonement theories, like Christus Victor, must include a backward and forward dimension, as it were; they must recognize that Christ has taken on the guilt, sin, and shame of past generations, while also understanding that God has already defeated the principalities and powers, and that reality will be fully realized when God becomes all in all.[35] In short, Wright's strategy for addressing the POE is centered on Christ's overcoming of evil and how Christians should live that out. Though he has explained that humans and supernatural entities are responsible for evil, he does not believe we can ever find a concrete answer to where evil originates in the first place, or why it is ultimately in God's good creation.[36]

IV

John Feinberg has answered the POE from a Calvinistic perspective. For Feinberg, God does not eliminate evil from the world because if he did, that would mean he would be unable to create "non-glorified human beings."[37] Feinberg rejects libertarian free will in favor of soft determinism, and acknowledges there is a price to pay for that: in doing so, it would appear that God could create a world in which people always freely do what is right, given the compatibilists' definition of freedom. This would seem to justify

33. Wright, *Evil*, 90.
34. Wright, *Evil*, 95.
35. Wright, *Evil*, 96.
36. Wright, *Evil*, 136.
37. Feinberg, *No One Like Him*, 781.

Mackie's famous objection that Plantinga dealt with above. But God has not done this, says Feinberg, because of what he calls the Integrity of Humans Defense.[38] God created human beings who are both metaphysically and morally finite, who are capable of emotion and desire and intentionality. In doing so, he created humans with the capacity for evil thoughts and desires and this is exactly where evil acts originate: in our desires. Given all of this context, yes, it is possible that God could remove all evil from the world, considering compatibilism and the nature of the universe/humanity that he has created. In doing so, however, God would contradict other goals that he has within the universe, and God cannot actualize a contradiction: "It is my contention that if God did what is necessary to rid our world of moral evil, he would either contradict his intentions to create human beings and the world as he has; cause us to wonder if he has one or more of the attributes ascribed to him; and/or do something that we would not expect or desire him to do, because it would produce greater evil than there already is."[39]

In order to demonstrate this, Feinberg looks at what it would take for God to remove all evil from the world. God could theoretically rearrange the circumstances of everyone in the world so that they would produce only morally positive desires. Given compatibilist freedom, this would allow people to be free and yet only produce moral good. But it would be much harder for God to do this than we may imagine, given how intricately connected everyone's circumstances are. And, given that humanity has inherited a sinful nature from Adam, it seems it may be impossible for God to rearrange everyone's circumstances in such a way that would result in moral perfection on earth.[40] Perhaps God could remove all desires from humanity, but then we would not be human, or free in any relevant sense of the term. So, God could remove all moral evil from the world, but that would require him to create humans that are not free, and that do not experience any kind of desires.[41] Thus, Feinberg concludes, his defense maintains the logical consistency of evangelical Christianity.

V

Greg Boyd has written extensively on the POE. The issue has yet to be resolved, he argues, because it is logically unsolvable within the paradigm of classical theism. If God's sovereignty is to be thought of as meticulous

---

38. Feinberg, *No One Like Him*, 787.
39. Feinberg, *No One Like Him*, 789.
40. Feinberg, *No One Like Him*, 790.
41. Feinberg, *No One Like Him*, 795.

control of all events, then it is inescapable that God is responsible for evil and thus cannot be all-loving.[42] Boyd cites R. C. Sproul as a modern example of the classical view of sovereignty:

> If there is one single molecule in this universe running around loose, totally free of God's sovereignty, then we have no guarantee that a single promise of God will ever be fulfilled. Perhaps that one maverick molecule will lay waste all the grand and glorious plans that God has made and promised to us.... Maybe that one molecule will be the thing that prevents Christ from returning.[43]

This view of sovereignty is contrary to Scripture and is not logically warranted; instead, it is the result of Hellenistic philosophical impositions on Christian thought.[44] The biblical and pre-Augustinian view of God's providence, however, was more similar to what Boyd terms the warfare worldview. As opposed to everything unfolding according to God's eternal decree, the biblical authors and early Christians viewed God as being engaged in a spiritual war against evil, and this spiritual war greatly affected life on earth. For this reason, they did not conceive of the POE in the way that the post-Augustinian church has, because they did not view pain and suffering as part of God's plan at all. In this warfare worldview, there is not a single divine will behind the evil that unfolds in the universe.[45] We should expect to see evil in the universe since God's will is not behind every event that transpires.

Boyd cites several biblical examples to substantiate these claims. In Dan 10, Daniel prays to God for three weeks but does not immediately hear from God. He is eventually told by an angel from Yahweh that his prayer was heard by God, but the angel had been caught up by a cosmic power referred to as "the prince of the kingdom of Persia." Thankfully, Michael, a "chief prince," came to help the angel in his fight against the prince of Persia, and because of Michael's help, the angel was finally able to deliver the message to Daniel from God.[46] Other similar biblical episodes are presented as proof of the warfare worldview. Job's affliction is ultimately not from God but is rather from Satan. Jesus himself taught that not all catastrophes are indications of God's will or action (Luke 13:1–5). At times, even deafness or muteness was not the result of God's will or a person's sinfulness, but rather

---

42. Boyd, *God at War*, 44.
43. Sproul, *Chosen by God*, 26–27, cited in Boyd, *God at War*, 39.
44. Boyd, *God at War*, 67.
45. Boyd, *God at War*, 20.
46. Boyd, *God at War*, 9–10.

the result of demonic activity (Mark 9:25). Paul himself could not reach Thessalonica, not because God did not will it, but because of the hindrance of Satan (1 Thess 2:18).[47] Most people, Boyd argues, never think that the reason a prayer was not answered is due to an angelic battle in the spiritual realm; in contrast, most think in terms of God saying yes or no, or God saying no and thus allowing evil for some greater purpose. Neither do people tend to think of sickness in these terms.[48] Even Arminian theologians and others who deny Calvinism often do not think in terms of the warfare worldview.[49]

The reason that most modern Christians, even non-Calvinists, do not think in terms of the warfare worldview is that they have a kind of "blueprint" view of divine providence wherein everything that happens is a part of God's plan, despite their supposed emphasis on human freedom. This is due to multiple factors. Augustinian influence in the West is primarily to blame in so far as, if everything unfolds according to God's plan, then the aforementioned spiritual war doesn't seem to be a war at all; it is more of a "sham" seeing as that it was all God's plan in the first place.[50] The other major reason for the abandonment of the warfare worldview in the Western Christian world is the belief in exhaustive divine foreknowledge. For Boyd, if God exhaustively knows the future as a concrete reality, if God knows with certainty what choices humans will make in the future, then creaturely freedom cannot be consistently maintained.[51] On the classical view of omniscience, it is difficult to see how the future is not exhaustively determined, which gives credence to the blueprint view of divine providence as opposed to the warfare worldview. This is not to say that one has to embrace the open view of the future in order to embrace the warfare worldview; it is just to say that if one adheres to the warfare worldview while also believing in the classical view of omniscience, then they do so inconsistently.[52]

Holding to an open view of the future will give the Christian an advantage in espousing the warfare worldview. Genuine freedom implies risk, says Boyd. And this notion of God taking a risk when creating seems incompatible with God having exhaustive definite foreknowledge of all future

---

47. Boyd, *God at War*, 52–53.
48. Boyd, *God at War*, 10.
49. Boyd, *God at War*, 49.
50. Boyd, *God at War*, 67. Here, Boyd says that the Augustinian view of divine providence was heavily influenced by the classical view of God. Namely, he cites immutability, timelessness, impassibility, and the view that God is *actus purus*.
51. Boyd, *God at War*, 49–50.
52. Boyd, *Satan*, 86–87.

events.[53] If God has exhaustive definite foreknowledge, then there are no open possibilities for God. For this reason, it seems implausible that we can ascribe genuine risk to God concerning his decision to create; if God only engages in activities in which he knows with certainty the outcome, then it doesn't seem as though there is any risk involved with his decisions. The classical Arminian view of foreknowledge certainly does nothing to mitigate these concerns, as that view states God can act in response to his foreknowledge and include those actions in his eternal decree. If God can alter his eternal decree by including divine permission for acts he knows free creatures will carry out, then certainly one cannot say there is risk on God's part in creating.[54] Simple foreknowledge, conversely, claims that God cannot act on his foreknowledge. In other words, he has exhaustive definite foreknowledge of the future, but this knowledge comes logically after his decision to create. In this view, God knows what will take place within creation, but cannot act on this knowledge to alter the course of events. This view, Boyd says, does away with some of the concerns regarding the compatibility of freedom and the classical Arminian view of foreknowledge.[55] At the same time, this view of foreknowledge still has some deficiencies when compared to the open view of the future. One such problem is that simple foreknowledge, or any other view of exhaustive definite foreknowledge, is simply not compatible with the biblical data, in that the Bible depicts God as facing a partially open future. Additionally, simple foreknowledge does not seem to allow God to intervene in the world at all. How can God respond to anything if he is unable to act based on his foreknowledge? And lastly, this view does not make any practical difference in the life of God or of humans. Everything proceeds as though God did not have any foreknowledge; thus, the view is irrelevant.[56] The open view, in contrast, holds that God faced the possibility but not the certainty that free creatures would revolt against him. Consequently, the open view allows Christians to affirm that God entered into a rather risky endeavor when creating the world; and this allows Christians to consistently argue that evil is the result of free will and that God is in no way responsible for evil.[57]

Free moral agents are responsible for evil in the world, whether they be humans or angelic beings. And in time, Satan became an immensely

---

53. Boyd, *Satan*, 86.

54. Boyd, *Satan*, 89.

55. Boyd, *Satan*, 89: "This view can ascribe genuine risk to God and is thus fully compatible with the trinitarian warfare theodicy."

56. Boyd, *Satan*, 89–90.

57. Boyd, *Satan*, 91–92.

powerful spiritual being who rejected God and his ways. The early Christian understanding was that Satan came to rule over the earth; he was the explanation for the pervasiveness of evil in the world. The New Testament recognizes Satan as the prince of the present age.[58] First John 5:9 tells us that the entire world is under the power of the evil one. Second Corinthians 4:4 goes as far as to say that he is the god of this world. This is the occasion of the ministry of Jesus: the world had been taken captive by evil cosmic forces and God was on a mission to defeat these forces and reconcile creation to himself.[59] The activity of Satan and lesser demonic forces is where the ultimate explanation for evil truly lies. This applies even to supposed "natural" evil. The New Testament views nature not as existing and operating on its own, but rather as being continuously influenced by invisible, spiritual beings. At times these beings influence it for the better while at other times they influence it for the worse.[60] For this reason, Boyd argues that there is no such thing as natural evil, only evil that we see in nature that is the result of the activity of demonic forces in rebellion against God. He asserts that Jesus himself did not agree that "natural" evil was simply the result of nature, nor the result of God's activity. Instead, he denies that natural evils were the result of divine punishment (Luke 13:4–5, John 9:1–4). Jesus also views natural infirmities and storms as being either the direct or indirect result of demonic activity (Mark 4:35–41, 9:25, etc.).[61] Many in the early church affirmed this view when they declared that God had appointed angels to oversee different parts of the world. Justin Martyr, for example, proclaimed that God had committed the care of men and nature to angels, but some angels had transgressed the appointment.[62]

At this point, one may be tempted to ask why God does not simply destroy the spiritual beings that are rebelling against him and causing so much harm in the world. Even if these creatures are genuinely free, as Boyd has argued, God could surely stop them given his omnipotence. However, the reason that God does not do this is because he cannot immediately terminate their existence.[63] This is not a denial of God's omnipotence, as the reason God cannot immediately destroy these beings is something intrinsic to himself. A metaphysical implication of God creating free moral beings is

---

58. Boyd, *Satan*, 35.
59. Boyd, *Satan*, 35.
60. Boyd, *Satan*, 247.
61. Boyd, *Satan*, 253.
62. Justin Martyr, *Second Apology* 5, cited in Boyd, *Satan*, 39–47. Boyd goes on to cite several others to substantiate this point, including Origen, Athenagoras, Tatian, and Tertullian.
63. Boyd, *Satan*, 181.

that he must allow them to exercise their influence over time, whether they be obedient to him or rebellious.[64] A rational nature does not truly possess the power to love or to rebel unless it has a temporal duration in which to exercise this capacity. If God were to immediately annihilate any being who turned against him, then the choice to follow his will would essentially be coerced, as opposed to being free: "The choice to love God or not (as well as every other choice between godly and ungodly alternatives) would have the same moral character as the 'choice' to breathe or not."[65] Thus it can be argued that God must endure the activities of these spiritual beings for some time if they are to be free moral creatures.

VI

Richard Swinburne has also written extensively on the POE. Like Boyd, he emphasizes the freedom of the will in order to explain why evil exists. Because of their free will and rational nature, humans are able to form various thoughts in their heads. They can form intentions to do good or to do evil. And they must be able to carry out these intentions at least to some degree, otherwise the world we live in would be deceptive, and a good God would not subject free creatures to a fundamentally deceptive world.[66] The opportunities that humans have to make a significant impact on the world inevitably lead to the possibility of evil. However, Swinburne argues that many of these opportunities for evil are necessary for us to have the opportunity to do good in the world. So, God is justified in creating a world in which evil is possible.

The chance to choose one's destiny, as it were, is inevitably a chance for evil to occur. In choosing one's own destiny, one must acquire knowledge, form habits that distinguish character, and determine to what we will give ourselves pleasure.[67] We have these choices as individuals, but humanity also has them as an entity. For example, as we discover more about the laws of nature, we have the choice to build rockets to go to the moon, to build atomic bombs, to cure cancer, or to not bother with any of it.[68] A good God would give humanity a plethora of choices so that we could be truly free to make decisions and, in some way, determine who we want to be. Swinburne contends that God, since he wanted a genuine relationship with

64. Boyd, *Satan*, 181.
65. Boyd, *Satan*, 183.
66. Swinburne, *Existence of God*, 219.
67. Swinburne, *Existence of God*, 220.
68. Swinburne, *Existence of God*, 222.

truly free creatures, would ensure that we are able to make decisions to the point of even shaping our own character. This would entail many small and large decisions over a decent span of time; consequently, we choose to form our own character intentionally instead of through mere impulse.[69] With all of these decisions to make, the possibility of evil is inevitable; but that is the metaphysical cost of genuine freedom.

Still, even if one accepts Swinburne's premise regarding freedom, a common question remains: what about death? Why does natural death in the world need to exist? Could not God have created a world in which all beings are immortal and yet still free? To this, Swinburne responds in a few notable ways. First, if all agents were to be immortal, then there is a type of negative action that they would not be able to take: they would not be able to end the existence of another free agent. If this were so, then it would demonstrate that God did not trust his creation to be truly free.[70] Second, if there were no death in the world, then ultimate sacrifice would not itself be possible. He quotes Jesus to say, "Greater love hath no man than this, that a man lay down his life for his friends." There would be no possibility of rescue from death and thus no possibility of supreme generosity.[71] Third, a world without natural death would take away from the seriousness of one's actions in so far as, if one had unlimited time to undo mistakes, then there would be virtually no consequence to one's choices.[72] Fourth, "a world with birth but without natural death would be a world in which the young would never have a free hand. They would always be inhibited by the experience and influence of the aged."[73] And lastly, perhaps the greatest value of a world with natural death is that it puts a limit on the amount of suffering a creature can inflict on another. Yes, creatures must be free to do evil things if they are to be genuinely free; however, this does not entail the ability to inflict unending suffering on others. Natural death, it seems, is a good God's way of limiting the scope of evil that free creatures are willing to partake in.[74]

Lastly, Swinburne's interaction with natural evil will be discussed. He finds some of the traditional responses to the problem of natural evil to be deficient. For example, some have asserted that natural evils such as disease and severe accidents serve the purpose of punishing someone for their sins. Though this could in theory account for some natural evil, it certainly cannot

---

69. Swinburne, *Existence of God*, 222.
70. Swinburne, *Existence of God*, 229.
71. Swinburne, *Existence of God*, 229.
72. Swinburne, *Existence of God*, 229.
73. Swinburne, *Existence of God*, 229.
74. Swinburne, *Existence of God*, 229–31.

explain natural disasters that impact children or animals.[75] Then there is the defense that says God uses nature to reward or punish the decedents of various people who are either obedient or disobedient to his will. Again, even if true, this could not account for all natural evil. A third defense is more robust, but still somewhat problematic: this is the idea that natural evils of all kinds are caused by supernatural agents such as fallen angels or demons. This defense is similar to Boyd's thesis regarding the POE, and Swinburne suggests it could theoretically account for all types of natural evil.[76] The deficiency lies in the fact that it adds an additional hypothesis to theism, in that it requires the existence of independent beings such as demons who have at least partial control over nature. There is little independent evidence of such a claim; in addition, theism does not require it to be true.[77]

With the traditional responses to the problem of natural evil being defective, Swinburne turns to two further reasons as to why God would bring about natural evil. This defense is termed the "higher-order defense."[78] The central claim here is that natural evil provides opportunities for valuable emotional response and free choice. Without natural evil, our ability to make free decisions would be significantly impacted. Something like the good of compassion can only be felt if others are suffering. A world with at least some amount of pain and compassion is at least as good as a world with no pain or compassion.[79] Ultimately, it is good to have a deep concern for others. Moreover, there are certain types of choices that are only possible if a response to evil is possible. Choices demonstrating sympathy and courage, for example, are only possible if there is evil in the world; and it is a good thing that we can choose to be courageous or sympathetic, or to perform an action of the sort.[80] In short, by bringing about or allowing natural evil to occur, God gives us the opportunity to choose to do good in ways that would not be possible in a world without suffering.[81]

The second substantiation of the higher-order defense is that natural evil helps to give humans the knowledge required to make significantly free choices. If a free agent is to have the ability to bring about evil or to prevent evil, then they must know how to do both.[82] Essentially, Swinburne argues

---

75. Swinburne, *Existence of God*, 238–39.
76. Swinburne, *Existence of God*, 239.
77. Swinburne, *Existence of God*, 239–40.
78. Swinburne, *Existence of God*, 240.
79. Swinburne, *Existence of God*, 240.
80. Swinburne, *Existence of God*, 241.
81. Swinburne, *Existence of God*, 243.
82. Swinburne, *Existence of God*, 245.

that in order for humans to have this level of knowledge, a good amount of data is needed regarding suffering and evil. For instance, someone may not take precautions against a house fire or disease unless they know of or have seen these things themselves.[83] Observing that one can suffer from a disease or house fire gives one the ability to choose whether or not they will inflict these disasters upon someone else.[84] And, if God normally unilaterally prevented disaster for those who could not help themselves, then it is unlikely that others would not step in to help those in need. A knowledge that disasters can occur and how exactly they occur is necessary for humans to be able to choose to do many different kinds of good or evil.[85]

VII

Process theologians will typically deny omnipotence, at least as it has been traditionally defined.[86] This has radical implications for their response to the POE. One such theologian is Thomas Oord. He has argued that although God is the most powerful being in existence, he is not omnipotent; rather, he is amipotent.[87] God does not control everything, nor is everything the result of his doing. He cannot act against his nature, override free will, change the past, or do what is logically impossible. Other theologians who believe God is omnipotent make similar claims, but Oord challenges these claims as he argues such qualifications render the term meaningless.[88] It is better to completely redefine what we mean when we describe God as powerful. In doing so, we should not only claim that God won't stop all evil, but that he cannot stop all evil.[89]

In recounting the 2017 Las Vegas mass shooting committed by Stephen Paddock, Oord says some struggle with why God did not stop such a horrendous event. Couldn't God have temporarily paralyzed the gunman, or jammed the rifles, or caused all of the bullets to miss their targets? All

---

83. Swinburne, *Existence of God*, 248.
84. Swinburne, *Is There a God?*, 94.
85. Swinburne, *Existence of God*, 252.
86. For one such explicit example, see Hartshorne, *Omnipotence*.
87. Oord, *Open and Relational Theology*, 81. Oord: "I coined this word by combining the Latin word for power—'potent'—with a Latin prefix for love—'ami.' From 'potent' we get words like 'potential' and 'potency.' We find the 'ami' prefix in love words like 'amity,' 'amigo,' and 'amicable.'"
88. Oord, *Open and Relational Theology*, 81.
89. Oord, *God Can't*, 17.

of these objections presuppose that God has the ability to do such things.[90] But, "to put it more precisely, God can't prevent evil singlehandedly."[91] This is a necessary belief if we are to maintain that God is truly loving. If God had the power to unilaterally prevent evil but chose not to do so, then God would not be loving in any meaningful sense of the word. Would a loving doctor allow a baby to die if he or she could prevent it? Would a loving mother freely allow her infant to drown? And would a loving uncle allow sex traffickers to kidnap his niece? If we say no to these questions, then on what basis can we say a loving God would allow such things? The word "love" would lose all coherence at that point.[92] Further, if Jesus is the perfect revelation of God, then Christians should not say that God allows evil when he otherwise could have prevented it. Could we imagine Jesus being physically present while someone is abused and him simply allowing the abuse to occur? No, says Oord, so if the perfect revelation of God is Jesus Christ, then this alone should be evidence that God would unilaterally stop all evil if he could.[93]

And this should not be a scandalous claim, as the Bible itself says there are many things God cannot do. For instance, God cannot lie (Titus 1:2), be tempted (Jas 1:13), grow tired (Isa 40:28), or deny himself (2 Tim 2:13).[94] Combine this information with the Bible's claim that God is love in his very essence (1 John 4:8, 16) and one can see that God would stop all evil if he could. Sure, there are some biblical passages, especially in the Old Testament, which give credence to the idea that God is not always loving or merciful. However, those passages are better considered to be cries of the oppressed; they are reflections of the suffering that the writers themselves experienced and oversaw. They are not accurate descriptions of the God who always loves. The majority witness of the Bible is that God is always loving, and Oord accepts the majority witness on the matter.[95] God's love is always empowering and is inherently uncontrolling.[96]

---

90. Oord, *God Can't*, 2.
91. Oord, *God Can't*, 17.
92. Oord, *God Can't*, 18–20.
93. Oord, *God Can't*, 21.
94. Oord, *God Can't*, 23.
95. Oord, *God Can't*, 25–26.

96. Oord, *God Can't*, 28. It is important to note here that Oord also says God is a bodiless spirit, with the implication being that he cannot do some things that one with a body could do. He cannot physically stop certain things from happening because he does not have a body. God is present and active in all situations, but his power is necessarily persuasive and not coercive. See pp. 30–34.

As well as being unable to unilaterally stop evil in the world, God also feels our pain. He is there to comfort us even when no one else may be. God relates on an intimate level with those who experience evil and feels what they feel.[97] To put it most precisely, God feels empathy toward us. He does not just pity us, as though he is vaguely aware of whatever suffering is going on in the world. Rather, he engages in emotional unity with us; he experiences what we experiences in his very nature.[98] Paul describes something like this when he says God consoles us in our afflictions (1 Cor 1:3). God never gets empathy fatigue. Instead, he responds to all pain and suffering with resilient hope.[99] Oord also points to Jesus's parable of the prodigal son to further validate his point. Jesus describes God in that parable as a Father who feels compassion, who is moved by his love for his son and is motivated by that love to act accordingly.[100] As opposed to being responsible for evil, God's relationship to evil is similar to ours: he endures pain and suffering along with us.

In addition to enduring evil with us, God also works to heal pain and suffering. Oord acknowledges what he calls the "problem of selective healing" which essentially objects to God's being good due to the fact that he does not heal everyone who asks it of him. If God has the power to heal everyone, then why doesn't he, especially when they ask him?[101] Some may blame the Devil or demonic activity, or even a lack of faith on the part of the one asking for healing, but these answers are unsatisfactory. God is more powerful than the demons, so he could heal someone even if those demons try to stop him. In addition, it is grotesque to tell an abuse victim or someone suffering from sickness or trauma that they just don't have enough faith for God to heal them. Why would a loving God wait until they built up enough faith to heal them anyway? Others appeal to divine mystery, as though God's mysterious plan includes forcing children and others to die from cancer, and this is somehow better than if they did not. For Oord, none of these answers demonstrate that God is loving in any significant sense.[102]

Since these more traditional sentiments associated with the problem of selective healing are incompatible with a loving God, Oord claims Christians must construct a new understanding of divine healing. This starts with an understanding that God is omnipresent. Yes, many Christians claim

---

97. Oord, *God Can't*, 48.
98. Oord, *God Can't*, 49.
99. Oord, *God Can't*, 53.
100. Oord, *God Can't*, 59.
101. Oord, *God Can't*, 81.
102. Oord, *God Can't*, 82.

they believe God is omnipresent, but they do so inconsistently, according to Oord. Seeing as that God is already active and involved with all of creation, we need not beg him to intervene in some scenario or another. This is what it means to say that God is love and that he is omnipresent: God is always working toward the good of all his creation and is present in every circumstance.[103] And God is already working to heal as much as he can: "God is always at work everywhere healing to the utmost possible, given the circumstances."[104] However, God is never the sole cause in any given situation as there are always other agents participating, whether they be good, or bad, or indifferent. The key here, somewhat obviously, is that although God is at work in every situation to heal as much as he can, the fact remains that he cannot heal single-handedly or unilaterally. This explains why some do not experience the healing that they need: "But when creatures fail to cooperate or the conditions are not right, God's work to heal is frustrated."[105] God's healing requires cooperation at all levels of reality because God always practices uncontrolling love. The woman who asks God to heal her from her depression may not be healed because she is the unwilling subject of an abusive relationship; and the teenager with cancer may not be healed because his cancerous cells may not respond to God's direct influence or to the influence that the physicians administer.[106]

VIII

John Cobb has expressed similar views to Oord's as they relate to understanding the power of God, albeit in a more academic tone. For Cobb, the Christian solution to the POE is to be found in a proper conception of divine power.[107] Some have said that perhaps evil can be explained by the presence of entities within the universe that God does not have control over. This is unsatisfactory, however, as his power is thus conceived as inconsequential and perhaps even nonexistent.[108] What the classical doctrine of omnipotence and the theory of limited power both miss is that they assume a faulty

103. Oord, *God Can't*, 89.

104. Oord, *God Can't*, 90. Here, Oord lists people like physicians, nurses, pharmacists, medical specialists, nutritionists, and "alternative" healers as those whom God works in and through to heal people in the world. God inspires them and works alongside them. The question, "Did God heal you or did a doctor do it?" is a false dichotomy. All healing has God as the ultimate source.

105. Oord, *God Can't*, 93.

106. Oord, *God Can't*, 95.

107. Cobb, *God and the World*, 87.

108. Cobb, *God and the World*, 88.

definition of power wherein it is understood as the ability to determine what is to be and what is not to be. If power is conceived in this way, then there can be no ultimately coherent answer to the POE.[109] Similar to Oord, Cobb then asserts that Christians must, on a very basic level, reconceptualize the very notion of divine power.

Due to classically prevailing definitions, power is often conceived by Christians in terms of compulsion or force. God has the power to force anything that is logically possible, and this is what makes him omnipotent. In following Charles Hartshorne, Cobb argues that this way of thinking about omnipotence leads to the conclusion that God is really the only power in existence. There is no competing power, and thus the power of God means very little. The power to lead an army of toy soldiers is given even to kids; but the power required to lead an army of men who retain their capacity to resist is comparably greater, given that their power competes with that of the leader: "The power that counts is the power to influence the exercise of power by others."[110] If power is reconceptualized in such terms, then God may still be described as omnipotent, given that Christians may say God is the most persuasive power in the universe.[111] With this understanding of power, Christians can fully account for the evil in the world without limiting God's goodness.

And since God's power is always persuasive in nature, it is inconsistent to say that he created the very matter in the universe from nothing.[112] This is not the kind of power that God possesses. God is limited by the nature and quantity of the matter and must act accordingly. God is always acting upon the world that is given to him, attempting to shape it for the good, but he did not unilaterally determine its entire evolutionary direction since the Big Bang. In fact, Cobb argues, "There is no reason to suppose that the world once came into being out of nothing, or that any precise goal or unalterable, specific purpose has guided its development."[113] Because of this, we must not ask why God caused the world to be just like it is; rather, we must ask why God seeks to persuade the world in the way that he does. This has implications for things like natural evil, for instance. Volcanoes

---

109. Cobb, *God and the World*, 88.

110. Cobb, *God and the World*, 89.

111. Cobb, *God and the World*, 90.

112. Process theologians typically assert that matter is coeternal with God and thus deny *creatio ex nihilo*. This is largely due to their understanding of the nature of God's power and has implications for Cobb's solution to the POE in particular. See further discussion in Cobb, *God and the World*, 89–93; Feinberg, *No One Like Him*, 160–61; and Oord, *Open and Relational Theology*, 62–64, 94.

113. Cobb, *God and the World*, 91.

and earthquakes indeed destroy life, but that could only have been avoided if life had waited until a higher degree of physical order was obtained. There is, however, a chance that if life had been postponed until such a point, the emergence of life on our planet may simply have become impossible by that time.[114] But it is better to have a world full of life with occasional devastating outbreaks than a world with no life at all. The ultimate point here for Cobb is that when God's power is understood as fundamentally persuasive in nature, then much of the evil in the world can be attributed to the incapacity of subhuman entities to be moved toward inclusive goals, which entail both their immediate and long-term satisfaction, as well as the maintenance of an order that enables other entities to do the same.[115]

As for humanity, it has been considered by some a viable complaint toward God that he made us with such a capacity to inflict harm on one another. But Cobb points out that we must understand God's creation of humankind from a process point of view. This entails that God has not created us as the highest form of conceivable being; if this were the case, then the complaint against God would be justified, as he could have easily made us into beings with a much greater tendency toward considering the welfare of others. Essentially, humankind should not be considered the result of God's direct willing us into being. On the contrary, God's creation of humanity should be conceived as his persuading nature toward "life, consciousness, maximum intensity, and freedom."[116] God is then not responsible for our seeming propensity toward violence and sin. He is still somewhat responsible for evil in the world though, as he is somewhat responsible for life itself. But he is only responsible for evil in so far as he has created the good, for evil can only exist where there is goodness; an earthquake or a tornado would be neither good nor evil in a world without life.[117] Only when there is value can value be taken away. The very possibility of sin and evil are the price paid for life, human freedom, and human consciousness: "Sin exists as the corruption of the capacity for love. Thus God creating good provides the context within which there is evil."[118] God is constantly working for the balance of good to triumph over evil. And the evil that we do endure God endures as well. God has not subjected us to evil that he himself is not willing to face with us; he feels the pain that we feel. The cross has long been a Christian symbol of this idea, but Cobb argues that it is only recently that

114. Cobb, *God and the World*, 93.
115. Cobb, *God and the World*, 94–95.
116. Cobb, *God and the World*, 95.
117. Cobb, *God and the World*, 96.
118. Cobb, *God and the World*, 96.

Christian theologians have taken the idea seriously.[119] God is more of a victim of evil than a propagator of it.

IX

David Ray Griffin has written the most thorough work on the POE from a process perspective.[120] He, like most process thinkers, has said that there can be no adequate answer to the POE if one attempts to do such a thing within the context of classical or traditional understandings of God.[121] Traditional ideas about God's role in the world and the nature of God's power must be reexamined. And when this is done from a process perspective, it is possible to provide an adequate theodicy while remaining faithful to the Christian faith.

What will ultimately separate traditional theodicies from a process theodicy is the traditional insistence that God is the actual or potential controller of all events that unfold within the universe.[122] Griffin argues that the nontraditional approach to the POE succeeds where traditional theism fails due to its willingness to undercut this fundamental assumption. Because of this, however, some have maintained that the process view of God portrays him as unworthy of worship. If one is to answer the POE from a process perspective, one must answer it in such a way so as to illustrate that God not only exists but is worthy of worship and praise. It is not enough to show that God's existence may not be contradicted by the presence of evil in the world; the theist must demonstrate that God's existence can better illuminate the totality of our experience than that of the atheist's interpretations of the world.[123] It may be said that the process view of omnipotence makes God weak but making a doctrine coherent is not synonymous with weakening it.[124] God is in some sense finite here, but since the world is actual, God cannot literally be the infinite or all that there is; though the accusation of belief in a finite God is typically a pejorative, it should be considered an implication of logical coherence. Traditional theism can verbalize its own notion of divine omnipotence, but this does not entail rational consistency. Thus, one cannot use the traditional view of God as a standard by which to

---

119. Cobb, *God and the World*, 97.
120. Griffin, *God, Power, and Evil*.
121. Griffin, *God, Power, and Evil*, 12.
122. Griffin, *God, Power, and Evil*, 251.
123. Griffin, *God, Power, and Evil*, 256.
124. Griffin, *God, Power, and Evil*, 272.

judge the logically consistent view of God given by the process theists.[125] If the classical view of God is in fact a contradiction given the existence of evil in the world, then as a logical contradiction it cannot be used as an adequate comparison to the process view of God. God is worthy of worship because he is the perfect reality who loves us; this simply does not entail the ability to unilaterally end evil. Since traditional theism's conception of divine omnipotence is logically incompatible with evil in the world, process theism's rejection of it cannot be considered a perversion of divine perfection.[126]

Having established that the process view of God does indeed lend itself to worshipfulness, Griffin moves to explaining how God's existence, properly conceived, is compatible with and makes sense of the evil we see in the world. There are three essential elements to the process solution to the POE. One has already been discussed at length: God's power is centrally persuasive, not controlling.[127] The second element of the solution is to recognize that there are two dimensions of intrinsic evil as opposed to one. These two criteria can be summed up as "disharmony" and "triviality" which are the opposite of Whitehead's two criteria for intrinsic good, which were "harmony" and "intensity."[128] Disharmony is an evil in and of itself, whereas triviality is evil only in a comparative sense, "i.e., if an experience is more trivial than it needed to be."[129] The recognition of these two criteria make it more difficult to rate an experience strictly in terms of intrinsic goodness in so far as a harmonious experience cannot simply be asserted to be better than an experience that is discordant. One must consider the triviality or intensity of such an experience. Thus, "encouraging the emergence of forms of experience which will be more intense but also more discordant than present ones is not necessarily inconsistent with moral goodness."[130] This will have radical implications for understanding God's involvement with the emergence of the evolutionary process within the universe. Griffin argues that while most focus on discord when dealing with evil, many ignore the fact that unnecessary triviality must also be overcome if the highest good is to be achieved.

---

125. Griffin, *God, Power, and Evil*, 272.

126. Griffin, *God, Power, and Evil*, 273.

127. Griffin, *God, Power, and Evil*, 276.

128. Griffin, *God, Power, and Evil*, 282. Disharmony occurs when two or more elements of an experience clash and create feelings of mutual destructiveness. Whitehead here was speaking of something like the feeling of pain or mental evils like horror or sorrow. Triviality refers to things like boredom and lack of zest or excitement.

129. Griffin, *God, Power, and Evil*, 284.

130. Griffin, *God, Power, and Evil*, 285.

If the only evil for God to avoid were that of discord, then the best way for God to avoid such evil would be for him to refuse to create. When thinking in these terms, one may expect a perfectly good God to refuse to bring any beings into existence who were capable of pain and suffering.[131] There is more to moral goodness than the avoidance of suffering, however. To be morally good is also to have the intention to bring about intrinsically rewarding experiences. This is vital to understanding how a morally perfect being could, in any way, bring about a universe wherein there is evil.

One of the reasons process thought can coherently claim God is good is that God has brought about social order from absolute chaos. It is true that within process philosophy, there have always been finite actualities; nevertheless, there is no reason to think that the types of universal order exemplified in our universe today have always been present. Outside of very fundamental principles that are seen as metaphysically necessary, there is good reason to believe that the forms of order we see in the universe have evolved from lesser forms. For this reason, Whitehead posited that there have been a series of cosmic ages, and they were not always as ordered and life producing as our current age is.[132] When a cosmic age dissolves, there is chaos that ensues; for this reason, the creation of our current cosmic age can be thought of as bringing order to chaos.[133] In a state of absolute chaos, there would be very few enduring entities. When God brings order to this chaos, he overcomes experiences that are incredibly trivial; by doing this, God increases intensity of experiences, which is a way to bring about goodness. Though there may be some forms of discord in our universe today, there is also certainly more intensity of experience than there would be in a universe without life. It can thus be said that God has brought about moral goodness by persuading nature toward a more ordered and lively end.

The third and final step of a process theodicy is "the explication of the correlations involving value and power that are implicit in the foregoing sketch of the evolutionary process by which the present state of our world was created out of a more chaotic state."[134] For instance, Griffin discusses the positive correlation between the capacity for intrinsic goodness and the

---

131. Griffin, *God, Power, and Evil*, 285.

132. Griffin, *God, Power, and Evil*, 285–86.

133. Griffin, *God, Power, and Evil*, 286.

134. Griffin, *God, Power, and Evil*, 291. "These correlations involve the following variables: (1) the capacity for intrinsic goodness; (2) the capacity for intrinsic evil; (3) freedom or the power of self-determination; (4) the capacity for instrumental goodness, or the power to contribute to the intrinsic good of others; (5) the capacity for instrumental evil, or the power to be destructive of the potential intrinsic goodness of others."

power of self-determination: one is not possible without the other, as most theodicies have stated in some form or another. There can be no significant degree of intrinsic value or goodness if conscious entities do not possess a significant form of freedom; if there is trivial freedom, then the value it produces is trivial.[135] The intensity of this reality is heightened by the fact that humans have a high degree of capacity to inflict both good and evil upon one another. Another correlation that Griffin discusses is that between the capacity for intrinsic goodness and the capacity for intrinsic evil. His comments are similar to that of the former correlation, in that the possibility of enjoying the good entails the possibility of enduring evil. If we have the capacity to enjoy various bodily, moral, and religious goods then we also have the capacity to reject these and make ourselves miserable.[136] He goes on, but the point is obvious: once the relationship between value and power are properly examined, it will become clear that God cannot unilaterally create a world in which there is no evil, and by creating the world we have, he has brought about goodness that would have otherwise failed to exist.

---

135. Griffin, *God, Power, and Evil*, 292.
136. Griffin, *God, Power, and Evil*, 294.

Chapter 6

Classical Theism and the Problem of Evil

I

CLASSICAL THEISTS HAVE PUSHED back against some of the more modern attempts to respond to the POE. Many contemporary classical theists have argued that some current approaches to the POE compromise the essentials of Christian faith, while offering less than satisfactory answers to the dilemma. Brian Davies is one such scholar who has done this. Perhaps some in contemporary theology have too hastily dismissed the idea that God uses evil in the world to bring about good that could not exist without the evil. We all acknowledge, Davies argues, that there are times when we must endure a temporary evil in order to enjoy an eventual good. A dentist must drill into or even extract a tooth to relieve a tooth ache from time to time.[1] Though some have claimed God's omnipotence should do away with the need for him to cause or permit evil in order to accomplish any particular good, this is ultimately mistaken. There are certain things God cannot do, such a lie, ride a bike to work, or even something as mundane as taking a bath. In addition, God cannot do the logically impossible.[2] This has, of course, been stated *ad nauseam* throughout the centuries. However, the implications of such realizations are still relevant for us today. God cannot bring about every X without also bringing about some Y.[3]

---

1. Davies, *Reality of God*, 112.
2. Davies, *Reality of God*, 113.
3. Davies, *Reality of God*, 115.

But can we really use this realization as a means to exonerate God concerning the existence of evil in the universe? Davies is not so sure. Though he does not deny the reality of human freedom, he does not view the typical free will defense as being adequate when it comes to answering the POE. It does not seem that libertarian human freedom is necessary for us to love our friends and families; if we accepted that we did not have such freedom, we would not love our families any less. Is a world with no human freedom, pain, or suffering any better than a world wherein we freely wreak havoc on one another? It does not seem so, given that we would not love our family members any less even if we lacked such freedom.[4] Moreover, the free will defense depends on the presupposition that people are able to act freely as though their freedom is independent of God's causal action.[5] The very existence of the world and the people in the world is constantly dependent on God continually sustaining it. Even if people do act freely, they do so within God's causal power. God is the source of all that is in existence, including one's free actions.[6] To deny this, Davies argues, is to assert that God is but one additional item in the universe that can distance himself from other items in the universe so as to allow them to act independently. This does not entail that human freedom is an illusion, but it does mean that even human free will choices fall under God's providence, as Aquinas argued.[7] Nonetheless, given that human freedom is dependent on God's causal power for its existence, Mackie's assertion that God could have made free humans who never sin seems to be correct. Some theists have rejected this premise. Davies, however, agrees with Mackie that there is strong reason to believe that God could have done this; therefore, the free will defense seems inadequate in responding to the POE.[8]

Concerning "nonmoral evil," the typical means and ends arguments from scholars such as Swinburne and Hick are rejected by Davies. For Swinburne, certain kinds of natural evil are necessary in order for various kinds of good to be achieved. Suffering from natural disasters is sometimes

---

4. Davies, *Reality of God*, 117–19. His point here is that we would not value any less the things that are most important to us if we lacked libertarian freedom.

5. Davies, *Reality of God*, 121.

6. Davies, *Reality of God*, 122.

7. Davies, *Reality of God*, 123. Davies asserts that Aquinas viewed human choice as an example of something that is not necessitated by anything in the universe. But that does not mean that human choice is not still dependent on God's causal power, given that God is the source of all being. God does not cause something like a creature may cause something; if he did, then his omnicausality may be a threat to human freedom. Conversely, God causes human freedom in so far as he makes humans to be creatures who act freely. See pp. 124–28.

8. Davies, *Reality of God*, 128–29.

necessary in order for someone to act heroically or empathetically. As for John Hick, he asserts that pain and suffering are essential for humanity to develop morally.[9] Each have their reasons, some of which have been pointed out in this book, but Davies says both are mistaken in their reasoning. If we were to morally justify God based on Hick's arguments, what would we have to say to the victims of evil? That they suffered so someone else could morally improve? This would in no way morally justify God, as he would be a God who would be acting in such a way so as to persuade us to concentrate on ourselves at the expense of others.[10] Moreover, we would be saying that evil is necessary for good to exist. Yes, there are certain kinds of good, perhaps, to which evil necessarily is a prelude. But it is quite an odd suggestion to argue that one is morally justified in putting someone in such dire need just so someone else can come help them.[11] For Davies, these arguments surely do not morally justify God in any meaningful sense.

Davies rejects other answers to the POE, such as evil being inflicted on us by God as just punishment for our sins, or the Leibnizian idea that God created the best of all possible worlds. For our purposes, there is one last idea that he rejects that is especially pertinent: that God suffers from evil just as humans do. Some names that Davies connects to this way of thinking are Jurgen Moltmann and Jon Sobrino. In essence, when this way of thinking about God is employed in response to the POE, God has nothing to answer to since he is himself a victim of evil.[12] Ultimately, this is a failure to distinguish between the Creator and the creature; Davies goes as far as to say it is "idolatrous."[13] God is the reason why there is something and nothing at all, so he cannot be on the receiving end of something external to himself. There are no good philosophical reasons for believing that God suffers along with creation. But Moltmann and Sobrino do not seem to be interested in philosophy at all, according to Davies. So, more to the point of their arguments, a God who suffers is not to be admired more than an impassible God. Suffering is not something to be admired in and of itself, despite the fact that some entities which suffer are to be valued over other entities which do not suffer.[14] Suffering is a restriction on someone. What is

---

9. Davies, *Reality of God*, 130.
10. Davies, *Reality of God*, 130.
11. Davies, *Reality of God*, 131.
12. Davies, *Reality of God*, 166.
13. Davies, *Reality of God*, 166.

14. Davies, *Reality of God*, 167. Here, Davies concedes that there may be instances where someone who suffers is to be valued more than someone or something who does not. For instance, someone dying in pain is to be valued more than a turnip or a desk lamp. However, this does not entail that suffering as such is an intrinsic good.

morally admirable is that someone would see suffering and do something about it; what is admirable is that someone would help someone else in need. God is in each of us, constantly sustaining our existence. Thus, God is with us in our suffering in a very intimate manner; but this could not be so if God were himself suffering from evil in his very nature. At that point, he would not be the source of all that is and would therefore not be within each one of us.[15]

These are some relevant critiques that Davies has leveled against various modern responses to the POE. He goes on to offer his own constructive response to the POE, which begins with addressing how God can be good if he is the creative cause of all existence. First, it must be said that evil does not exist in a real sense in so far as evil does not exist as a substance or as an entity; evil is simply how we describe the degradation or corruption of something that is good: "Evil suffered occurs as existing things fail to be as good as they could be."[16] Thus, Davies concludes that the evil in evil suffered cannot be caused by God. Since evil has no real being, God cannot be responsible for it, seeing as that God is the cause of all that is real other than himself.[17] It is not a creature or entity that God creates. God's causality should be thought of in terms of "making things to be" which would, of course, exclude evil.[18] We may suffer something that we call evil, and it may very well be a corruption of the good; however, even evil suffered is due to the goodness of God, not because God sustains or brings about the existence of evil, but rather because evil requires goodness to even be conceived. God brings about every good thing, as goodness has real existence which God sustains. Evil may degrade this, but God certainly does not sustain its existence or bring it about.[19]

One may reply to such lines of reasoning that, even still, God has a moral duty to prevent his creation from falling into sinful behavior or from suffering from such behavior given that it is within his power to do just this. But Davies pushes back against this charge of neglect against God, arguing that the argument presupposes God is a kind of particular thing that is subject to duties and obligations.[20] Given his classical theism, Davies rejects this premise, as he believes it makes God out to be a kind of psychological subjectivity that is subject to something outside of himself. Of course, God

15. Davies, *Reality of God*, 168.
16. Davies, *Reality of God*, 177.
17. Davies, *Reality of God*, 177–78.
18. Davies, *Reality of God*, 178.
19. Davies, *Reality of God*, 180–81.
20. Davies, *Reality of God*, 191.

would still be evil by any definition of the word if he directly caused evil as an end unto itself; nevertheless, God has not done this. Perhaps one could say that God should have created even more goodness than he has. But, in doing so, we would be placing God under an obligation to create, something that would obviously undermine his sovereignty; it would make a law that God is obligated to be transcendent of God himself, which would mean one is no longer talking about God at all. When Christians speak of God as being good, it is not as though he is good in a moral sense because he has participated in goodness. Rather, he is goodness itself.[21] God's goodness is not dependent on creation in any way; he would be the same even if all of creation did not exist.

II

James Dolezal largely agrees with Davies's Thomistic approach to the logical POE in his endorsement of Davies's work on the POE. At the most fundamental level, what makes something good is its existence: "Whatever is desirable for a thing to be or become in accord with its nature is 'good' for that thing."[22] Seeing as that evil only exists as a degradation of the good, then God has only made and sustained the existence of what is good. God is the cause of the existence of creatures and consequently their sinful acts, so in some way God is responsible for evil. But even the sinful acts of creatures can be good in some way, so long as their existence is desirable according to their nature. Ultimately, as Aquinas argues, God causes the existence of free creatures as well as the existence of their sinful acts, but God does not choose what those actions will be.[23] Some may argue that God is morally culpable for the existence of such sinful actions, but moral standards cannot be applied to God as God is not a moral agent. God does not behave well or poorly, as God does not behave at all; he is *actus purus*.[24] This is Davies's best contribution to the discourse surrounding the POE, Dolezal asserts. In the end, it is a mystery why God created a world with evil in it when he could have done otherwise. Nonetheless, this is not a problem for God's existence, as subjecting him to such moral categories is simply an anthropomorphism.[25]

---

21. Davies, *Reality of God*, 192.
22. Dolezal, Review of *Thomas Aquinas*, 492.
23. Dolezal, Review of *Thomas Aquinas*, 492.
24. Dolezal, Review of *Thomas Aquinas*, 493.
25. Dolezal, Review of *Thomas Aquinas*, 493.

III

Edward Feser has further elucidated the Thomistic approach to the POE. The alleged logical POE that people like Mackie and James Sterba have invoked against the existence of God is a simple category error.[26] Much of the discussion surrounding God and evil in modern philosophy is centered in theistic personalism as opposed to classical theism, and this is the main culprit as to why such category errors are so prevalent today.[27] Those like Mackie and Sterba seek to assign moral virtue, or a lack thereof, to God as though God was a finite agent participating in some more fundamental and transcendent moral laws. The logical POE presupposes that God is a part of this natural and moral order, but classical theism teaches that God is completely distinct from it.

As opposed to God being subject to the natural and moral order, Thomists argue that God is the reason why the natural order can exist in the first place. God is the source of its being. God is the first cause not merely temporally, but fundamentally in so far as the natural order could not continue to exist without God maintaining its existence. So, God is not simply an agent-cause or a temporal cause of anything else, he is rather the grounding for all that is in existence. When a finite substance exercises causal power, it does so in accordance with the laws of nature.[28] God, however, does not act within these laws and thus is not subject to them. For Feser, the consequence of such a realization is that the language humans use about God must be analogical in nature as opposed to univocal. This means that when Thomists or other classical theists speak of God causing the world to exist, they do so in an analogical sense.[29] For some in the modern world, this has not been fully appreciated. God's causing of the universe is analogous to a human's building of a house, though the two are not the same sort of thing. A failure to realize this proper approach to language regarding God is part of what underlies the alleged logical POE, wherein those like Mackie and Sterba expect God to be good in the same sense as a finite moral agent and expect him to cause the universe to exist in the same way that a human would cause the existence of a new house.

Feser then turns to Sterba's work particularly. For Sterba, the logical POE is rooted in what he calls the "Pauline Principle" that states one may

---

26. Feser, "Thomistic Dissolution," 1.
27. Feser, "Thomistic Dissolution," 2.
28. Feser, "Thomistic Dissolution," 7.
29. Feser, "Thomistic Dissolution," 8.

not do evil for the sake of a good outcome.³⁰ Though the Thomists typically distinguish between God causing and permitting an action, Sterba claims that in some cases the Pauline Principle would still apply even when an evil is permitted. Such examples are easy to conceive, such as a parent being morally culpable for their child hurting themselves if they could have easily stopped them from doing so but chose not to. The problems with Sterba's argument here are twofold. For starters, Thomists suggest that the rewards for the blessed in the afterlife are of infinite worth in comparison to temporal suffering (Rom 8:18). Thus, "and God permits the moral evil that exists precisely because he draws this infinite good out of it."³¹ Moreover, humans are social animals with a free will who are directed by their nature toward shaping their destinies. If God were to systematically prevent free choices from having their natural effects, then that would render the natural order meaningless. In that case, God would be giving humans the power to shape their destinies without actually allowing them to do so.³² Feser argues that this helps to makes sense of the sin and suffering we see around us, but it should not be thought of as an exoneration of God, because God is not subject to the laws of nature and is thus in no need of exoneration.

The second problem with Sterba's invocation of the Pauline Principle as a standard by which to judge God by is that, again, he presupposes God is a finite moral agent. Yes, humans may be obligated to stop horrendous evils if they have the power to, as they are governed by natural and moral laws of which the Pauline Principle is a part. Yet God is not subject to such natural law as he is not a part of the finite group that is governed by those principles.³³ This is all simply a category error: "To claim that, by permitting horrendous evils, God is violating the Pauline Principle, is like claiming that, by creating the natural order *ex nihilo* he is violating the law of the conservation of mass, or like claiming that the doctrine of divine concurrence conflicts with the law of inertia."³⁴ God transcends this natural order; he is its cause. When Sterba compares God to a superhero who should intervene

30. Sterba, *Is a Good God*, 2–4, cited in, Feser, "Thomistic Dissolution," 12.
31. Feser, "Thomistic Dissolution," 12.
32. Feser, "Thomistic Dissolution," 12.
33. Feser, "Thomistic Dissolution," 13.

34. Feser, "Thomistic Dissolution," 13. This does not entail that God could arbitrarily make something evil actually to be good. He could not morally obligate humans to torture babies for fun, for example. God is not subject to natural laws, but he is their grounding for existence. His commands for humans will be consistent with those very laws of nature and morality because they flow from him. Thus, the typical Euthyphro dilemma seems to be a false choice because if God creates human beings and the natural laws that govern them, then what he commands will be consistent with the nature of humans. See Feser, "Thomistic Dissolution," 10.

to prevent evil, or when he compares him to a political state that has a duty to protect its citizens from criminals, he operates within a theistic personalist understanding of God that leads him to make such category blunders.[35]

IV

David Bentley Hart has expressed concern that certain forms of Thomism, namely Baroque Thomism championed by philosophers such as Reginald Garrigou-Lagrange and Domingo Bañez, could logically make God culpable for the sin in the universe. Garrigou-Lagrange, for example, claimed that God is either determined by something external to himself or he is the one who determines all things; there can be no alternative.[36] Bañez had similarly claimed that if God is the primary cause of all causing then he has to be the first efficient cause of all human actions, including sinful actions.[37] The claim is always, of course, that this does not infringe upon the human's freedom or responsibility. Finite wills cannot help but err due to their intrinsic deficiency of inherent nothingness; if God does not uphold them by his grace, they will naturally gravitate toward sin. And so, the inclination toward evil may not be ascribed to God. Further, since God is not obligated to give the rational will any grace at all, he cannot be implicated in the creature's sin.[38] The human's action is free, so long as the action is not contingently determined. That is, so long as the action is not determined by a contingent cause, then the action is free. This does not entail, however, that the cause cannot be determined by a primary cause; this only means that so long as the action taken by a human is not determined by a sequence of antecedent secondary causes, then the action is considered contingent,

---

35. Feser, "Thomistic Dissolution," 14.

36. Garrigou-Lagrange, *Predestination*, cited in Hart, "Impossibility as Transcendence," 168. This would make sense, Hart says, if the formula were applied to two causes which have real relation to one another; however, this formula cannot be applied to God as God's being is entirely beyond the finite contrast between being and nonbeing. Both finite act and potency only exist within God's infinite actuality: "God is absolute, that is to say, in the most proper sense: he is eternally 'absolved' of finite causality, so much so that he need not—in any simple univocal sense—determine in order to avoid being determined. His transcendence is not something achieved by the negation of its 'opposite.'" Hart, "Impossibility as Transcendence," 168–69.

37. Bañez, *Commentaria in Summa Theologiae*, cited in Hart, "Impossibility as Transcendence," 172.

38. Hart, "Impossibility as Transcendence," 172–73. Here he is drawing broadly from the Baroque Thomist tradition, and more specifically from the work of Diego Alvarez.

and therefore free.[39] If the creature's act is considered contingent, then the creature can logically be said to have the ability to act in a different manner, though this possibility will never be realized: "For the creature's act is contingent in its own mode, it is necessary as eternally decreed by God."[40] God does not physically determine the will, but rather he predetermines the will by creating its power to choose and causing the moral sequence of choices he intends. Within this understanding of human freedom and God's eternal decree, it is asserted that God is absolved of any responsibility for the existence of sin or evil and that the human will remains free.

For Hart, this construction of God's relationship to the world is "absurd" and "repellent."[41] This "Bañezian" view portrays God as evil.[42] This view of causality, with its reliance upon the concept of premotion or *praemotio*, divides the primary causality of God into creation and then an additional predetermining of the will.[43] For the Bañezian view is not satisfied with God as a metaphysical or moral first cause; he must also exert a kind of physical causal influence into physical secondary causes, else those physical causes might escape his providence. But, Hart argues, this places division in God's primary causality. The act of *creatio ex nihilo* cannot be thought of as giving existence to static entities which then must be acted upon in a further manner in order to function. Rather, God's donation of being must be conceived as creating secondary causes which possess actual being, so much so that they can be genuinely described as "not God" in some way. These secondary causes, since they possess real existence, impart actuality to potentiality in a way that is proportionate to their powers.[44]

A further problem is that the Bañezian view of human freedom reduces the question of freedom to one of logical contingency. This is an insufficient view of freedom. If a person will inevitably carry out in action in accordance with God's eternal decree, then that action cannot be considered free merely due to its being logically contingent. What makes an act free is not simply the logical conditions of the action, but the action itself. If the action is causally necessitated or eternally predetermined, then it is not free in any meaningful sense.[45] If indeed the Bañezian view of God's relationship to creation is correct, then moral evil is God's work. What is needed, then,

---

39. Hart, "Impassibility as Transcendence," 173.
40. Hart, "Impassibility as Transcendence," 173.
41. Hart, "Impassibility as Transcendence," 175.
42. Hart, "Impassibility as Transcendence," 184.
43. Hart, "Impassibility as Transcendence," 176.
44. Hart, "Impassibility as Transcendence," 176.
45. Hart, "Impassibility as Transcendence," 177.

is a view of God's providence as being transcendent in so far as God's providence must be thought of in terms of his being present in all things, including actions he does not predetermine, but also that cannot determine him in any way.[46]

Can God's act of creation be considered so transcendent that he is capable of creating rational wills that are able to resist him? Hart argues that within a proper understanding of God's transcendence, the answer is yes. God's omnipotence is perfectly revealed when he does this, as everything within that freedom comes from God: the being of the creature, act, potency, the primordial movement of the soul toward the good, the natural law within the creature's intellect and will, the continual permission of finite autonomy, and, yes, the indetermination of the creature's freedom.[47] All of these are dependent on God for their existence and are a participation in the mystery of God's infinite freedom. Ultimately, to say that God creates dependent freedoms that he does not determine is the same thing as saying God creates dependent creatures that are in some way genuinely something other than God.[48] Admittedly, one cannot describe the mechanism by which God creates genuinely free creatures. Yet this is simply an implication of the doctrine of *creatio ex nihilo*. God causing creation must be thought of in analogical terms, as creation from nothingness is not a kind of cause that we can compare anything to, nor is it something we are remotely capable of duplicating.[49]

One of the Thomistic concerns regarding God's causality is that if God creates being which acts in ways that he does not predetermine, then he becomes dependent on those actions for his knowledge of them. In short, God becomes dependent on something other than himself in order to be fully who he is, the omniscient creator of the universe. Additionally, God could be susceptible to pathos if he gives being to actions he does not predetermine. To these concerns, Hart again appeals to the logic of transcendence. God's knowledge in creation goes beyond the realm of the determined and the determining.[50] Everything the creature does is within the possibilities that God has created. Hart agrees with Thomas in that God can know evil by way of its degradation of the good that God wills. In the same way, God can know the free sinful acts of creatures through the good that he wills by way

---

46. Hart, "Impassibility as Transcendence," 178.
47. Hart, "Impassibility as Transcendence," 180–81.
48. Hart, "Impassibility as Transcendence," 181.
49. Hart, *Experience of God*, 139. Here, Hart explicitly says this is why we can reject a mechanistic determinism and think of God's act of creation as a timeless donation of being to truly free secondary causes.
50. Hart, "Impassibility as Transcendence," 181.

of the freedom of the rational soul he creates.[51] Further, "God can 'suffer' the perfect knowledge of the free acts of his creatures not as a passive reaction to some objective force set over against himself, but as the free, transcendent act of giving being to the world of Christ—an act to whose sufficiency there need attach no mediating 'premotion' to assure its omnipotence."[52]

The providence and sovereignty of God must not be thought of in terms of direct, meticulous control over the course of history. This age in which we live is certainly not God's ideal for creation. Rather, Hart sees the New Testament as depicting creation as fallen and corrupt, and the consequences of this are that God should not be seen as unilaterally dictating all events within the universe. Paul describes this age as "the present evil world" (Gal 1:4).[53] Rebellious spiritual powers are often depicted as being responsible for the rule of this world (Col 1:6; 1 Cor 2:8; Eph 1:21, 3:10).[54] John even goes on to say that Satan is the "prince of this world" (John 12:31, 14:30, 16:11) and that the whole world lies under his control (1 John 5:19). Meanwhile, Paul goes as far as to say that Satan is "the god of this world" (2 Cor 4:4).[55] Concerning the picture the New Testament portrays regarding God's reign over the world and his conflict with evil, Hart claims there is essentially a kind of "provisional cosmic dualism."[56] This is not an absolute dualism, as God is the source of all that is; there are not two sources, one being good and the other evil. Still, Hart says this temporary dualism of the New Testament cannot be avoided by serious readers of the New Testament. And this should make it clear that however one thinks about the picture the New Testament provides us relating to God's sovereignty, it is at least abundantly clear that the writers had no conception of God as directly governing or willing all that comes to pass.[57] Nor is there any moral justification for how things are; instead, the New Testament writers focus on God's eventual

---

51. Hart, "Impassibility as Transcendence," 181–82.
52. Hart, "Impassibility as Transcendence," 182.
53. Hart, *Doors*, 65.
54. Hart, *Doors*, 65.
55. Hart, *Doors*, 65–66.
56. Hart, "Devil's March," 80. This makes one think of similar statements made by other prominent theologians from various backgrounds. This was essentially the premise of Greg Boyd's work on the POE that we examined earlier. In addition, in the midst of World War II, C. S. Lewis said, "But I freely admit that real Christianity (as distinct from Christianity-and-water) goes much nearer to Dualism than people think. . . . The difference is that Christianity thinks this Dark Power was created by God, and was good when he was created, and went wrong. Christianity agrees with dualism that this world is at war. But it does not think this is a war between independent powers." Lewis, *Mere Christianity*, 45.
57. Hart, *Doors*, 66.

victory over Satan, sin, and death. And most certainly, when one looks at the life of Christ, where God is most perfectly revealed, one does not see any occasion for believing that Christ thought of sin or suffering as part of God's eternal plan. Conversely, when Jesus confronts sin and suffering, he forgives the sin and overcomes the evil therein.[58]

The difference between understanding God's providence as God's willing good in creation despite their rebellion as opposed to believing that God directly and eternally willed all that comes to pass is the difference between believing in God's providence or believing in determinism.[59] And to believe in determinism is to believe that God is evil. Again drawing from Aquinas, Hart says that providence must be understood as primary causality, and God's primary causality transcends secondary causality. Thus, God can create genuine freedom while at the same time ensuring that his eternal purposes will be accomplished in creation. Moreover, Hart argues that this is comparable to understanding that although creation is a result of God's timeless donation of being, creation is still something logically contingent and thus something different than the divine essence.[60]

For Hart, this understanding of primary causation and God's providence is only part of the necessary response to the POE. In the end, "all causes are logically reducible to their first cause."[61] Though it is important to accurately portray God's relationship to secondary causes, those causes are still dependent on him for their existence. Because of this, it does not matter how much freedom one ascribes to contingent causes, all secondary causes are entailed within God's decision to create. Because Christians believe in *creatio ex nihilo*, we believe that God created freely in so far as he was not forced or even influenced to create by something external to himself. Therefore, all actualities and possibilities are logically reducible to him as their first cause. Moreover, because the act of creation is infinitely free, the end of that action is its "whole moral truth."[62] Thus, Hart argues that if there is to be a solution of sorts to the POE, it must be found in eschatology. And this eschatology must be nothing less than universalism. If we are to say with any coherence that God is good or that he is love, then there cannot remain any unredeemed evil in the cosmos. If the end of a person's existence is to be evil, then God would be evil himself for bringing that person into existence, as the end of an eternally free action will determine its moral

58. Hart, *Doors*, 87.
59. Hart, *Doors*, 82.
60. Hart, *Doors*, 83–84.
61. Hart, "Devil's March," 81.
62. Hart, "Devil's March," 81.

truth. A distinction is to be drawn, of course, between an eternal reality and a temporal reality. God does not directly dictate how all temporal events will unfold; he does, however, give temporal reality its existence, and if he does so knowing that will result in eternal suffering, then he can in no way be considered love in his very essence. Perhaps God's eternal kingdom, perhaps God becoming all in all wherein all rational wills return to him can be considered a morally acceptable reality given the price of temporal evil and suffering. But eternal suffering could never be considered an acceptable price for anything that is good in any cogent sense.[63] Thankfully, Hart says, God has not brought anything into being that will suffer eternal torment: "For if anything were to be eternally lost—the least little thing—then the goodness of creation could never be more in the end than a purely conditional goodness, a mere relative evaluation, rather than an essential truth. And then neither could God be the Good as such."[64] All will eventually be saved; all will be redeemed. The little girl who was once tortured, in the end, will ultimately be made to be a partaker of the divine nature. She will be made to love as God loves; she can thus overcome all evil by God's grace.[65]

V

This concludes my overview of how adherents to different models of God respond to the POE. Both moral and logical aspects of the problem have been identified and addressed from various points of view. The next chapter will inquire as to how the underlying metaphysical beliefs of the theologians, Bible scholars, and philosophers impacted their approach to defending God concerning the existence of evil. Again, this chapter primarily focused on the existence of temporal evil, though there were brief mentions of God's eventual victory over evil. For the most part, the goal has been to keep the focus on temporal evil as most Christians agree that God will finally overcome evil. As we saw with Hart's appeal to universalism, however, the nature and terms of that victory may differ depending on the theologian. Those eschatological issues could be their own book, however, so what has been written will suffice for the current purposes of this work.

63. Hart, "Devil's March," 92.

64. Hart, "Devil's March," 96. He goes on: "But because they say God creates freely, they must believe that his final judgment shall reveal him for who he is. If God creates souls he knows to be destined for eternal misery, in himself he cannot be the good as such, and creation cannot possess any true moral essence: it is from one vantage an act of predilective love, but from another vantage, and one every bit as logically necessary, it is an act of prudential malevolence."

65. Hart, "Devil's March," 96.

Chapter 7

Analyzing the Differences Between the Paradigms

I

THIS CHAPTER WILL PROCEED by contrasting the various approaches to defending the existence of God that have been summarized in the previous four chapters. Specifically, it will explore how the underlying metaphysical beliefs of the theologians and philosophers impacted their efforts. We will begin with the more metaphysically oriented arguments for the existence of God, and then move to the different methods of responding to the POE. Again, the goal here is not to simply determine which arguments are used by theologians from different theological traditions, but rather to examine how their metaphysical beliefs determined which arguments they used and how they implemented those arguments. As for the analysis of the arguments in chapters 3 and 4, this chapter will focus on the more fundamental differences. Some of the other discrepancies are still important, but they were made more explicit within the arguments themselves. For example, when Swinburne defends the logical possibility of an omniscient God, he does so by rejecting the classical definition while opting for the open theist understanding of omniscience. Something similar can be said for Launonen's and Mullins's argument that an open theistic interpretation of the cognitive science of religion can be seen as evidence for theism. Part of the purpose of the overviews in chapters 3 and 4 was to lay out these more evident differences, so they won't be revisited here.

II

Perhaps the most important conclusion one can take from reading chapters 3 and 4 is that the competing paradigms logically designate God's existence in different ways. For a majority of theistic personalists that were examined, God may possess the property of necessary existence, and he may be metaphysically necessary, but he is not logically necessary. For O'Connor, God's necessity cannot be that of formal logical necessity, as there is no logical contradiction in denying that he exists.[1] Plantinga and Swinburne also describe God as a contingent being in some sense.[2] Plantinga goes as far as to say that most modern theologians now agree with the sentiment that God is logically contingent. And he is correct in that assessment.

The most apparent consequence of the more modern inclination to describe God as logically contingent is that arguments for his existence are usually now framed in terms of probability. If God is not logically necessary, then it is at least possible, though it may be highly unlikely, that he does not exist. Therefore, the most that can be said of his existence is that it is highly probable. Yes, often theistic personalists will believe it is so likely that God exists that one would have to be a radical skeptic in order to deny his existence; nonetheless, his existence is still ultimately probable as opposed to logically necessary. This can be seen when Craig, for instance, describes the fine-tuning of the universe to point to an ultimate designer: "unless the design hypothesis can be shown to be even more implausible than its competitors."[3] Craig is clearly working within the framework of plausibility and implausibility here. In the same way, Swinburne constantly frames his arguments for God's existence as being probable or more probable than the alternative. When speaking on the cosmological argument, he says that it cannot be a valid deductive argument; if it were, then the existence of a complex universe apart from the existence of God would be logically impossible. This cannot be the case for Swinburne, so he says the cosmological argument fails as a deductive argument; what is more interesting for him is whether it is a valid C-inductive or P-inductive argument.[4] In other words, Swinburne rejects that the cosmological argument is a proof of God's existence and instead investigates whether or not it makes God's existence more probable than atheism. Plantinga's frequently utilized possible-world semantics further illustrate this point: there are possible worlds in which

---

1. O'Connor, *Theism and Ultimate Explanation*, 66.
2. Swinburne, *Coherence of Theism*, 101; Plantinga, *God, Freedom, and Evil*, 39.
3. Craig, *How Do We Know*, 57.
4. Swinburne, *Existence of God*, 136–37.

God does not exist, which obviously entails that when speaking of God's existence in the actual world he is speaking in terms of probability. In the work of Plantinga's that we primarily examined, he concludes his work on the ontological argument as follows: "What I claim for this argument, therefore, is that it establishes, not the truth of theism, but its rational acceptability."[5]

It seems that the metaphysical catalyst for the "probability approach," as it were, for the theistic personalists is their denial of the DDS. Existence is possible apart from God, even if it is highly unlikely. God is not the ground of all being or being itself. Therefore, there is no reason to assume that God is logically necessary in the grand scheme of existence. John Feinberg, the reader will recall, in responding to classical theist Paul Tillich, explicitly said there is no value in arguing that God is being itself or the ground of all being; conversely, God must be a distinct being among other beings.[6] This denial of simplicity, and the modern understanding of God, have led many to assume that the existence question, or the question as to why anything at all exists or how existence is even possible in the first place, is unanswerable. This is precisely how O'Connor described the contemporary state of affairs concerning the existence question.[7] Now, O'Connor himself does attempt to answer the existence question, since he is ultimately unsatisfied with the notion that we do not have or cannot know the ultimate explanation for why anything at all exists. In doing so, he understands that a necessary being cannot possess a complex nature; he argues this in response to Spinozian pantheism, which asserts that the universe itself is a necessary being and that there is no such thing as contingent existence. The problem for the Spinozians is that the property of necessary existence cannot result from the rest of the necessary being's essential nature; a necessary being's property of necessary existence cannot be contingently related to its essential nature.[8] Again, if this were the case then there would be no explanation for the property of necessary existence being related to the rest of the necessary being's essential nature. Due to this realization, O'Connor admits that the medieval scholastics posited that

5. Plantinga, *God, Freedom, and Evil*, 112.
6. Feinberg, *No One Like Him*, 207–8.
7. O'Connor, *Theism and Ultimate Explanation*, 66. He did not say this was explicitly due to the denial of divine simplicity. I simply mean to say that O'Connor asserted that the existence question was unanswerable for many contemporary philosophers. The reason he gives is that when one gets into the existence question in sufficient depth, one is forced to say there is a relationship between contingent reality and a necessary being. This is exactly what much of classical philosophy concluded. Many modern philosophers, however, scrutinize the idea of a necessary being and conclude that such a being is incoherent and thus the reasoning that may lead one to the existence of a necessary being loses its force. See his discussion of this on p. 66.
8. O'Connor, *Theism and Ultimate Explanation*, 87.

the connection between the various aspects of the necessary being's essential nature is that of identity: God's omnipotence is his omniscience, which is his mercy, etc.[9] This is the DDS. O'Connor, however, sees the doctrine as problematic, so he argues that although God's essential nature has numerically distinct properties, they must be internally and necessarily connected to one another. As far as theistic personalists are concerned, this is the closest one may get to arguing that God is the ground of all being. Nonetheless, a classical theist may still argue that O'Connor's conception of God makes him a composite being which would mean he cannot possess aseity and thus cannot be the ultimate explanation for existence as such. To use the language of the analytic tradition, O'Connor's conception of God makes him metaphysically necessary, but not logically necessary.[10] In the end, the result is the same: God's existence is highly probable but not certain.

The classical theists argue for God's existence in a different way. They mostly do not argue in terms of probability, but rather in terms of logical necessity. David Bentley Hart, for example, has ridiculed the modern conception of God as well as the modern approach to apologetics that has followed. The ID movement has been made possible precisely because Christians have largely abandoned the classical tradition. It is no coincidence that ID theory followed from the rise of theistic personalism, in that what is at stake for its advocates is the question of why our particular universe exists the way that it does. The very possibility of existence as such is not the question at hand for this particular movement within Christianity. Hart's disdain for ID ideas comes out in his arguments against Stephen Hawking, who claimed that if there was a type of quantum vacuum wherein the physical laws of nature resided, then God would not be necessary to explain our existence seeing as that universes could endlessly spawn from that quantum vacuum.[11] Of course, for Hart, God is the ground of all being. Thus, even the existence of such a quantum vacuum or the physical laws of nature are dependent on God for their existence. Nothing can possibly exist without him. Hawking's argument then is left with the same ineptitude: the existence of the laws of nature themselves that "run" the universe, as it were, is in need of explanation. And more to the point concerning arguments from probability, ID theory may be able to prove that God's existence is highly probable, but it

---

9. O'Connor, *Theism and Ultimate Explanation*, 88.

10. The reason for this modern tendency, says Hart, is that analytic philosophers tend to think of necessity as a logical property possessed by certain propositions or universals, such as mathematical numbers or formulae. This is not, Hart insists, the same as claiming God is "necessary being" or being itself. See his discussion of this in Hart, *Experience of God*, 114–15.

11. Hart, *Experience of God*, 40.

also may not accomplish such a thing, depending on one's background and worldview presuppositions. As Hart argues, probability is itself a tricky concept and difficult to prove one way or another when dealing with something as complex as biology or something as large in scope as "distinct geographical epochs."[12] The classical tradition was more concerned with proving that the very possibility of existence itself is dependent on God, whereas more modern models of God assume that existence is possible apart from God, and then try to argue that given our set of circumstances, it is likely that God exists.

The classical arguments for God then mostly are concerned with proving the logical necessity of his existence. When looking at Feser's *Five Proofs of the Existence of God*, this is easy to observe. Every proof of God's existence that Feser offers is in some way dependent on the notion of divine simplicity. Whether it is an argument from contingency, or composition, or scholastic realism, or the differentiation of essence and existence, or even the PSR, all arguments are dependent on God as the ground of all being. And this is perhaps why these types of arguments are not always popular with theistic personalists. We observed in chapter 3 that the theistic personalists would often ridicule and critique traditional arguments for God's existence. At times they would rework the arguments in an attempt to prove the probability of God's existence, while at other times they would completely deny that the arguments have any merit. One may think of Swinburne concluding that the cosmological argument makes it "likely" that God exists, and that the existence of a complex universe apart from God is "unlikely."[13] Plantinga called both the cosmological and teleological arguments "unsuccessful."[14] The classical arguments for God's existence relied on classical metaphysics, so it is no surprise to see the denial of the DDS lead to a rejection of the classical arguments.

This realization is key to understanding the modern movement away from something like scholastic realism and even the rationalist proof of God's existence. It is common, though not universal, for theistic personalists to deny God's aseity, or at least to deny it as it was classically understood.[15] As we saw in chapter 3, for example, some theistic personalists assert that abstract objects and moral truths exist independent of God's will. On the "extreme" end, process theists will even deny *creatio ex nihilo*. For

12. Hart, *Experience of God*, 38.
13. Swinburne, *Existence of God*, 152.
14. Plantinga, *God, Freedom, and Evil*, 84.

15. Some may opt for an alternative route. William Lane Craig, for example, has argued for an outright rejection of realism. See Craig, *God Over All*. It is argued that God's aseity remains coherent, as there are no real properties that he is dependent on.

the process theists, the world is not independent of God, nor God of the world.[16] Further discussion concerning this point will be had later in this chapter when examining the process approach to the POE, however. As for the non-process theistic personalists, Plantinga and Feinberg said similar things on the subject of abstract objects and universals.[17] For Feinberg, this isn't to deny God's aseity; rather, God's aseity must be defined as his self-existence. The reason for God's existence lies in his very nature and he is not dependent on anything external to himself for his existence. This is to be contrasted with the classical definition of aseity, wherein God is not dependent on any distinct properties for his existence; God does not depend on universals for his existence, but they rather depend on him for their existence.[18]

Regardless, this understanding of God's relationship with abstract objects has led some theistic personalists to be dissatisfied with the traditional moral argument for God's existence, and seemingly perhaps to deny the PSR. Swinburne is a good example of this. He distinguishes between the existence of moral truth and humanity's awareness of the truth of moral propositions. He does say that humanity's awareness of moral truth points to the probability of God's existence, but he does not think that the existence of moral truth itself is evidence of God's existence. Fundamental moral principles, for Swinburne, are logically necessary, whereas God's existence is not; therefore, the existence of fundamental moral principles does not depend on God's existence.[19] Nothing necessarily grounds the existence of these moral principles; they are observed and reasoned toward and are true whether or not there is an ultimate explanation for existence as such. This leads to my second point, which is to say Swinburne and others seemingly deny the PSR. Swinburne in particular, when addressing Leibniz's argument for God from the PSR, asserts that "there can be no 'absolute explanation' of the existence of the universe."[20] Moreover, Swinburne says we have "no general reason" for accepting the claim that everything has an ultimate explanation.[21] It is important to point out that Swinburne does suggest that intellectual honesty demands we postulate the smallest number of brute

---

16. Whitehead, *Process and Reality*, 343–45.
17. Plantinga, *Does God*, 35; Feinberg, *No One Like Him*, 335–37.
18. Feinberg, *No One Like Him*, 239–40.
19. Swinburne, *Existence of God*, 214.
20. Swinburne, *Existence of God*, 148.
21. Swinburne, *Existence of God*, 149.

facts that is conceivably possible.[22] Obviously though, this does not change his rejection of the PSR nor his reworking of the moral argument.

This is all in stark contrast to the Augustinian proof that Feser offered for God's existence. For the classical tradition, everything must have an explanation if it is to be intelligible. Abstract objects such as mathematical numbers and universals such as moral principles must have a grounding for their existence. And the grounding for these logically necessary truths, for the scholastics, was the divine *logos*. The grounding for the existence of such objects and propositions, Feser argued, must be God, as the grounding for universals cannot be finite. Even if there were no physical, finite universe, fundamental moral principles and mathematical objects would still exist; thus, the necessity of their grounding in the infinite, eternal, and immutable divine *logos*. Here, it is not just the human awareness of such truths that points to the probability of God's existence; it is the very existence of such truths that points to the logical necessity of God. This is related to the classical tradition's commitment to the PSR: if the PSR is false, then there is no reason to believe in the intelligibility of anything.[23] So, for classical theists, if moral truth can exist with no grounding or justification to answer why it exists, then rational inquiry into anything is no longer possible. The universe, or God for that matter, cannot simply be a brute fact and neither can the existence of moral truth. All that exists is ultimately grounded in God.

What has been described so far in this chapter is the core of the difference between classical theists and theistic personalists when it comes to their differing metaphysical ideas and how those ideas influence their argumentation for God. Having said that, there are still a few smaller but important differences between the two camps that need more attention before moving on to the POE. These differences are related to the ontological argument. Now, it is difficult to say that the ontological argument that was original to Anselm has been a cornerstone of classical theism. It has in fact been a matter of great dispute in the classical tradition. For instance, it was outright rejected by Aquinas since he thought one could not prove God's existence strictly via a priori reasoning. Hart acknowledges that although it has had its share of defenders, generally speaking the philosophical consensus has been that it is a failed argument. He does, however, think it could be a successful argument if interpreted in a certain way. If, say, instead of Anselm speaking of God as a distinct being he is rather speaking of God as Being itself, then the argument is successful: "That than which it is impossible to conceive

---

22. Swinburne, *Is There a God?*, 44–45.

23. Feser, *Five Proofs*, 150. We also saw this come out in Ron Highfield's arguments. See Highfield, *Great Is the Lord*, 77.

anything greater is not a being among other beings, not even the greatest possible of beings, but is instead the fullness of Being itself, the absolute plenitude of reality upon which all else depends; and manifestly it would be meaningless to say that Being lacks being or that Reality is not real."[24]

Nonetheless, as we saw in chapter 3, the ontological argument has been modified and used by theistic personalists as different as Plantinga and Hartshorne. Plantinga in particular uses exercises in modal logic to derive God's actual existence from his logical possibility. Because Plantinga views existence as a type of predicate that is assigned as a logical category of sorts to different properties that have at least one instance of a concrete instantiation, he seeks to prove that the property of maximal greatness is in fact instantiated in at least one possible world. Logical possibility does not alter regardless of which possible world one conceives. And if it is indeed possible that maximal greatness be instantiated in a possible world, then it is instantiated in at least one possible world, which means that it would necessarily be instantiated in every possible world, as the property of maximal greatness entails necessary existence. This is certainly different than Anselm's original argument as well as Hart's charitable interpretation of it. Again, we are left ultimately with an argument from probability, as Plantinga himself says the entire line of reasoning hinges on whether or not one believes it is possible that the property of maximal greatness be instantiated in a possible world.[25] Thus, the most that can be said is that this argument provides a basis for the rationality of theism. To prove God's existence here, one would need to prove that it is logically possible for the property of maximal greatness to be instantiated in a possible world; this would entail defending the properties of omnipotence, omniscience, moral perfection, etc., all individually, which is obviously beyond the scope of the ontological argument. This can also be contrasted with the classical arguments for God's existence on the whole so far as they concern the great making properties: many classical arguments seek to prove the logical necessity of an uncaused cause; then when the nature of that cause is examined, things like omnipotence, omniscience, and moral perfection will be logically entailed. Concerning the ontological argument specifically, the difference here largely is centered on the analytic understanding of existence as a type of predicate. Since existence as such is a kind of brute fact or a given in much of modern philosophy and theology, Plantinga's modal ontological argument doesn't seek to shed any light on the existence question. Hence his focus on the logical possibility of a property

---

24. Hart, *Experience of God*, 122.
25. Plantinga, *God, Freedom, and Evil*, 112.

called "maximal greatness" being instantiated. God's necessary existence is a property that he participates in; it is not his very essence.

Hartshorne is similar to Plantinga regarding his understanding of the nature of existence as a predicate, though he does distinguish between what he calls "simple existence" and contingent existence.[26] Where he differs from Plantinga is that his offerings of modal and ontological proofs for the existence of God are somewhat predicated on an alternative understanding of perfection and maximal greatness. Of course, Plantinga differs from classical theists in his understanding of God's relation to his properties and essential nature; however, he largely agrees with them concerning God's omnipotence and omniscience. Hartshorne, as a process theist, departs radically from the classical understanding of God's omnipotence and omniscience. Thus, when he considers God's perfection, he articulates it differently. If forced to defend God's perfection as classically understood, then Anselm's argument ultimately fails as it forces one to defend a logically incoherent view of perfection and God.[27]

Due to his understanding of God as temporal and process as being most fundamental to reality, he rejects the idea that God is *actus purus*. Instead, Hartshorne insists that we should be able to differentiate between the divine individual and different divine states. It is incomprehensible to say that God is loving while at the same time asserting that he remains unchanged; to love is to care about differences or tragedy and to respond to them differentially, depending on the circumstances.[28] This is a common claim from theistic personalists: for God to be loving, he must be able to respond to and be affected by others. To have the potential to be able to respond to others should be considered a divine perfection. God must have divine potential if he is to be perfect. Anselm did not consider divine potential to be a part of maximal greatness, but Christians today should, says Hartshorne.

---

26. Hartshorne, *Logic of Perfection*, 63. God's existence in different divine states would be considered contingent existence. Ogden concisely describes the process understanding of the nature of existence, which Hartshorne will employ in his line of argumentation: "Here it is important to understand a distinction between existence and actuality, which is one of the distinctions quite obscured in the metaphysical tradition. A person may be said to 'exist,' provided the essential characteristics by which he or it is defined are somehow actualized. . . . 'Existence,' in short, properly functions as an abstract variable. Hence, to say that anything 'exists' requires that the variable 'actuality' have some specific value." He goes on to say this entails that a proper conception of God is "two-sided or bipolar." In that, God is both supremely relative and absolute. Ogden, "Reality of God," 47–48.

27. Hartshorne, *Logic of Perfection*, 33–34.

28. Hartshorne, *Logic of Perfection*, 35.

This differentiation between divine states and the divine individual is crucial to another aspect of Hartshorne's argument as well: in order for Hartshorne's ontological argument to work, one must be able to differentiate between the necessity of perfection and the concrete instantiation of perfection itself. The reasons for this were discussed in chapter 3. If a being or property is contingent, then it is logically possible that it either does or does not exist in actuality. However, the property of necessary existence logically entails actual existence; it is a contradiction to say that the property of necessary existence is contingent and yet that God necessarily exists in all possible worlds. It is also a contradiction to assert that God is contingent in so far as he has potential and goes through change, while simultaneously arguing that he necessarily exists. Further, Anselm argued that it must not even be conceivable that perfection could be conceived to be nonexistent. If one is to be able to intelligently speak of the possibility of the nonexistence of perfection, or the necessity of perfection, one must be able to apply a property-instance distinction in God. And this is possible for process theism, but not necessarily for classical theism. The necessity of perfection is of a higher or more abstract type than its contingent instantiation: Hartshorne thus argued on the basis of Anselm's argument that the existence of perfection is logically necessary while the states in which it exists are contingent concrete instantiations. God is divine perfection, in a sense, whereas the different states in which God exists are contingent and involve potential, but this is consistent with Hartshorne's understanding of divine perfection.[29]

It is then easy to see how Hartshorne's process theism impacts his implementation of the ontological argument. By agreeing with Anselm's argument, despite his revisions, he is essentially arguing for the logical necessity of God's existence. This sets him apart from some of the other theistic personalists whose work has been examined. He actually concludes that if theologians and philosophers contend that God's existence is logically contingent, then by virtue of the "Anselmian Principle" they have proved that God's existence is logically impossible.[30] This is a keen insight, and consistent with his commentary on Anselm's original argument that said Anselm disproved both empirical theism and empirical atheism.[31] God's existence, for Hartshorne, is either logically necessary or logically impossible; and he believes his reworking of the ontological argument is proof of God's logically necessary existence.

29. Hartshorne, *Logic of Perfection*, 65–66.
30. Hartshorne, *Logic of Perfection*, 89.
31. Hartshorne, *Anselm's Discovery*, 3–4.

III

Though there are some exceptions that will be discussed later in this section, most responses to the POE are at least somewhat dependent on the concept of free will. This is at times applied to humans, while at other times it is relevant to supernatural beings such as angels or demons or even God. The doctrine of free will is in some ways a metaphysical doctrine, to be sure, but it does not appear that one's doctrine of God fully determines one's understanding of human freedom. It does, however, seem that one's doctrine of God will impact how one's understanding of human freedom is implemented into the argument, and that will be explored below. For now, this section will begin by examining those with more of a compatibilist understanding of human freedom. This includes some classical theists and theistic personalists.

The neo-Calvinist tradition within theistic personalism and certain portions of the Thomistic tradition have some significant overlap concerning human freedom and the POE. John Feinberg represented the neo-Calvinist tradition in this book. He admits that it would be possible, given his understanding of freedom, for God to create a world in which humans do not commit any evil. In giving his defense as to why it would be difficult and perhaps impossible for God to arrange the world in such a way that people always do what is good, he focuses on the nature of human desires. Moral evil originates in human desires; it is not a substance that God creates and has no existence in and of itself. These are similar semantics used by Davies; he agrees with Mackie as well that it was within God's power to create free creatures who never do anything wrong. Though not as explicit in his terminology, by agreeing with Mackie Davies has rejected libertarian free will. The freedom of the creature then is to be found in the logical conditions of the action the creature partakes in. Where Davies the classical theist and Feinberg the theistic personalist part ways then is in their explanation of how they exonerate God for not doing something it was logically possible for him to do. Feinberg gives a plethora of defenses to specific objections, but they center around the idea that evil originates in human desires.[32] Ultimately, for God to create humans who never choose to do evil would require him to create humans without desires or to miraculously restrain

---

32. Feinberg, *No One Like Him*, 787–96. Some examples here are that humanity inherits a sinful nature from Adam, and that even without the sin nature, Adam sinned. For God to create humans who always freely do good, it is asserted that he would need to create humans that do not have desires or to miraculously constrain them from doing evil when they come into a desire to do so. This would contradict human freedom, however. Thus, for Feinberg, it is a contradiction to say that God could create humans with compatibilistic freedom who do not ever choose to sin.

humans from producing evil when they acquire an evil desire. People are stubborn toward God, and it may be "more difficult than we suppose" to rearrange the world in which everyone's desires produce exclusively good deeds, given the interconnectedness of humanity.[33] The obvious defect here is that according to Feinberg's soft determinism, God is the one who causally determines which desires all individual humans will have in their lives, so though it may be "difficult," his omnipotence should make that more than feasible. Davies, as we saw in chapter 6, does not believe that the free will defense against Mackie's objection is adequate, given that he is correct in his assertion that God could have created free humans "such that they would always freely choose the good."[34] And when humans act freely, they cannot do so independently of God's causal action anyway since God is the source of all being. Thus, God is ultimately responsible for all of creation, even free human actions that occur within God's providence. Instead of exonerating God as though he were a psychological subjectivity participating in moral actions as humans do, Davies argues that God is not really in need of that kind of exoneration. God is not subject to anything external to himself, and he is not a moral agent who participates in moral good or evil. He is goodness as such, and his goodness is not dependent on creation. God does not behave in a moral or immoral manner; God is *actus purus* and so to attempt to assign his act of creation as moral or immoral is simply an anthropomorphism. Dolezal said this was Davies's best contribution to the discourse surrounding good and evil.[35]

Though they shared in a compatibilist understanding of human freedom and thus agreed that a free will defense cannot answer Mackie's famous objection to theism, Davies and Feinberg nonetheless did not agree on how exactly to solve the issue apart from human freedom. Davies's classical theism causes him to see God not as a kind of relational person at all, whereas Feinberg seeks to exonerate God in a similar way that he might exonerate a human being. By subjecting God to his nonconsequentialist ethics, Davies would argue that Feinberg is committing a massive category error and is subjecting God to something even more transcendent than himself.[36] Feser

33. Feinberg, *No One Like Him*, 790.
34. Mackie, *Miracle of Theism*, 165.
35. Dolezal, Review of *Thomas Aquinas*, 493.
36. See Feinberg's discussion in Feinberg, *No One Like Him*, 783–87. By nonconsequentialist ethics, he means to say that an action is not determined to be good or bad by the end result of the action; what makes an action good or bad is something else, which could be obligation, duty, or because God commanded it. Particularly, Feinberg claims he holds to a kind of modified command theory wherein moral norms are determined by God, but he doesn't determine those moral norms arbitrarily; rather, he does so in

said something similar regarding the theistic personalist approach to the POE.[37] For Davies, God's goodness is not moral goodness.[38] It would seem that their understandings of divine transcendence cause them to approach the issue in very different ways, despite their agreement concerning the nature of human freedom. This is at the heart of the difference between classical theism and theistic personalism that has been demonstrated throughout this book.

This leads us to a deeper discussion regarding divine transcendence. The classical theists tend to appeal to God's transcendence, as they understand God's causing of the universe to exist in a strictly analogical manner, whereas the theistic personalists tend to have a more univocal understanding of God as the cause of the universe. This does not, however, mean that even all of the classical theists agreed with one another in their application of divine transcendence to the POE. Hart, for instance, said that the logical conditions of an action cannot be what make it truly free; if a temporal action was ultimately determined by God and could not have been otherwise, then it is not a free action, regardless of its logical status.[39] No amount of semantics or wordplay can make divine determinism compatible with genuine human freedom, according to Hart. In addition, though Hart would agree with his fellow classical theists on God's goodness being different than moral goodness, he disagrees as to whether that means God can predetermine sinful actions and still be goodness as such. To him, this deterministic tendency within various strands of Thomism makes God out to be evil. Where transcendence needs to be employed is in explaining how God can create wills that are dependent upon him for their existence, while those very same wills or desires are not predetermined by him. The Bañezian concern was that if God does not determine all secondary causes, then they are determining him, seeing as that they are dependent upon him for their existence. Hart invokes divine transcendence here to suggest that God's timeless donation of being transcends such categories: *creatio ex nihilo* is so radically unlike any finite cause that we can conceive. God is the ground for why there is any potency at all for secondary causes, thus he is the ground of free actions that he does not predetermine. To put it simply, Hart believes that a proper understanding of divine transcendence can account for the

---

accordance with his nature and attributes.

37. Feser, "Thomistic Dissolution," 1.
38. Davies, *Reality of God*, 128.
39. Hart, "Impassibility as Transcendence," 177.

belief in what he calls "genuine" human freedom, wherein humans have the power of contra choice.[40]

This is related to Hart's articulation of divine providence. There is in the New Testament a kind of temporal dualism, so God's providence cannot be conceived as a unilateral determination of all that comes to pass. This has significant overlap with some of the more free will-oriented theistic personalist understandings of divine providence. Outside of Hart, this approach was especially utilized in the works from Boyd and Wright. For Wright, evil is not so much something to be explained as it is something to be dealt with. Evil is something that God overcomes, not something that he causes or is responsible for. As we saw in chapters 5 and 6, both Wright and Hart have given ample biblical examples to explain this type of dualistic approach to evil that the New Testament authors in particular have. Where Wright differs from Hart is that for Wright we may go as far as to say that God is a victim of sorts regarding evil in so far as God suffers along with his creation,[41] an idea that became popular among twentieth-century theistic personalists. Hart, of course, rejects this approach to the issue due to his commitment to divine immutability and impassibility. Boyd has a similar dualistic understanding of God's relationship to evil, though he is more concerned with the metaphysics of evil than Wright is. Boyd's *God at War* lays his understanding of providence out concisely. His approach to providence has many similarities to Hart's. Where he differs considerably is in his understanding of divine foreknowledge. For Boyd and other open theists, neither God nor humans could be truly free if God has exhaustive foreknowledge of all future choices. Thus, when he articulates his theodicy in the sequel to *God at War*, he states that although one does not have to hold to open theism to employ his warfare theodicy, adherence to a classical view of omniscience makes one do so inconsistently.[42] The move toward theistic personalism, for some, has been motivated by a desire to articulate a logically coherent view of free will; this entails a denial of classical omniscience for open and process theists. Swinburne, the reader will remember, agreed with Boyd that an action cannot be genuinely free if God knows with certainty what a rational agent will do in the future.[43]

Hart conversely argues that divine transcendence, and not a view of God as temporal, is the solution to what may be deemed "the foreknowledge

---

40. Hart insists that although his view of freedom is a rejection of determinism, it is not a purely libertarian model. Rather, his model is what he calls an intellectualist model, which will be discussed further below.

41. Wright, "Christianity Offers No Answers."

42. Boyd, *Satan*, 86–87.

43. Swinburne, *Is There a God?*, 9.

problem." God's knowledge of dependent wills and what those wills may or may not do in the future goes beyond human understandings of knowing or not knowing, of determining or not determining. God knows the evil of what creatures may do simply by that evil's degradation of the good that he eternally wills through the freedom of his creatures.[44] For Hart, this is similar to how the Logos suffers via a free act as opposed to a change in his nature:

> Just as the incarnate Logos really suffers torment and death not through a passive mediation of his nature, imposed by some exterior force, but by a free act, so God can "suffer" the perfect knowledge of the free acts of his creatures not as a passive reaction to some objective force set over against himself, but as the free, transcendent act of giving being to the world of Christ—an act whose sufficiency there need attach no mediating "premotion" to assure its omnipotence. And that eternal act of knowledge is entirely convertible with God's free intention to reveal himself in Christ.[45]

Plantinga also appeals to a type of warfare theodicy, at least in so far as he is dealing with natural evil. This is related to his free will defense relating to the POE, as he claims natural evil then can largely be conceived as being the result of Satanic and other demonic activity.[46] Here, however, he does not necessarily point to the logic of divine transcendence to deal with the issue of God's foreknowledge; he rather illustrates the compatibility of God's exhaustive foreknowledge by using modal logic:

> (49a) Necessarily, if God knows in advance that X will do A, then indeed X will do A.
>
> (49b) If God knows in advance that X will do A, then it is necessary that X will do A.[47]

For Plantinga, though the atheist's attack on classical omniscience demands that (49b) is true, only (49a) is true, thus the atheist's attack fails. God's foreknowledge of future creaturely acts does not entail that creatures lack the power of contra choice; their actions are not themselves necessary. This is ultimately a relatively simple argument: God's foreknowledge does not

---

44. Hart, "Impassibility as Transcendence," 181–82.

45. Hart, "Impassibility as Transcendence," 182.

46. Plantinga, *God, Freedom, and Evil*, 58–59.

47. Plantinga, *God, Freedom, and Evil*, 67. This approach is not necessarily exclusive to Plantinga or the neoclassical theists. Aquinas makes a similar argument. See Aquinas, *Summa Theologiae* 1a.14.13.ad.3.

causally necessitate all human actions. Hart, however, may conclude that Plantinga falls into the crosshairs of the Bañezian concern that human actions would be determining a part of who God is by refusing to appeal to transcendence. Regardless, here we have two different ways of dealing with the epistemic issues regarding God's foreknowledge and human freedom that are clearly influenced by their neoclassical and classical theism.

Both of these approaches differ from the open and process theist defenses of God's omniscience. Swinburne is one of the clearest examples of this alternative. Aside from human freedom, his primary motivation for embracing the open view of God's omniscience is the freedom of God. God is said to be unable to be genuinely free to act in one way or another if he has exhaustive foreknowledge of his own actions.[48] God must be able to act successively as time passes in such a way that would allow him to adapt to a particular set of circumstances. Alternatively, Hart has argued that God's freedom is not to be derived from an arbitrary choice of whether or not he will create a universe, or even from deliberations as to exactly what kind of universe he will create. In God, possibility does not exceed actuality, so there is no meaningful distinction between freedom and necessity.[49] Of course, a phrase like creation "might not have been" can still be true, so long as it is understood as a modal qualifier in so far as the statement must refer to creation's dependence on God for its existence as opposed to it being a declaration asserting that God arbitrarily chose to create instead of choosing not to create.[50] The logic of the doctrine of omniscience is routinely asserted by atheists to be absurd. But here we have seen several different ways of addressing such concerns, each clearly influenced by the given scholar's model of God.

Process theists have responded to the POE in perhaps the most distinctive manner. One of the perceived advantages of process theism is its ability to give satisfactory answers to the numerous questions people have about God and the world as a result of the POE. The downside for some Christians, obviously, is its denial of omnipotence as classically understood, as well as its denial of *creatio ex nihilo*. Regardless, process theism's denial

---

48. Swinburne, *Coherence of Theism*, 182–83.

49. Hart, *You Are Gods*, 105, 117.

50. Hart, *You Are Gods*, 116. Hart asserts that creation may be necessary in some sense, as for God to act rationally—that is, freely according to his nature—then he must create. There is no metaphysical difference between *creatio ex nihilo* and emanation; the difference between the two doctrines is that *creatio ex nihilo* ensures creation is wholly logical as it is the result of an infinitely free act of God. In both instances, all that exists comes from one divine source and is sustained by divine grace. See discussion in Hart, *That All Shall Be*, 71.

Analyzing the Differences Between the Paradigms 139

of classical omnipotence and *creatio ex nihilo* allows for process theists to give answers to the POE that are not and have not typically been given. Let us start with the implications of a denial of classical omnipotence. Oord coined the term "amipotent," with "ami" being the Latin prefix for "love" and "potent" being the root for words like "potency" and "potential." Thus, to describe God as amipotent is to say that his power is the power of love, and love is always persuasive as opposed to coercive.[51] Though the other process thinkers we examined do not use this term to describe God's power, it essentially captures the essence of what they say, as can be seen in chapter 5. This conception of God's power pushes Oord to say most explicitly that God cannot unilaterally stop evil. This realization, it is argued, fully solves the POE. Previously, this was impossible for Christians due to their adherence to classical omnipotence. Though this is somewhat oversimplified, most Christian responses to the POE have, for Oord, essentially been centered on the idea that God merely allows evil as opposed to causing it. For some in the process tradition, however, this answer will just not suffice. Oord compares this to an uncle simply allowing his niece to be kidnapped, or a mother freely allowing her baby to drown.[52] He even invokes Jesus, as he claims Jesus did not allow evil but rather confronted it when he was in its presence.[53]

One of Oord's points of emphasis is that God is a bodiless spirit, so he cannot unilaterally stop physical evil. Again, this is further reason God's power must necessarily be conceived as persuasive as opposed to coercive. If one is to conceive of entities other than God truly being able to resist his will, then divine power cannot be thought of in terms of coercion: if classical omnipotence is true, then God is essentially the only power in the universe.[54] And obviously, if God is the only power in the universe, then there can be no genuine resistance to his will, which means the evil in the universe is ultimately his doing. This is at the heart of the process understanding of divine power as it relates to the POE: traditional theodicies fail because there can be no true resistance to God's will and power in the universe, thus rendering it a contradiction to say that God is loving.

The process understanding of divine power is directly relevant to process theists' understanding of creation. Because God's power is always persuasive, *creatio ex nihilo* is logically impossible; for God to act, he must do so in conjunction with something else. He cannot persuade "nothing."

---

51. Oord, *Open and Relational Theology*, 81.
52. Oord, *God Can't*, 18–20.
53. Oord, *God Can't*, 21.
54. Cobb, *God and the World*, 89.

As opposed to a more traditional Christian doctrine of creation, process theologians believe that God created the present universe from a more previous chaotic state.[55] And process theism's understanding of creation is an integral part of their dealings with the POE. It is a common atheist objection that since God could create any world he wanted, he should have created a universe that is more friendly toward life and that produces more good than it does. Specifically regarding humans, it is often said that God should have created in such a way that humans would be significantly less prone to subject one another to violence and general harm. We saw that Feinberg, given his neoclassical theism, responded to such an objection by claiming that God desired to create "non-glorified human beings." In that, God wanted to create humans, not super humans, so that we could have genuine relationships and desires. John Cobb replies to this objection in a different way. As we saw in chapter 5, Cobb said the world as we have it is not the result of some immutable, eternal decree from God in eternity past. Rather, God has persuaded the world to eventually bring about life, but he cannot unilaterally determine what the world looks like. The creation of humanity in particular should be articulated as God persuading the world towards "life, consciousness, maximum intensity, and freedom."[56] So God is not to blame for humanity's propensity toward sin seeing as that humanity, as it is, is not the result of God's creation out of nothing but rather God's persuading the universe to produce life.

For Christians who hold to *creatio ex nihilo*, God's creating the universe is not in any way influenced or impacted by anything external to himself. This entails that the universe, regardless of how one understands the relationship between primary and secondary causality, is logically reducible to God as its primary cause of existence. Hart says this is a logical truism.[57] Process theism, however, does not share this view of God as the universe's primary cause for existence, which allows process adherents to approach the POE in radically new ways.

Christian apologetics can never be completely separated from Christian faith or from Christian metaphysics. So, while some may welcome these new and different approaches to the POE, other Christians may see such views as unacceptable given their understandings of Christian orthodoxy.

The last aspect of the Christian responses to the POE that will be discussed is the invocation of God's victory over evil. Though this has not been the primary focus of this book, it has been an element of the Christian

---

55. Griffin, *God, Power, and Evil*, 285–86.
56. Cobb, *God and the World*, 95.
57. Hart, "Devil's March," 81.

response to the reality of evil in the universe throughout history. In the works that have been examined, it was occasionally brought up by scholars from both classical and modern persuasions. For Wright, God's final and permanent victory over evil should be the central point of a Christian's response to the POE.[58] When Christians preach Christ crucified, the Christus Victor atonement theory should be emphasized, as the preaching of the cross itself can be seen as a vital part of a Christian's approach to the POE. Evil is not something the Bible fully explains; it is far more concerned with telling the story of God overcoming evil than explaining why evil exists in the first place. If Wright had his way, it seems that he would have others stop trying to explain evil and focus more on explaining that God has overcome it in Christ. This defense principally asserts that God is good even though there is evil in the world because he will eventually defeat it and be eternally all in all. Though explained somewhat differently, something similar is said by Feser. He refers to Rom 8:18 to explain that Thomists believe God's eternal rewards make temporal suffering insignificant in comparison. For Feser then, God is good despite temporal evil precisely because God will eventually bring infinite good from it and will reward his people with a glorious eternity. Even some process theists make God's victory over evil and a subsequent afterlife a part of their theodicy. Though not all process theists agree on what exactly an afterlife will look like, some see the possibility of an afterlife as something that helps to prove God's goodness in light of temporal evil. Griffin, for example, in the newest edition of *God, Power, and Evil* said that if he were to rewrite the book, he would put more of an emphasis on the reality of an afterlife as he now believes it to be a more important part of a Christian's response to the POE than when he originally wrote the book.[59]

Clearly, an appeal to God's final victory over evil and the reality of an afterlife is a part of how most Christians respond to the POE. This transcends the differences Christians have due to their adherence to various models of God. Yet how exactly one parses the intricate details of an appeal to the afterlife will somewhat differ, and those differences can be influenced by one's metaphysical beliefs. Obviously, atheists will often object to this appeal to an afterlife by claiming that the concept of eternal conscious torment in hell is unjust. This is an enormous subject and answers to such claims have differed drastically throughout Christian history. Even if one just considers the contemporary Christian responses, there are still a plethora to choose from. For those who believe in eternal conscious torment, the reality of hell is not necessarily something they appeal to in order to exonerate God,

---

58. Wright, *Evil*, 41.
59. Griffin, *God, Power, and Evil*, 10.

though they may defend the doctrine in response to criticism. One may think of the Thomistic tendency to justify God's goodness in light of the eternal conscious torment of the damned on the basis of divine justice and vengeance. For Thomas, the saved shall rejoice at the sight of the torments of the damned; this is not because the saved are rejoicing at the torments of the damned per se, but rather they are rejoicing that God's justice is being realized.[60] I suppose a Thomist could say that this is a part of Thomas's theodicy in a sense. Regardless, it is typically argued that God is good in spite of the reality of eternal conscious torment and not because of it.

Some scholars have found it necessary to reject eternal conscious torment in order to properly respond to the POE. Boyd and Hart are two such examples. For these two, an understanding of God's final victory over sin cannot include the eternal conscious torment of the damned. And their respective views of hell were implemented in their responses to the POE. In *Satan and the Problem of Evil*, Boyd advocates for a version of annihilationism, though not as zealously as he does today, years after that book was released.[61] He notes that an increasing number of biblical scholars and theologians are opting for annihilationism as opposed to eternal conscious torment.[62] Ultimately, though creation was a risky endeavor, annihilationism enables God to trivialize Satan's evil efforts by making him the god of nothing. And God's victory over evil is absolute given annihilationism: "All suffering endured in the probationary period will be behind us. Satan and all the humans and angels who followed him will be in the past."[63] God's risky creation will have been worth it given his victory over evil and the magnificence of the eternal kingdom. Most relevantly, given Boyd's open theism, when God creates someone, he does not know with certainty whether they will be eternally reconciled to God or annihilated. If they are annihilated in the sense Boyd argues for, it is because they have chosen this reality; they have let their actions become their very being (or lack thereof).[64] God must allow for someone to choose what their ultimate destiny will be. Perhaps most importantly, God does not create someone knowing that they will

---

60. See Aquinas, *Summa Theologiae* Suppl.94.2–3.

61. Boyd has since become a more convinced annihilationist, so it is difficult to read *Satan and the Problem of Evil* without this in mind, for those of us who listen to his teaching and read his more current works. In this book particularly, he argues that in so far as everything external to the nonbeliever is concerned, the nonbeliever will be annihilated. Their rebellious will continues to exist, but only via "the existence of utter negation." See Boyd, *Satan*, 342.

62. Boyd, *Satan*, 327.

63. Boyd, *Satan*, 357.

64. Boyd, *Satan*, 189.

eternally reject him, so the atheist charges that hell is unjust are dealt with by Boyd's open theism and annihilationism.

As was observed in chapter 6, Hart's universalism is at the forefront of his theodicy in so far as for Hart, although it is important to understand the proper relationship between God's primary causality and truly free secondary causes, in the end, all of these free secondary causes are logically reducible to God as their primary cause. Thus, if God is to be good and an ultimate answer to the POE is to be found, it must be found in eschatology. God is good precisely because he reconciles all to himself. And this universal reconciliation is a metaphysical necessity, given Hart's Christian monism, which he argues is just a fully developed classical theism. Nature has no existence in and of itself; it is entirely dependent on supernature for its existence. Hart puts it in Aristotelian categories: "Nature stands in relation to supernature as (in Aristotelian terms) prime matter is to form."[65] Because of this, nothing within nature could fail to achieve its "naturally supernatural end" unless God was the moral cause, which would contradict the notion that he is the goodness as such. Ultimately, everything that exists does so via God's timeless donation of being, so "God is all that is. Whatever is not God exists as becoming divine, and as such is God in the mode of what is other than God. But God is not 'the other' of anything."[66] If creation was in fact made for the glory of God, then universalism is a "necessary premise for any coherent account of spiritual creation."[67]

Universalism is also the result of an intelligible articulation of human freedom. Genuine freedom does not only consist in the power of contra choice; such freedom would be little more than spontaneity. Though the power of contra choice is an important component to human freedom, it alone cannot define human freedom. Conversely, Christian thought that was nondeterminist has historically fallen under what Hart calls the "intellectualist model."[68] An action is free only if it is fully rational. That is, the action must not be coerced, but it also must be in accordance with one's nature and own proper good. If an action is not coerced and yet is carried out in ignorance, it cannot be said to be genuinely free. Thus, for Christian theology, an action is only fully free if it conforms to the Good that our natures were originally made for.[69] And considering that God is the goodness as such, it is thus logically incoherent to suggest that humans can freely reject him for

65. Hart, *You Are Gods*, xvii.
66. Hart, *You Are Gods*, xviii.
67. Hart, *You Are Gods*, 122.
68. Hart, *That All Shall Be*, 172.
69. Hart, *That All Shall Be*, 173.

all eternity. Yes, humans may temporally reject God in part out of ignorance or hatred, but to eternally reject him would mean that those humans are not free in any meaningful sense.[70] For Hart, God is the goodness as such, and the goodness of creation is realized in the end of the action: and the end of creation is universal reconciliation of God, with nothing left outside of or lacking that goodness.

Though this is far from a thorough discussion on the afterlife as it relates to the POE, this demonstrates how some metaphysical assumptions affected various scholars' beliefs on the nature of God's victory over sin. For Boyd, the possibility of suffering—this includes perhaps even an element of eternal suffering—is a metaphysically necessary truth of God's creation.[71] We must be free to accept or reject God and God must allow us to experience those consequences in order for our actions to be genuinely free. On the contrary, Hart's Christian monism causes him to see universalism not simply as being entailed by creation or morally necessary given *creatio ex nihilo*, but as metaphysically necessary. Other scholars have responded to criticisms of the doctrine of eternal conscious torment, but as has been previously stated, those responses fall outside the scope of the current work.

---

70. See Hart's discussion in Hart, *That All Shall Be*, 192–93.
71. Boyd, *Satan*, 25.

Chapter 8

A Classical God in a Modern World

I

Up to this point, I have attempted to be objective in providing an overview and analysis of the contemporary intersection between metaphysics and apologetics. The material has hopefully been somewhat helpful or at least mildly entertaining. From this point on, however, I am dropping the objective descriptions and offering my own thoughts on the importance of believing in classical theism. I write from the perspective of someone who regularly deals with many such questions related to the material, from "deconstructing" Christians who were fed evangelical fundamentalist theology growing up to skeptical college students who understand that materialism provides their lives no greater meaning, yet are not convinced Christianity has anything better to say. Some of these ideas may seem academic and abstract; but that does not stop many people from pondering such difficulties.

As a theologian first and foremost, I cannot help but admit that theistic personalist construals of the nature of God are quite puzzling to me. Classical Christian theology proper was crafted in such a meticulous way that it is impossible to separate early Christian doctrinal formulations from their underlying metaphysical beliefs. Modern scholars do not always appreciate this to the degree that they should. When the pro-Nicenes formally articulated their understanding of God, they did so through an unabashedly classical paradigm in so far as when they discussed the divine processions, for instance, they understood them to be timeless actions within the Godhead. They would have never imagined that Christians would later attempt to formulate a doctrine of the Trinity without believing in divine timelessness.

What would this lead to? Well, one answer is social trinitarianism.[1] Some adherents to social trinitarianism even deny the doctrine of divine processions outright.[2] And what is the difference between this and Arianism in so far as creedal orthodoxy is concerned? Both would reject parts of the Nicene Creed. Or what would it mean to say one believes in the Nicene Creed while simultaneously believing that God is temporal? Hasker has done just this, asserting that the Son is always being begotten of the Father. This is a rather idiosyncratic view, and leads one to wonder what exactly the implications are for God's very essence to always be in process. Does God's essence change, given that the generation of the Son is a temporal act?[3] Is what is most foundational to reality in fact process or change? Are we encroaching on the territory of process metaphysics now? Further, one would seemingly be forced to deny the DDS if one believes in social trinitarianism. Of course, as we have seen in this book, there are those who are more than happy to do this. If God is made up of three persons, and that term is used in a univocal sense, then God is made up of three distinct centers of consciousness and three distinct wills. This is flatly incompatible with divine simplicity,[4] which is of course one of the reasons why the Cappadocians were not social trinitarians. It would also seem to indicate that the Trinity is more of a quartet, seeing as that there is one entity we call God, which is composed of the Father, Son, and Spirit, yet each of these three are fully God in that they have their own center of consciousness and will, so one wonders how we do not have four divine entities. And without the DDS, God as Trinity himself is a composite being. What grounds the existence of the Father, Son, and Spirit? Are they "just there"? If there are three distinct principles that are uncaused, then again, do we not have three Gods? One may say the divine essence is the uncaused cause which they all share in. So is the divine essence more fundamental than the persons? And if so, it would again appear that we have four divine agents as opposed to three. There would also

---

1. This term is somewhat ambiguous in the literature, as Mullins has pointed out. See Mullins, "Hasker," 182. Here I use the term to refer to models of the Trinity that assert each of the divine persons have their own will and center of consciousness. To refer to the divine persons as "persons" is to do so in a univocal sense.

2. Here it should be noted that adherence to divine timelessness does not entail one will embrace the divine processions. Kevin Giles has identified over a dozen scholars with prominent followings who deny the divine processions, including Wayne Grudem and Paul Helm. See Giles, *Eternal Generation*, 30–33, cited by Hasker, *Metaphysics*, 214.

3. Hasker obviously argues to the contrary. He claims that for God there is no "causal gap" between God willing something to happen and it happening. Thus, God can will the Son to exist everlastingly. See Hasker, "'God's Only Begotten Son,'" 219–21.

4. Hollingsworth, "Mere Social Trinitarianism," 33–36.

be no basis for the Father being the Father, and the Son being the Son. They would be more like brothers, ontologically speaking.

One may recall that the Nicene Creed begins with "We believe in one God, the Father." The one God just is the Father, because the Father is the only uncaused cause. The term "God" here refers to an uncaused cause: "There is one God because there is one Father."[5] Monotheism is thus predicated on the Father. The Son and the Spirit share in the divine nature precisely because the Father is their principle. There is not one essence that transcends the persons;[6] the Father grounds the existence of the Trinity, as he grounds the existence of the Son and the Spirit. To suggest that the Son and the Spirit share in the divine nature is to say that they proceed from the Father and thus derive their divinity from him. The Son is "true God from true God." They are coeternal with the Father, as they are not created beings. When the Nicene party argued this, they meant to say that the Son and Spirit are timeless with the Father, and that everything else is created and thus temporal. Everything else experiences sequence. This is how the creed explains their being *homoousios* with the Father. Moreover, the divine essence is not a composite entity because the Father, Son, and Spirit do not together combine to form the divine essence. Rather, the pro-Nicenes were committed to a kind of simplistic unity as opposed to a composite unity of persons. Again, the Son and the Spirit proceed from the uncaused cause by nature, thereby sharing in the divine essence. The doctrine of the *monarchia* (μοναρχία) of the Father was essential to Nicene theology and its implications were explicated via classical metaphysics. To my mind, a rejection of classical metaphysics entails an abandonment of Nicaea.

A denial or modification of Nicaea may not be considered the worst thing in the world for some modern theologians. I personally don't think someone is a God-hating heretic if they have disagreements with Nicaea, given my admittedly "low" view of the role of ecclesial authority. I happen to believe Nicaea was correct in its understanding of God, but it is also evident that many God-fearing Christians today have their skepticisms of the Nicene formulation. What is most strange to me is when certain scholars will deny classical theism, but insist we must believe in Nicaea, as though its

---

5. Basil, *Homily Against the Sabellians* 3. (*On Christian Doctrine*, 294). Also: "There are not two gods because there are not two fathers. Whoever introduces two first principles preaches two gods." Basil, *Homily Against the Sabellians* 4 (*On Christian Doctrine*, 295).

6. Again, Basil makes this clear: "But when I say 'one substance,' do not think that two are separated from one, but that the Son has come to subsist from the Father, his principle. The Father and Son do not come from one substance that transcends them both. For we do not call them brothers, but confess Father and Son." Basil, *Homily Against the Sabellians* 4 (*On Christian Doctrine*, 295).

doctrinal formulations can be separated from the underlying metaphysics. But alas, this is not principally a theology book, so I will return to the issue of apologetics now. These theological disputes have been discussed at length elsewhere, with many fervently disagreeing with my conclusions. Suffice it to say that, from a theological standpoint, I find the quest to integrate some form of theistic personalism with classical Christian theology proper to be less than a fruitful endeavor. To my mind, the process theists are most consistent in their willingness to reconsider all facets of the Christian doctrine of God in light of their rejection of classical metaphysics.

II

There is little doubt that theistic personalist scholars are on the offensive today. A rejection of classical theism is popular for biblical, philosophical, and theological reasons. Post-Enlightenment thinking in general and analytic philosophy and theology in particular are not friendly towards analogical predication and negative theology. When scholars today reject the DDS, they do so with an almost giddy demeanor. They attack it proudly and confidently. And to be sure, there are a number of extremely sophisticated arguments against the DDS. This would include disagreements with the doctrine per se, as well as doubts as to its compatibility with core Christian teachings like the incarnation. If one is a serious thinker, one cannot read literature from the likes of Plantinga or Mullins and conclude that there is nothing there to consider. Due to the erudition of these modern scholars, and given the general abandonment of the classical view of God in our culture, it is at times easy to see why theistic personalists feel so comfortable being on the offensive. The rules of the game, as it were, are firmly set in their favor, and some are able to play it well.

In the midst of all this, however, there is an overlooked yet extraordinarily important detail missing from the discussion: theistic personalists often do not fully appreciate just how much they are giving up when they denounce the DDS. Sure, it is easy, given the rules of analytic philosophy and theology, to criticize the doctrine. But it should not be so easy to ignore the negative consequences of disposing with a metaphysical idea that has been central to all of the philosophically reflective theistic faiths for the last two thousand years. There is a reason philosophers and theologians maintained the truth of divine simplicity even when it proved difficult while hashing out the implications of the doctrine for revealed theology. Without the DDS, God loses his fundamentality. God becomes dependent on something else to be what he is: metaphysical parts, nature, time, etc. When one denies the

DDS, despite the perceived theological advantages of doing so, one loses an ultimate explanation for why there is anything at all. Existence as such becomes a brute fact due to God existing as a being among other beings within the continuum of reality.

This was easily seen in chapter 3. Without the DDS, there is no rationale for the PSR, as one is eventually forced to conclude that some entities—whether they be fundamental moral truths, mathematical formulae, or other universals—simply exist as brute fact. If God exists and is made up of parts, where did those parts come from? If there are truths independent of God, where did they come from? Swinburne was most explicit about his ultimate rejection of the PSR, but this realization was implicit in most of the theistic personalist arguments for God's existence. O'Connor said as much when he observed that the existence question has been deemed unanswerable by most of modern philosophy. Of course, this is to be expected from atheists; but for a Christian to engage in such reasoning is an entirely different matter. What is to separate an atheist's assertion that existence as such is a brute fact from a Christian's? If fundamental moral truth, or abstract objects, or necessarily true mathematical formulae do not need any grounding for their existence, then can a Christian really tell the atheist that their proposition of a "just there" universe is fanciful or intellectually incoherent? I would say not. On what basis could Christians tell an atheist, say, Sam Harris, that his moral realism is incoherent if fundamental moral propositions are independent of God's nature? After all, a 2020 PhilPapers survey indicated that a majority of modern philosophers are moral realists, to the tune of 62.07 percent either accepting or leaning towards moral realism.[7] This makes for a large amount of atheist philosophers affirming moral realism, given that 66.95 percent either affirmed atheism or leaned towards affirming atheism, with another 7.18 percent claiming to be agnostic. These atheists largely consider morally true propositions to be metaphysically necessary brute facts. They have no grounding for their existence beyond their metaphysical necessity. They are the epitome of "just thereness." The classical theist can confidently say the atheist, no matter how badly he may want objective moral truth, has nothing in which to ground such propositions. Conversely, a denial of the DDS leaves the theistic personalist playing the same game as the naturalists; they propose the existence of brute facts because they have rejected God as the ground of all being.[8]

---

7. "Survey Results." These numbers were limited to the responses of philosophy PhDs.

8. I will reiterate a point made earlier: some theistic personalists will attempt to deal with this objection, such as Craig or O'Connor. For O'Connor, his proposal concerning God's essential nature is thoughtful, but inadequate. It would still be subject to

The DDS is what enables us to say that God is the end of reason's journey. If there exists truths that are independent of God, then we are left looking beyond God for truth. I am inclined to agree with Feser and Pruss when they claim that a rejection of the PSR ultimately leads to a radical skepticism about even our perceptions, as they may not have any coherent reason for being the way that they are.[9] If unintelligibility is possible, then the atheist is justified in saying the existence question is unanswerable. If Swinburne is correct in his contention that we are forced to acknowledge the existence of brute facts, then the atheist can simply assert one more brute fact than Swinburne; the physical universe as a whole or the laws of nature or quantum phenomena can be "just there." No, if the universe is ultimately intelligible, then the DDS is indispensable. Once the Christian gives away the fundamentality of God, he gives away the answer to the existence question. From there, it is a sparring contest with the atheist to see who can convince the other that their naturalism/theism is more probable. And apparently the atheists are winning, at least concerning professional philosophy. When the understanding of God shifted from a classical paradigm to the modern analytic paradigm, it did not bode well for Christian philosophy. When God went from being as such to a being among other beings, the philosophical cost of rejecting his existence became much less punitive. Though the Christian analytic philosophers find themselves on the offensive against classical theists, their betrayal of classical Christian metaphysics has cost them dearly against the atheists.

III

But what about popular-level apologetics? That is where most apologetic efforts are carried out, so one may be tempted to argue that it is rather irrelevant what happens at the professional level. To that, my response is twofold. For starters, it is never irrelevant what happens in academia. I know it may seem that way to those not embedded in the minutiae of professional

---

the same criticism that classical theism employs against all composite realities: they are dependent on their parts to be what they are. No matter how it is posited, if God has numerically distinct properties, he is dependent upon those properties to be what he is. This is especially true given O'Connor's belief that God is temporal. Since he is temporal, God is thus made up of a combination of potentiality and actuality. He is subject to potentiality—something external to himself—to be what he is. As for Craig, he is content to deny realism: "The overriding point, however, is that there is just no compelling reason to be a realist." This is, of course, a denial of divine conceptualism, which he calls the "historic Christian position." See Craig, *God Over All*, 206–7.

9. Feser, *Five Proofs*, 149; Pruss, "Leibnizian Cosmological Argument," 28.

philosophical and theological debate. To the average Christian, the language of these debates seems so abstract and arbitrary. In some ways I am sympathetic to such attitudes. Nonetheless, ideas that prevail in academic settings have a tendency to find their way into the everyday lives of that society's citizenry. Take Critical Theory and its derivatives, for example. When Herbert Marcuse was marrying Critical Race Theory to civil rights initiatives in American universities, the average person may have been unaware. They were simply concerned with the debates that were taking place concerning racial equality in public life. This is understandable, of course. Little did the average person know that sixty years later, however, their fifth-grade grandson would be determining whether he is an oppressor or an oppressed citizen by surveying his immutable traits in the classroom. Sure, Critical Race Theory is a graduate level social theory used to evaluate the relationship between societal structures and ethnicity, so it is not explicitly taught to fifth graders. But the ideas and the consequences of such a paradigm are felt even in grade school. The same can be said for HR departments, popular television, and national politics. The point is: what prevails in academia often finds its way, in one form or another, to public life.

Metaphysics and apologetics are no different in this regard. Academia helps to shape the theology of clergy, and clergy help to shape the theology of their congregations. There is no doubt that theistic personalism has won the day among the average churchgoer, and even among the typical person who utilizes apologetics to share and defend their faith. Classical theism seems foreign and strange to many Christians today. And more importantly for them, it appears to be flatly incompatible with the biblical data, given the modern propensity toward univocal readings of the Old Testament especially. To dare to suggest one must read the biblical text with classical metaphysics in mind borders on a heresy in today's day and age.

Additionally, the consequences of theistic personalism's prevalence within academia have been vividly manifest in popular level apologetics. Movements such as Young Earth Creationism (YEC) and ID theory have dominated the discourse in our culture in recent decades. This has been detrimental to Christian apologetics. We are frequently left discussing the physical origins of the universe or what kind of (if any) evolution of species has occurred. I vividly recall attending a large youth group conference as a teenager, and the entire theme was explaining how dinosaurs and humans had certainly been alive at the same time on earth. It is difficult to exaggerate the vanity of such an event or how much damage events like it have done to the faith of American teenagers. If we are going to discuss God's existence, we should be talking about the nature of consciousness, or the need for an ultimate explanation for existence, or Thomas's five ways. Yes,

I'm quite confident that a youth conference on Thomas's five ways would be much more beneficial to teenage Christians. Regrettably, YEC and ID keep us talking about dinosaurs and evolution.

Obviously, to be fair, not every theistic personalist would endorse such movements or the types of arguments they provide for God's existence. In fact, most theistic personalists in academia would have plenty of negative things to say about YEC in particular. Yet it is the consequences of various academic ideas that have made such movements possible. Consider YEC. Principally, its core idea is that God created the world roughly six thousand years ago via successive temporal interventions for six consecutive days. Such an idea combines a lack of understanding concerning the genre of Genesis—the assumption being that Gen 1 was intended to convey a material history of the universe—with a rejection of classical Christian understandings of creation.[10] As for the former, any exegesis of Genesis that would entail allegory cannot be tolerated. Genesis 1–3 must be taken as an explanation of the material or scientific origins of the universe. God gave us the details of the creation of the world in Genesis, says Ken Ham.[11] And if one does not take this creation account "literally" then one cannot use it in any kind of authoritative manner when it comes to something like the historic Christian understanding of marriage between a man and a woman.[12] To call this an anachronism would be a gross understatement. Nonetheless, it is Ham's conviction that the text must be read in a "straightforward" or univocal sense. He is simply following the guidelines laid out by "The Chicago Statement on Biblical Inerrancy," which is a product itself of modernity. Gone are the days of, say, Origen and Augustine allegorizing the days of creation in Genesis precisely because the univocal sense of the text seems to contradict the scientific knowledge of their day. Origen and Augustine recognized that it would be an absurdity for there to be light on the first three days before the creation of the sun on the fourth.[13] Gregory of Nyssa made the observation, long before the advent of historical-critical studies, that there seemed to be two separate creation accounts in Gen 1–3.

---

10. One can see the mistake in such a viewpoint even if one does not adhere to classical metaphysics. One simply needs to understand Genesis's place among contemporary ancient Near Eastern literature. John Walton, for example, has said, "Analysts of the ancient Near Eastern creation literature often observe that nothing material is actually made in these accounts" and "They show little interest in material origins." See Walton, *Lost World*, 33, 34.

11. Ham, *Lie*, 17.

12. Ham, *Lie*, 101.

13. O'Keefe and Reno, *Sanctified Vision*, 95–96.

In his *On the Making of Man*, he sees this as a need to invoke a "nonliteral, spiritual interpretation."[14]

The crux of the matter here is obviously not to say that Ken Ham represents the only logical conclusion of modern biblical interpretative methods. As I said earlier, one can understand Gen 1–3 in such a way that does not lead to YEC without appealing to classical biblical exegesis. Rather, I simply mean to say that it is a tendency towards univocal understandings of the biblical text that have enabled something like YEC to become so popular in evangelical culture today. Even before the church fathers had a grasp on ancient Near Eastern literature that was contemporary with the Old Testament, they were able to understand the Genesis creation accounts in ways that were conducive to their scientific knowledge of the day. Augustine and Origen utilized these classical tools in order to further their apologetic efforts. In fact, that was Origen's primary concern, as he felt if people were limited to a "literal" reading of the Scripture, they would see it as nonsensical.[15] Though many in academia may be capable of more careful nuance in their integration of modern science with their univocal readings of the biblical language, it is not so easy for others to follow suit. This is not, needless to say, a reason to abandon academic inquiry into such matters. An academic cannot always control how his or her ideas will be received by the masses. My only contention here is that if Christians had a classical understanding of the Bible, and if we read it and treated it like the aforementioned fathers did, then the masses would have no reason or incentive to invent something like YEC. This does not require agreement with the particular theology of Augustine, Origen, or Gregory; this simply entails commonality in approach to the text generally.

A rejection of a classical Christian understanding of creation also makes YEC possible. As Hart has noted, many of the Christian theologians of the patristic era understood creation as a timeless donation of being. Basil, for instance, thought of God's creative act as timelessly bringing into being past, present, and future.[16] This is vital. If *creatio ex nihilo* was not timeless, it would introduce sequence into God's existence. More pertinent for present purposes, if creation was thought of as a timeless act, there would be no need for certain Christians to ascertain from Gen 1 that God created the universe through sequential physical interventions. For those who adhere to this patristic view of creation, something like evolution shouldn't be considered to rival God's creative act. Hart points to John Henry Newman,

---

14. O'Keefe and Reno, *Sanctified Vision*, 96.
15. O'Keefe and Reno, *Sanctified Vision*, 95.
16. Hart, *Experience of God*, 25–26.

a contemporary of Darwin's and a patristics scholar in his own right, as someone who could find nothing in the theory of evolution itself that would prove to be antithetical to the Christian understanding of creation.[17] This is because if creation is understood to be timeless, then God's act of creation is conceived as the totality of existence, regardless of how exactly physical realities developed or over how long of a period of time this occurred.

Yes, if one understands creation as a temporal act(s), then one can still conceive of creation in such a way so as to be consistent with observable data. God's temporal act of creation could have taken place over thirteen billion years ago. However, so long as one conceives of creation as a temporal act, then YEC is possible in principle. Conversely, if creation is timeless, then YEC's central premise—that God created via six successive cosmic interventions throughout the course of a literal week—is false *in principle*. I suppose a classical theist could in theory believe in a young earth. He could believe that God's timeless act of creation unfolded within time, and that time only goes back roughly six thousand years into the past. There would, however, be little reason for him to believe that, given the geological and biological evidence we have today. And considering the fact that the text of the creation accounts is being allegorized by the classical theist, there is even less reason for those accounts to form the basis for any beliefs regarding the material history of the unfolding of various geographical epochs. Creation conceived as temporal, combined with a preference for univocal conceptions of biblical language, sets the stage for YEC.

IV

This goes beyond particular movements fueled by a rejection of classical metaphysics. The view of God that these movements exemplify, a God who exists within the continuum of nature, can be seen throughout popular-level discourse with the new atheists. At times the level of dialogue is beyond parody. One may think of the famous instance of Yuri Gagarin going into orbit and claiming that he did not see God above earth. Whether or not he actually said this is disputed, though the fact that such an utterance could be believably fabricated is telling enough. Or one could think of a more modern example. As was mentioned in the introduction to this book, Sam Harris was being interviewed in 2022 by a popular YouTube channel called Triggernometry. During the interview, he questioned why people still believe in God, given that we haven't been able to see heaven or God yet. Harris asserted that if God or heaven existed, we would have been able to see them

---

17. Hart, *Experience of God*, 26.

by now! We have telescopes that have been looking into deep space giving us billions of years of data. If you don't laugh, you have no sense of humor. But as funny as this was, it demonstrated quite clearly that even someone with a PhD in cognitive neuroscience can have absolutely no conception of classical theism. What Harris is arguing against is often a caricature of even theistic personalism. Again though, it is a belief in God as a being among beings that makes such absurdity possible. There is an expectation that God is "out there" somewhere; he exists as an object among objects so if we just look hard enough, perhaps we can find him.

Admittedly, this is an extreme example. Though the level of discourse is usually poor, it rarely reaches those depths. Most churchgoing theistic personalists are able to explain that heaven and God perhaps do not exist within the same dimension as we do, or that God is an incorporeal being.[18] Few expect to be able to actually see God with a telescope. And yet, the question must be asked: where would Sam Harris get the idea that God is "out there" somewhere within the confines of nature? Clearly, it is an intuition he has garnered from listening to people talk about God. For those with no understanding or concern for classical theism, God is a being among beings, though he may be the supreme being in that class. To say that God exists is to essentially say that he exists in the same way you or I might exist. As Ogden explained, existence is an abstract variable attached to something that has actual existence in some definite state.[19] This is very different from saying that God is existence as such. For the classical theist, God does not instantiate the property of divinity or necessary existence or what have you; rather, God is the source of all being, the reason why any property can be instantiated in the first place. Hart puts it this way: God is "at once both the *superior summo meo* and *interior intimo meo*; and that he is not merely the supreme being set atop the summit of beings, but is instead the one who is transcendently present in all things, the ever more inward act within each finite act."[20] With this understanding of God's existence, it would be impossible for one to even conceive that God can be "found" with a telescope. If, however, one conceives of God's existence in similar terms as the existence of finite entities, then it is easy to see how such a conclusion could be reached within the cultural discussion.

18. Though this idea itself is increasingly being challenged by some adherents to open theism, as the understandings of the biblical descriptions of God become increasingly univocal. The reader will recall that Clark Pinnock openly questioned the historic Christian idea that God is incorporeal precisely on these grounds. See Pinnock, *Most Moved Mover*, 33–34.

19. Ogden, "Reality of God," 47–48

20. Hart, "Impassibility as Transcendence," 170.

This may still seem rather silly to most readers of the theistic personalist persuasion. If it does, I would submit to you that these examples from Gagarin and Harris are not all that different from the idea that "science can disprove God." And this is, of course, no different than saying, "science proves God exists." Both are egregious category errors, but are nonetheless repeated *ad nauseam*. To suggest that science has anything directly to say about the existence of God is to make the same mistake that Gagarin and Harris made, though on a slightly less explicit level. Such an attitude presupposes that God is a part of nature, and that he exists in the same way that finite realities exist. Science observes finite reality, but God cannot be observed in that way. God transcends existence and nonexistence, in so far as we use those terms to describe the existence of natural phenomena. He is not a force among other forces to be observed and quantified. God's act in creation does not rival any observable scientific realities. On the contrary, he is the source of the very possibility of such realities, and such observation. It is wholly irrelevant to the question of God whether or not, or to what extent, evolution of species occurred. God would be the source of their being regardless of how exactly we measure the material history of their coming into the forms they are now. It is likewise completely extraneous to the question of God as to how old the universe is. The universe could be six thousand years old, or it could be thirteen billion, or twenty-seven billion (a number that is becoming increasingly popular in the aftermath of the latest James Webb telescope photos)[21], or it could be without temporal beginning or end, and God would still be its source of being. These scientific questions are admittedly fascinating and worthy of pursuit. They do not, however, shed any light on the question of God's existence.

At most, general observations about the physical universe tell us something about, say, the nature of causation. We know from observing natural phenomena that in order for any potentiality to become actuality, something actual must cause this to occur. Hence, Aristotle's argument for God's existence based on the need for something devoid of potential to exist, lest there be an infinite metaphysical regress. Paul uses similar reasoning in Romans when he claims that we can know the divine nature simply by contemplating creation. But this is not science proving God's existence; this is simply taking phenomenological concepts and applying them to the realm of metaphysics. When someone like Stephen Hawking says that science has proven God does not exist, he means to say that God is not needed to explain why this particular physical universe exists. That can, after all, be explained via cosmological speculations such as his theorized quantum

---

21. For example, see Gupta, "JWST Early Universe."

fluctuations. Here, God's creative act is alleged to be some specific temporal event that took place in the distant past; and there is no need for that to explain the physical universe we have now, given the Big Bang or Hawking's quantum fluctuations or whatever other speculative cosmological model is fashionable on a particular day. Thus, when the new atheist says, "Science has disproven God," they essentially proclaim that certain specific scientific observations have proven, in and of themselves, that God does not exist. This is impossible given classical theism, but as has been demonstrated, classical understandings of God are not what is being discussed in such conversations.

To assert that science has proven God exists is equally ludicrous. The entire ID movement embarks on a similar journey to that of the new atheists. They seek to find instances within nature that cannot be explained by an unguided process of evolution—"irreducible complexity"—and proclaim that these scientific discoveries have proven the existence of an intelligent designer. This is the exact same category error that the new atheist makes. And really, what does this prove? That God's design of nature had a flaw so he was forced to interject? Paul Tillich described this as *argumentum ex ignorantia*: specifically the ignorance of scientific and historical knowledge that God could fill. For Tillich, this is an "undignified procedure" that discredits everything associated with apologetics.[22] I tend to agree. But more importantly, to reiterate an extremely helpful point of emphasis made by Hart in chapter 4, this view of science and God makes it possible that science could in principle disprove God's existence one day.[23] If there is a scientific observation about a particular organism that one deems unguided evolution cannot be responsible for, then what happens when a scientific advancement is made and that instance of irreducible complexity is now explainable via evolution? Or what happens if one day we arrive at a point where there are no more instances of irreducible complexity? This is the entire problem with the dominant view of God in popular Christian-atheist conversation: God's action in creation is seemingly a rival to that of natural processes. The fact that Christians may get nervous in the pews if their pastor mentions "the Big Bang" in a positive or neutral tone means they see natural explanation as a rival to God's work in the universe, when they should view God as the reason why any natural processes are possible in the first place.

22. Tillich, *Systematic Theology*, 6.
23. Hart, *Experience of God*, 41.

V

There is an old story that has its roots in Hindu mythology concerning the problem of infinite regress. Essentially, it is said that the earth is flat and is supported by seven elephants; and those elephants do not sink and are thus on stable ground due to the fact that they stand on a giant tortoise. If one asks what the giant tortoise then stands on, only mystery abounds. This story has been discussed at length throughout the centuries by philosophers such as John Locke, David Hume, and Bertrand Russell in dealing with issues surrounding epistemology. Hume and Russell claim that this story cannot be used as a proof for God's existence, since God himself would require a cause. This, of course, misunderstands the claims of classical theism, but their discussion of the story is nonetheless noteworthy. There are also modern articulations of the story, some with more of a scientific orientation. One such version goes something like this:

> *There was a professor giving a lecture in the 1700s about the structure of our solar system, explaining that the sun is positioned in the center with a round Earth orbiting around it. Upon listening to the conclusion of the lecture, an older woman approached the professor to offer a critique.*
>
> *"Professor, your presentation was riveting and your theories provocative. However, they are still wrong, despite their thought-provoking nature."*
>
> *"I appreciate the kind words, ma'am. Where exactly was I in the wrong?" replied the professor.*
>
> *"Well, Earth is not round at all. You see, Earth is a flat plain that is held up by four giant elephants."*
>
> *"What are those elephants standing on?"*
>
> *"The back of a giant turtle," said the older woman.*
>
> *"What does that turtle stand on?"*
>
> *"An even bigger turtle!"*
>
> *"And what about the even bigger turtle?" asked the professor.*
>
> *The older woman smiled with a sense of triumph. "Don't you see, professor? It's turtles all the way down!"*

As I alluded to, this story can and has been employed in different ways to demonstrate various points of view. Nevertheless, I believe it effectively portrays some of the larger points of emphasis in this chapter. The elderly woman proves the inadequacy of brute facts and infinite regress to provide us with a rational framework with which to view our own existence. When a philosopher asserts that objective moral facts have no need to be grounded in anything more fundamental, or when one claims the universe just is itself a proper explanatory stopping point, they are making the exact same move that the elderly woman makes in the story. They are appealing to unintelligibility, regardless of their desire to do so. Classical theism solves the problem of brute facts and infinite regress.

It should be clear at this point why adherence to classical theism is so imperative from a metaphysical standpoint. The "God of the philosophers" is the result of rigorous philosophical reflection. The ability to reason toward God in such a manner can also be considered revelation from God himself. All revealed theology must be consistent with what is logically entailed in such metaphysical investigation. No matter how cogent a particular theological idea may seem, if it entails that the world is ultimately unintelligible, then it must be false. It is my contention that if the world is to be comprehensible, then classical theism must be true. Philosophers from various faiths, including Christianity, have known this for thousands of years. By forsaking classical metaphysics, Christians have unwittingly made the new atheism a palatable philosophical position. Paradoxically, a recovery of these classical principles can help to make Christian faith a more intellectually persuasive option for those who feel they cannot believe in the God they have so often heard about.

Chapter 9

The Problem of Evil and Monism

I

THE CONTENT IN THE PREVIOUS chapter is, to my mind, fairly straightforward. The existence of God as classically defined is the only way to make sense of our own existence; it is the only way that our world, and our experience of it, can be intelligible. And for theistic personalists to do away with God's fundamentality is a catastrophic error. This is simple enough. But when it comes to the POE things get a bit more complex. As Boyd pointed out, the post-Augustine church has spent more energy on the POE than any other single issue. I confess the reason for this is that there has never been produced a fully satisfactory answer to the problem. We long for the issue to be "solved" but, as it turns out, that simply is not fully possible for our finite minds. Yes, some answers and general approaches to the issue are better than others, but any honest person can concede that proving God's goodness is more difficult than proving God is the ground of all being. When speaking of ontology, the task is rather simple. When speaking of God's goodness, however, one should be more understanding of those who struggle to reconcile a good God with a universe filled with death and suffering.

This should make it all the more important for Christians to respond adequately to questions surrounding the POE. And it is in responding to the POE that some theistic personalist portrayals of God's relationship to creation are most understandable. Augustinian inclinations towards determinism are largely responsible for the standard "God works in mysterious ways" sentiment that is often present when some terrible evil or suffering occurs. The implication, then, is that the evil originated in God's will before it became manifest to us. Consequently, a large part of the reason for the emergence of openness and process theology was to more suitably respond to questions concerning God's goodness. Admittedly, I have a fondness for process theology particularly when it comes to this issue. Though the process approach is not consistent with historical Christianity, its answers are more satisfying than much of what has been offered by either classical theists or non-process theistic personalists. The move to deny omnipotence and *creatio ex nihilo* makes it as though one can expect for evil to exist. If God is always creating out of chaos then a battle between good and evil is more or less foundational to the fabric of reality. God can hardly be implicated in the same way that he is when considering other systematic responses to the POE. It almost makes one think of the creation myths of old, before the days of highly developed philosophical reflection. Bronze Age worshipers of the gods didn't necessarily have a "problem of evil" to solve because they did not conceive of a perfectly good and omnipotent deity from whom all things flow. Creation was often the result of a battle between deities. The existence of evil was essentially to be expected. Process theism, of course, has its differences with these myths, as process philosophy contains a highly developed metaphysical system of thought in its own right. This is true. But the idea that chaos is a part of the structure of existence has much in common with these old myths, at least in so far as the question of evil is concerned.

To be sure, this is a large point of emphasis of this book: apologetics and metaphysics cannot be separated. So although some theistic personalist responses to the POE are admirable, at least on the surface, they ultimately cannot be true in their totality because they lead to metaphysical absurdities. As fond as I am of certain aspects within process thought, it is still subject to the basic criticisms of classical theism. Where did this chaos that God is creating from originate? What is the basis for the existence of universals given that God is a composite being himself? No matter how much we may try to escape it, divine simplicity is a nonnegotiable if the world is to be intelligible. Thus it seems that the only coherent metaphysic must be some type of monism.[1]

---

1. There are different varieties of monism that philosophers can reference. The type of monism I am referring to in this chapter specifically and the book more broadly is distinguished in the contemporary literature as priority monism. Other kinds of monisms may have kernels of truth in them, but they won't be discussed here. For our purposes, a Christian priority monism simply refers to the belief that everything exists only derivatively from a singularity, that being God. The Father is the only thing that exists in and of himself; all else derives its existence from him. Nothing can exist independently of God, as he sustains all that has been, is, or ever will be.

II

The second indispensable truth to establish relating to the POE is that a strong view of free will is absolutely necessary for Christian apologetics. This is undoubtedly the area in which theistic personalism has made its most positive contribution to Christian apologetics. Free-will oriented theistic personalists have forced the classical tradition to reconsider and rearticulate a view of freedom of the human will that is consistent with God's goodness. Though there are formidable responses to the POE within the classical tradition, the further removed from patristic theology, the seemingly worse these responses become. Medieval and Reformation era explications of God's relationship to the world in light of classical theism were not always faithful to God's goodness. The easiest way to demonstrate this is simply to look at Calvin's writings. Following in the later Augustinian tradition, Calvin envisaged God's sovereignty in terms of raw power. His conception of God's relationship to the world led him to completely eradicate any semblance of decency in his construal of God's relationship to evil. God predestines everything that occurs; even the thoughts and inclinations of man are a result of this eternal, irrevocable, and comprehensive predestination of all that will come to pass:

> The devil, and the whole train of the ungodly, are in all directions, held in by the hand of God as with a bridle, so that they can neither conceive any mischief, nor plan what they have conceived, nor how muchsoever they may have planned, move a single finger to perpetrate, unless in so far as he permits, nay unless in so far as he commands, that they are not only bound by his fetters but are even forced to do him service.[2]

This includes, most egregiously, the eternal reprobation of the nonelect. For Calvin, some are given salvation, while others are barred access from it.[3] To be clear, then, God predestines all evil that will ever occur, including even the thoughts and plans that would lead to that evil being carried out. Not only that, God also predestines for the reprobate to be eternally tormented for the evil that God ensured they would commit.

It is impossible to construct anything like a Christian response to the POE given Calvin's theology. The problem is that Calvin's God is just evil. Most rational people are able to see this. Nevertheless, Calvin was only being more explicit about what theologians before him had concluded concerning the nature of God's relationship to the world. The baroque Thomist tradition

---

2. Calvin, *Institutes*, 1.17.11.
3. Calvin, *Institutes*, 3.21.5.

that Hart spoke about earlier had more or less established a similar theology by the time of Calvin. They are to be commended, I think, for at least having the moral aptitude to realize the need to attempt to articulate God's sovereignty in ways that would not directly implicate him in the atrocities of humankind. They failed though, of course. If a temporal action is made inevitable by God's decree then it cannot be free, regardless of its logical designation.[4] I agree with Hart, in that so long as we are speaking of a specific act of the will that has its origins in God's eternal decree, it cannot be considered free in any way that would make sense of God's relationship to it. It may be admirable for the Bañezians to describe sinful actions as logically contingent in an endeavor to make God's eternal decree consistent with the claim that he is perfectly good; but it is still nonetheless true that such an elucidation is ultimately little different than Calvin's.

All denials that humans have the power of contra choice, whether they be forms of compatibilism or hard determinism, inevitably make God the author of evil. This is a point that many theistic personalists have successfully emphasized. A strong view of free will must include the ability for one to have the capacity to choose or not to choose to do a particular thing. That is not all it must include, needless to say. We instinctively understand this, but Christians don't always have the easiest time conveying this intuition. I am inclined to agree with the intellectualist model of freedom as opposed to the libertarian model. Freedom is not merely to be ascertained simply by the power of contra choice. If one is truly free, one must also act rationally according to one's nature. A child may be "free" to walk in the middle of a busy street, in so far as there is nothing external nor internal to the child that is prohibiting her from doing so. From a purely libertarian point of view, she is free. Yet we would not consider her to be truly free, as she is acting, on some level, out of ignorance and irrationality when doing such a thing. She has the ability to walk into the busy street or to abstain from doing so, but this is not the true extent of freedom. In this scenario, one would blame the parent of the child as opposed to the child herself due to the fact that she is not really acting freely at all, even though she has the power of contra choice. Thus, freedom is best understood as acting in accordance with rationality, free from external or internal restraint.[5] Having said this, though freedom

---

4. Hart, "Impassibility as Transcendence," 177.

5. Of course, so long as we are speaking of freedom in this life, we are speaking in terms of degrees of freedom. Though we may rarely be restrained from acting in a certain way, we do not often experience a measure of perfect rationality. Especially with respect to God, there is some level of ambiguity. In the same vein, I am reminded of 1 Cor 13:12, where Paul says we will see love perfectly one day, but now we view love as though we were looking through a mirror in obscurity.

is more than the power of contra choice, it is not less than that. If one's desires are predestined by God, and one inevitably acts in accordance to one's strongest desires, then one is not free. Swinburne correctly argued that the Christian understanding of human freedom has largely been understood as having the power of contra choice, or to act independently of causes that are influencing them. The reason for this understanding, says Swinburne, was in part due to the fact that moral responsibility necessitated such an understanding of human freedom.[6]

Because of their denial that the human will maintains the power of contra choice, compatibilism and hard determinism simply do not allow for humans to have moral responsibility. Their adherents argue to the contrary, naturally. Compatibilists, for instance, agree with the hard determinists that everything that will ever happen is causally determined. However, they view the agent as free, considering that they are acting in accordance with their greatest desires.[7] And this entails moral responsibility, since the "free" agent is doing what they desire to do. This is, to put it bluntly, moral idiocy epitomized. Compatibilism does nothing to quell concerns over the obvious incompatibility of determinism and moral responsibility. If people are predetermined to sin, that is still true regardless of whether they are physically compelled to act by God, or if they are compelled to act in accordance with their strongest desires, especially considering that God is the one who predestined the desires they would have in the first place! The compatibilist simply kicks the can down the road, as it were; but that road still ends with God as the author of all evil that occurs.

No, if God is to be good, then a strong view of human freedom is categorically indispensable. Few have put this as succinctly as Erasmus did in his battle with Luther over the freedom of the will, which he viewed as essentially a conflict regarding the goodness of God. For Erasmus, the human will is free only if an individual has the ability to embrace or turn away from Christ for salvation.[8] If God commands us to do something, but does not give us the capacity to do that very thing, then one is compelled to ask, among other questions, "Why blame me, when it is neither in my power to preserve what you gave me, nor to keep away the evil you implant in me?"[9] There is no sense in which we would ever ascribe moral responsibility to someone who cannot help but do otherwise. It would be tyrannical of God to command us to do something, without giving us the ability to fulfill

---

6. Swinburne, *Coherence of Theism*, 183, 185.
7. Feinberg, *No One Like Him*, 635–37.
8. Erasmus, *Free Will*, 26.
9. Erasmus, *Free Will*, 40.

the command. God would be fundamentally unjust if he did such a thing. Erasmus gives the example of a lord who commands a servant to run to a certain location, but has tied him up in chains. We would universally consider that lord to be cruel and merciless if he punished the servant for not obeying his orders.[10] This is directly relevant for compatibilism, given that on this analogy, the servant would be tied down with the desires that God predestined him to have. For God to command him to do something that is contrary to those desires would be brutal and tyrannical. Thus the moral responsibility in this scenario would belong solely to God.

Some in the classical tradition, such as Davies, would be quick to assert that God is not a moral agent engaged in making decisions that will either conform to or not conform to some set of moral propositions that are external to himself.[11] While perhaps helpful within the context of the doctrine of God debates with theistic personalists, the sentiment verges on an unhelpful, banal truism in so far as it relates to the POE. God is the Good as such, and anything that proceeds from him as its source must also be good, lest there be a logical contradiction in the claim that God is the Good. He may not be a finite moral agent, but it is still incoherent to suggest that Goodness as such can directly will moral evil, or predestine it via some medium such as human desires. That is not a paradox; it is a contradiction.

III

The patristic era of Christian theology understood the importance of human free will as it relates to moral responsibility and the goodness of God. Greg Boyd has said that Augustine's classical theism significantly influenced his later determinism,[12] but it is evident from other patristic sources that they were able to maintain both classical theism and a strong view of human freedom. This is not to suggest that Boyd is completely wrong here; it is clearly possible for one to extrapolate their classical theism in such a way so as to become a determinist. My contention here is that the pre-Augustinian church clearly did not feel as though they had to do so. In fact, it was their understanding that God is perfect Goodness that motivated them to advocate for a strong view of human freedom.

Hippolytus, in his *Refutation of All Heresies*, argues that God alone is the source of all existence; there was nothing coeternal with him, whether that be "infinite chaos, nor measureless water, nor solid earth, nor dense air,

10. Erasmus, *Free Will*, 89.
11. Davies, *Reality of God*, 191.
12. Boyd, *God at War*, 67.

nor warm fire, nor refined spirit, nor the azure canopy of the stupendous firmament. He was One, alone in Himself."[13] And yet,

> Now the world was made from nothing; wherefore it is not God; as also because this world admits of dissolution whenever the Creator so wishes it. But God, who created it, did not, nor does not, make evil. He makes what is glorious and excellent; for He who makes it is good. Now man, that was brought into existence, was a creature endued with a capacity of self-determination.... But man, from the fact of his possessing a capacity of self-determination, brings forth what is evil, that is, accidentally; which evil is not consummated except you actually commit some piece of wickedness.... Evil had no existence from the beginning, but came into being subsequently. Since man has free will, a law has been defined for his guidance by the Deity, not without answering a good purpose. For if man did not possess the power to will and not to will, why should a law be established?[14]

Here we see what can be described as an early Christian example of monism, wherein there is nothing that does not have its source in God. He makes specific mention of chaos and dangerous waters, which were commonly present in creation myths of old. Still, evil exists only derivatively via the free choices of man; and this free will is defined as "the power to will and not to will."

One may also think of Origen, who said nothing existed apart from God, and that all things which now exist have been called into being by him.[15] Simultaneously, he argues that it is a well-defined teaching of the church that all men possess free will:

> This also is clearly defined in the teaching of the Church, that every rational soul is possessed of free-will and volition; that it has a struggle to maintain with the devil and his angels, and opposing influences, because they strive to burden it with sins; but if we live rightly and wisely, we should endeavour to shake ourselves free of a burden of that kind. From which it follows, also, that we understand ourselves not to be subject to necessity, so as to be compelled by all means, even against our will, to do either good or evil. For if we are our own masters, some influences perhaps may impel us to sin, and others help us to salvation;

---

13. Hippolytus, *Refutation of All Heresies* 10.28; text in Robertson, *Ante-Nicene Fathers*, 5:150.

14. Hippolytus, *Refutation of All Heresies* 10.29; text in Robertson, *Ante-Nicene Fathers*, 5:151.

15. Origen *First Principles* preface.4; text in Robertson, *Ante-Nicene Fathers*, 4:240.

> we are not forced, however, by any necessity either to act rightly or wrongly, which those persons think is the case who say that the courses and movements of the stars are the cause of human actions, not only of those which take place beyond the influence of the freedom of the will, but also of those which are placed within our own power.[16]

The freedom of the will is articulated in such terms by Origen as the ability to act against desires and influences that compel us to either sin or do good. We are not forced to act in accordance with these desires. Instead, we are our own masters. He utilizes this principle in his argument against the likes of Marcion, Valentinus, and Basilides. For those individuals and their followings, God the Father of Jesus cannot be the creator of all that is, because there are such a variety of different circumstances that numerous beings find themselves in. As well, there is far too much evil in the world for God to be its creator.[17] Origen responds to such concerns:

> We have frequently shown, by those declarations which we were able to produce from the holy Scriptures, that God, the Creator of all things, is good, and just, and all-powerful. When He in the beginning created those beings which He desired to create, i.e., rational natures, He had no other reason for creating them than on account of Himself, i.e., His own goodness. As He Himself, then, was the cause of the existence of those things which were to be created, in whom there was neither any variation nor change, nor want of power, He created all whom He made equal and alike, because there was in Himself no reason for producing variety and diversity. But since those rational creatures themselves, as we have frequently shown, and will yet show in the proper place, were endowed with the power of free-will, this freedom of will incited each one either to progress by imitation of God, or reduced him to failure through negligence. And this, as we have already stated, is the cause of the diversity among rational creatures, deriving its origin not from the will or judgement of the Creator, but from the freedom of the individual will.[18]

This section of Origen's work contains speculation on why exactly some people find themselves in certain positions in this life that are seemingly not their choice. Discussion about such matters goes beyond the scope of this

---

16. Origen, *First Principles* preface.5; text in Robertson, *Ante-Nicene Fathers*, 4:240.
17. Origen, *First Principles* 2.9.5; text in Robertson, *Ante-Nicene Fathers*, 4:291.
18. Origen, *First Principles* 2.9.6; text in Robertson, *Ante-Nicene Fathers*, 4:291–92.

book. What is vital to note here is Origen's insistence on two things: God is the source of all being and rational natures possess a genuinely free will. Yet there are certain things, says Origen, that originate not in the will of the Creator, but in the free will of created rational natures.

And lastly, there is Gregory of Nyssa. He on multiple occasions described God as the source of all being, and yet maintained that God had created genuinely free rational wills. When grappling with the reality of premature infant death, he writes,

> Now, that everything that exists, after God, in the intellectual or sensible world of beings owes that existence to Him, is a proposition which it is superfluous to prove; no one, with however little insight into the truth of things, would gainsay it. For everyone agrees that the Universe is linked to one First Cause; that nothing in it owes its existence to itself, so as to be its own origin and cause; but there is on the other hand a single uncreated eternal Essence, the same forever, which transcends all our ideas of distance, conceived of as without increase or decrease, and beyond the scope of any definition; and that time and space with all their consequences, and anything previous to these that thought can grasp in the intelligible supramundane world, are all the productions of this Essence.[19]

Yet, in his *On the Making of Man*, he insists that human nature possesses a free will. This is, in part, due to the fact that God created us "for no other reason than that He is good." It is because of his goodness that he creates humans with "all good gifts."[20] And it is the free will that God gives man that makes possible a plethora of good in the created order, not least of which are virtue and wisdom:

> Thus there is in us the principle of all excellence, all virtue and wisdom, and every higher thing that we conceive: but pre-eminent among all is the fact that we are free from necessity, and not in bondage to any natural power, but have decision in our own power as we please; for virtue is a voluntary thing, subject to no dominion: that which is the result of compulsion and force cannot be virtue.[21]

---

19. Gregory of Nyssa, *On Infants' Early Deaths*; text in Schaff and Wade, *Nicene and Post-Nicene Fathers*, series 2, 5:375.

20. Gregory of Nyssa, *On the Making of Man* 16.10; text in Schaff and Wade, *Nicene and Post-Nicene Fathers*, series 2, 5:405.

21. Gregory of Nyssa, *On the Making of Man* 16.11; text in Schaff and Wade, *Nicene and Post-Nicene Fathers*, series 2, 5:405.

The result of such sentiments among the patristic writers was often what may be described as a general view of God's sovereignty. God was providential over all, yes, but this did not mean that God's providence was described in ways that, say, a Calvinist today would describe it. Origen, for example, said that depending on how one describes the reality, God may not be providential over all that is. If we say that God's providence regulates all things, that is only true if we are referring to God providentially willing all that is good. If we mean to say that God providentially regulates all things, including evil, "then it is no longer true that the providence of God regulates all things, unless we refer directly to God's providence things which flow as results from His arrangements."[22] He even goes on to argue that we cannot say transgressors are regulated by the providence of God, because we cannot say that they follow God's law when they transgress.[23] For Origen, God can be said to have delegated numerous providential duties to spiritual beings. Some of these spiritual beings rebelled against God, while some are faithful to God. So, for natural blessings like clean air or water, the angels are responsible for overseeing and controlling those things. Conversely, seemingly natural disasters like famine or pestilence among humans can be attributed to the work of demons.[24] Justin Martyr said something very similar.[25] Athenagoras reiterated this sentiment, claiming that God had created angels so they would carry out his providence throughout existence. God is said to exercise universal and general providence, while the particulars are handled by the angels. Unfortunately, some of those angels rebelled against God.[26]

I could go on with such examples from the patristic era, but this should suffice for the time being. Naturally, this is not to say that everyone in the patristic era described God's relationship with evil in exactly the same terms. Certainly there were differences in how precisely one would describe the finer details or rationale for as to why God allows evil to exist. The assertion here is simply that while the details may differ, the fundamental assumption was the same: classical theism is true while determinism is false. God is the source of all that is, and this includes his creation of dependent yet free

22. Origen, *Against Celsus* 7.68; text in Robertson, *Ante-Nicene Fathers*, 4:638.
23. Origen, *Against Celsus* 7.68; text in Robertson, *Ante-Nicene Fathers*, 4:638.
24. Origen, *Against Celsus* 8.31; text in Robertson, *Ante-Nicene Fathers*, 4:651.
25. Justin Martyr, *Second Apology* 5; text in Robertson, *Ante-Nicene Fathers*, 1:190.
26. Athenagoras, *Plea for the Christians* 24; text in Robertson, *Ante-Nicene Fathers*, 2:142 It should be noted, to give one more example of the patristic commitment to both classical theism and free will, that Athenagoras earlier in this same work described God as impassible. He also says God timelessly generates the *Logos*. See Athenagoras, *Plea for the Christians* 10; text in Robertson, *Ante-Nicene Fathers*, 2:133.

rational wills. Thus, while Boyd may be correct that Augustine's classical theism eventually led him to be a determinist, this principle simply does not hold for all classical theists. Most probably, Augustine's determinism should be considered idiosyncratic within the patristic era of the church.

IV

The question then remains: given classical theism's understanding of *creatio ex nihilo* and divine conservation, how might God create a free universe or free rational natures? As was seen with Bañezian thought, if one conceives of God's creative act in similar terms to that of finite causality, then it would be impossible for God to create genuine freedom. Hart was correct to argue that the logic of transcendence must be appealed to if one is to perceive of God's creation as a creation of truly free secondary causes. For Hart, it is no different to declare that God can create dependent rational freedoms that he does not determine than it is to declare that he can create dependent beings that are something other than God.[27] How exactly God does this is admittedly mysterious. This is not, however, an ad hoc appeal to mystery. *Creatio ex nihilo* is a kind of cause that we cannot duplicate via science or experience or what have you. Finite causality is fundamentally incapable of bringing matter into being from nothing. When we speak of God causing the universe to exist, we inevitably speak in analogical terms. Unless one denies *creatio ex nihilo*, one is forced to speak of this type of causation via analogical and even apophatic terminology, regardless of one's desire to do so.[28]

So yes, it is entirely possible to reconcile classical theism with a strong view of freedom by invoking the goodness of God, negative theology, and

---

27. Hart, "Impassibility as Transcendence," 181.

28. The same logic can be applied to the foreknowledge problem. God does not foreknow in the same way that we foreknow something. In fact, God's knowledge is mysterious in itself, considering that he does not observe an act and process it as we would, given that he is pure act. Hart appeals to Thomas to argue that God "knows" evil only through a privation of the good that he wills to happen through the freedom of his creatures. See Hart, "Impassibility as Transcendence," 181–82. He also points out that God's knowledge of something finite is not different than his act of creating the finite, given the DDS. He's not changed by such knowledge in the way that we would be changed by it. See Hart, *Experience of God*, 137. Thus, God does not look down the corridors of time, process the decisions that people will make, and then decide whether or not it is still a good idea to create that specific possible world. His foreknowledge just is his timeless creation and sustaining of free secondary causes, including all of their potentiality and actuality. It does not determine what free choices the creature will make but rather enables their possession of freedom.

analogical predication. The result inevitably must be the sort of provisional dualism spoken of by those such as Lewis, Boyd, and Hart (as well as the early church). It is at this point that different forms of theistic personalism have much in common with that of certain classical understandings of God's providence. There are scholars from both camps who understand that this is how God's providence needs to be expressed to properly explain his relationship with evil. When one examines the work of Boyd and Hart from chapters 5 and 6, one easily can find significant areas of agreement between the scholars. For both, God's providence should not be thought of in terms of unilateral dictation of every event that ever unfolds within the created order. Both also ascribe vast influence within the world to angelic and demonic activity. And both point to the New Testament and the early church as having emphasized this activity when attempting to explain why there is so much evil in the world. Ultimately, Boyd's "warfare worldview" is immensely comparable to that of Hart's construal, in that both see the temporal unfolding of the universe as being largely the result of sinful influence on what is otherwise a good creation. God's providence then is not direct dictation of all that comes to pass, but is rather his sustaining of existence and eventual victory over sin, Satan, and death.

V

As has been alluded to, modern classical theists can implement some of the insights from free will-oriented theistic personalists into their own responses to the POE. For instance, Boyd's work proposed that it is of metaphysical necessity that God allow free agents to exercise their freedom in a significant way if they are to be truly free.[29] This is speculative, as one can never know exactly to what extent a rational nature would need to exercise its free will in order to be "truly" free. Nonetheless, the principle seems solid enough. It is one thing to say that a rational nature is free; but it is an entirely different matter for the rational nature to actually be free in any meaningful sense. The same can be applied to some elements of what process theology has provided in this area. For process theists like Cobb, the universe should not be conceived as the result of God's unilateral will in all its detail. The classical theist should be able to say the same, given the general view of God's providence. Brutal animal death within nature, or extinction level events that occurred millions of years ago on earth, or a tsunami that kills thousands, or a child being diagnosed with cancer can all be envisioned as privations of the Good. God knows them as such, and they are contrary to

---

29. Boyd, *Satan*, 181.

his will. They are not direct results of his will, but are rather the result of truly free secondary causes. And these free secondary causes do not have to be limited to the human will; as the process theists assert, there are free nonhuman secondary causes. For the classical theist, this should be a point of emphasis, just as it was in the early church. Such ideas certainly help to illuminate why there is an abundance of evil in the world. Classical theism must become comfortable once again with this provisional cosmic dualism.

So long as the dualism is provisional, however, theistic personalism has no advantage over classical theism when addressing the POE. For in affirming that God will inevitably gain a complete and total victory over Satan, sin, and death, the theistic personalist is asserting God's omnipotence. And if God has omnipotence, then it matters not if he has exhaustive divine foreknowledge, nor if he has a real relation to the world; if God is omnipotent, then he can *in principle* prevent any and all evil that occurs. The open theist must admit, as they often do, that God can stop evil, even if he doesn't have exhaustive divine foreknowledge, as he has dynamic omniscience, thus he knows everything that is currently happening and could intercede at any point. Of course, they usually will appeal to the freedom of the creature, as at least some evil must be allowed if the creature is to be free; but the classical theist can do the same! The issue of foreknowledge turns out to be rather irrelevant to the core issue surrounding the POE. Whether or not God has this exhaustive foreknowledge is superfluous to the question of his omnipotence. To reiterate, God can intervene to stop evil given his omnipotence, regardless of one's view of foreknowledge. This is why I say that the process theists are the only theistic personalists with any real advantage here. By denying omnipotence, they are striking at the heart of the POE in ways that neither open theism nor neoclassical theism can. Therefore, while many modern classical theists can learn from their emphasis on free will and constructions of God's providence, non-process theistic personalist responses to the POE have no feasible benefit in principle to that of the classical theist's.

We are forced to conclude that while emphasizing a strong view of freedom is helpful, and while properly understanding the nature of God's providence is essential, we still must submit that God could prevent at least some evil that occurs within the universe while allowing a significant amount of human freedom. Mackie and William Rowe have pointed this out: while some moral good may require God to allow for genuine human freedom and thus the possibility of evil, not all moral good requires this and thus not all evil can be accounted for by claiming that God must allow free agents to make free choices. So, while Mackie later admits the POE doesn't fundamentally disprove God's existence,[30] the existence of evil makes it unlikely that God exists, given that a good God would stop any evil that he can, so long as he is not annihilating human freedom or destroying a greater good. Rowe has put forward one of the most forceful articulations of this line of thinking, arguing that an omnipotent and perfectly good God would be able to stop at least some of the evil in our universe since there most likely cannot be a greater good that is achieved by allowing its existence.[31] Some evil may be necessitated by freedom or a greater good, but surely not all, or so the argument goes. This has been commonly deemed "the evidential argument from evil" (EAFE). While the process theist can simply contend that God is unable to unilaterally stop evil, most other theists are unable to do this. Christians then are forced to say that God must have some greater purpose for allowing evil. One could invoke God's eventual victory over evil as many Christians are apt to do, but that still does not fully explain the existence of temporal evil in the world.

The POE then is, as I have said, answerable but not "solvable" in the same way that we might solve a math problem. Does this mean Rowe and Mackie are correct in their invocation of the EAFE? The answer is a resounding "no" and this is precisely why one cannot separate apologetics and metaphysics. If the EAFE does indeed make it less probable that God exists—and if considered in a kind of intellectual vacuum, it does—then it would seem to be a fairly decisive blow against the existence of God. After all, for the theistic personalist, God's existence can only be demonstrated in terms of probability; so as long as we are having the discussion within that paradigm, then the atheist appears to have the upper hand when they invoke the EAFE. However, the classical theist is not discussing God's existence in terms of probability. If God's existence is indeed necessary on logical and metaphysical grounds, then we have independent reason for knowing that God exists apart from considerations surrounding the existence of evil. This is where Feser has made his greatest contribution to the discussion. The EAFE is only compelling if we do not already have sufficient reason for knowing that God exists.[32] God as the ground of all being logically entails

30. Mackie, *Miracle of Theism*, 176.
31. Rowe, "Problem of Evil," 335–41, cited in Feser, *Five Proofs*, 297.
32. Feser, *Five Proofs*, 298. I do disagree with Feser in so far as he agrees with Davies that God could have created a world with free rational natures who only choose to do good. God does not deliberate between an infinite number of universes that he could create, which may include a world with free creatures who can make morally significant choices while choosing only to do good. Rather, God creates the world of the *Logos*, and this world includes the existence of free rational natures and other free secondary causes. This freedom by definition entails the possibility and apparent actuality of sin. It is as Hart argued, drawing from Maximus the Confessor: God wills all to salvation,

that he is omnipotent, omniscient, omnipresent, and perfectly good. Given the privation account of evil that is standard in classical philosophy, God is perfectly good because he is purely actual. And actuality in accordance with one's nature directly corresponds to goodness, while badness corresponds to unrealized potentiality.[33] Since God's goodness is logically entailed in his existence, the classical theist has intellectually significant grounds for arguing that there is a greater good that God would jeopardize should he prevent certain evils in the world. I would personally lean on Boyd's assertion that if a secondary cause is to be truly free, God must allow it to exercise its freedom in significant ways for significant amounts of time. No, we cannot fully understand what exactly constitutes "significant freedom," but we have reason for believing the principle is true. The theistic personalist like Boyd could utilize this principle, but they would be doing so within the context of countering the EAFE on the basis of probability, whereas the classical theist can exploit it in light of the logical necessity of God's existence.

VI

Two truths must be maintained in Christian apologetics. The first is that the only coherent metaphysic is some type of monism, which logically entails belief in the DDS. Without this, one must look beyond God for truth, while often one is left to posit brute facts as inevitably existence as such becomes unintelligible. I suppose one could become a nominalist, but that would be a departure from not only historic Christianity, but also from sound philosophy more generally. There is a reason many of the theistic personalists discussed in this book want nothing to do with nominalism! The second essential truth is that a strong view of free will must be maintained; and this emphasis on freedom should be extended to nonhuman secondary causes. Without this freedom, God becomes the author of evil and humans lose any meaningful moral responsibility. When either of these truths are abandoned, as happens too frequently in both the modern and classical camps, only catastrophe remains for Christian apologetics. If, however, these truths are successfully emphasized, then atheism will be crushed and God's goodness will be demonstrated.

---

but the nature of that cause must inevitably involve a permission of the will. Thus, God's creation of the good and permission of evil are one and the same act. See Hart, "Impassibility as Transcendence," 182. Nonetheless, Feser is correct in his assertion that the EAFE is only convincing if we isolate the POE from other logical considerations.

33. Feser, *Five Proofs*, 221.

Chapter 10

Winning and Losing

I

IN POLITICS, THERE ARE WHAT political analysts generally refer to as winning issues and losing issues. For Republicans, an example of a winning issue would be tax cuts, while a losing issue would be a decrease in entitlement spending. Conversely, Democrats can champion abortion (up to a certain point) as a winning issue while something like increased immigration is a losing issue. What defines a winning issue or a losing issue is the level of public support for such policies. Political parties and candidates will—if they are decent political strategists, that is—campaign on whatever winning issues their political platform adheres to. Republicans will promise tax cuts and Democrats will promise abortion access precisely because a majority of American voters support these policy positions. Now it should be obvious, but a policy's status as either a winning issue or losing issue does not determine its truth, political effectiveness, nor its moral acuity. Nevertheless, political entities will tend to emphasize winning issues on the campaign trail while they avoid too much public discussion about a position they hold that is not popular with the public. If one is attempting to persuade people to their political party or at least to vote for them in the upcoming election, this reality is inevitable.

Something similar can be said for Christian apologetics. We do not necessarily have polling data readily available to us as do the politicians and their lackeys, but we do have other ways of identifying winning issues for Christian apologists in twenty-first century America. The basic question we can begin with is, "How convincing is this argument to a non-Christian?"

Obviously, even if it were true, convincing an atheist that, say, there was a worldwide flood where a pair (or seven?) of every animal on earth boarded a giant ark and stayed there for around a year until they exited would be rather difficult. This would apparently include animals from Arctic climates who found their way back to their natural habitats once they exited the ark. Not exactly a winning issue for Christians, yet some are convinced this must be defended as a literal historical event. No, if Christians wish to win over atheists or agnostics or whomever, a good strategy would be to focus on positive answers to the proposed question. This doesn't mean one should compromise one's deepest convictions; it simply means that it is prudent tactics to focus on debates in which your opponents are going to be more sympathetic to your point of view. The "losing" issues can always be discussed later once the skeptic is more inclined to accept Christian teaching. Sure, discussion of losing issues is eventually inevitable, but a priority should be placed on topics that highlight the rich intellectual heritage of the Christian faith, as well as its pragmatic utility. In other words, it would be wise for Christians to shift the discussion, in so far as they are able, to matters that portray Christianity as rationally convincing and practically relevant for building up individuals, families, and societies.

One thing I cannot help but notice, however, is that theistic personalism has led Christian apologists to focus heavily on losing issues. And these losing issues are often on the wrong side of truth regardless, so it's especially egregious that Christians should concentrate on such discussions. Take the relationship between Christianity and science, for example. The theistic personalism of the twentieth and twenty-first centuries made most explicit what had been evident in the years leading up to the Enlightenment: the classical Christian understanding of God and his transcendence had been forsaken by large swaths of society, Christian or otherwise. This led to a clash between faith and science, given that God was now understood to exist within nature and as a force among forces to be quantified. This conflict still exists, at some level, in the minds of most people in Western cultures today. Numerous magazines and books and even entire organizations have been produced and founded in an effort to either harmonize faith and science, or to argue for their incompatibility. It should be abundantly clear to anyone paying attention at this point that so long as the tension persists, the topic will be a losing issue for Christians. Once the modern understanding of God was adopted, the need to "prove" his existence via science was unavoidable. As it turns out, an increasing number of people are not convinced this can be done. And it can't, of course. If empirical observation is thrust to the forefront of epistemology, as has happened in modernity, then when something that is supposed to exist within reality cannot be measured and observed in some way, its existence as such will be doubted. Explanations that involve matter or forces that can be physically quantified will be considered more likely to be true or even the only possible options. When Christian apologists write about how evolution isn't true, or how the earth is actually six thousand years old, or that instances of irreducible complexity can be detected in certain organisms, they are simply playing a game that they cannot win in an era of empiricism. So long as physical explanations in any way rival God's creative act or providence, Christianity will be considered to be at odds with scientific observation by the masses, and thus untrue.

II

The entire ID movement and its emphasis on "fine-tuning" epitomizes the losing nature of apologetics based on science. There is no shortage of apologists that in some way employ the fine-tuning line of argumentation against atheists. Some have been observed in this book. This particular argument commits what I consider to be the cardinal sin of modern apologetics: it presents God's creative activity as something to be scientifically measured. Whether it is irreducible complexity or the seemingly improbable (and incredibly complex) conditions that sustain our reality, these scientific observations have long been considered proof by ID advocates that an intelligent mind constructed the universe as we know it. I am sympathetic towards this type of reasoning; I see it as an understandable attempt to articulate the classical intuition that the rational coherence of nature as a whole is a reflection of God's infinite intelligibility. But the ID movement, generally speaking, is not arguing from the concept of intelligibility per se; to do so would be to argue for God's existence from the PSR. What the ID theorists are doing is starting from specific observable scientific facts, and contending that these entail God's existence is probable. To reiterate Hart's point from chapter 4, the classical intuition was to speak of "universal rational order" as pointing towards God.[1] We expect to observe this universal rational order because of the PSR. We should not seek to scientifically perceive specific causal gaps within nature or even particular instances of mathematical improbabilities and thus conclude that God exists. For the Christian, these individual instances of immense complexity may indeed spur us to think fondly of God's creative power; but for the atheist who is committed to naturalism, they will often be happy to explain them away with some kind of material explanation.

1. Hart, *Experience of God*, 38.

And this is why even something as understandable as arguments from fine-tuning are losing issues for Christian apologists. Physical observations cannot rival God in any way. But this is implicit in making the assertion that God is the explanation for why there is a particular instance of irreducible complexity, or for the mathematical improbability of various cosmic wonders. The implication then is that God's activity is physically observed; and it is different than mere natural causation, given that certain realities within nature can be explained with purely physical explanation, while others require a divine explanation. When natural elucidations and God in any way compete, it will be easy for skeptics to side with science over God, seeing as that they can physically observe natural phenomena, while expecting that there will one day be further physical justification for supposed divine explanations. If God's existence is probable, and science is said to point to this probability, then in principle it can be argued that science proves God's existence is improbable. So long as proving God's existence is at least in part grounded in the scientific method, his existence can and will be demonstrated to be suspect by that same scientific method. In short, if science can prove that God exists, then it can disprove that God exists. One could argue that this means we just need to be better scientists than the atheists. To that I will simply ask: How has that gone for the last one hundred years?

III

The existence of objective morality was long considered a winning issue for Christian apologetics. It was most famously C. S. Lewis's favorite argument for God's existence. Thomas's fourth way contains what could be considered a variation of the moral argument. Moral arguments have been successful largely because it is self-evident to a vast majority of people that objective morality exists on some level. Moreover, it is easily demonstrable that any theory of morality which does not depend on the transcendent is ludicrous. Naturalistic accounts of morality are especially asinine unless, that is, the atheist is "allowed" to posit objective moral propositions as brute facts. As we have seen, this is becoming increasingly common among atheistic philosophers; and I would say this trend is beginning to make its way to popular-level atheism. At the same time, there are prominent Christian philosophers like Swinburne declaring that fundamental moral truth exists independent of the nature of God. The result is that this once winning issue is being turned into either a nonissue or a losing issue for Christians. Again, once it is considered intellectually acceptable to postulate brute facts, there is nothing to stop the atheist from doing this within their own ethical theories. Swinburne and others can then argue that our awareness of such moral truths is evidence that we were created by God all that they want, but in the end such arguments are only probabilistic in nature. And because they are probabilistic, they inherently admit to the fact that humans could conceivably have this awareness of moral truth in a world in which God does not exist. This undercuts the reason why moral arguments were winning arguments in the first place: in the past, God was needed in order to make sense of the existence and our awareness of moral truth. Now, he is merely a possible explanation for our awareness of such truth, and is increasingly seen as unable to ground the existence of fundamental moral truth even if he does exist.

When an atheist considers the POE in conjunction with this understanding of God's relationship to morality, moral arguments for God quickly become insufficient. In fact, if the POE is considered through a theistic personalism paradigm, then the existence of evil is perhaps the most obvious losing issue for Christians. And the primary difficulty here is that it is inevitably the most discussed topic relating to religious faith. It is certainly not a losing issue that can be tabled for later discussion. If the existence of God is not necessary to explain existence as such—that is, if there are possible worlds in which God does not exist—and objective morality can exist without God, then the absolute abundance of evil in the world makes God's existence increasingly improbable. One can see how the atheist would arrive at such a conclusion, anyway. Even if something like fine-tuning arguments make it appear that the ID theorists are correct, and even if Swinburne is correct in his assertion that our awareness of moral truth makes it probable that God exists, the POE tends to erase any inroads that theistic personalists make in their endeavor to convince the atheist that the existence of God is more probable than not.

IV

If Christians desire to persuade atheists to believe, we must focus on winning issues. Classical theism enables us to do this far more effectively than any variation of theistic personalism ever could. The POE, for instance, will likely never be a winning issue for Christians. However, classical theism can mitigate the losing nature of the discussion, as it were. By examining the POE from the perspective that God's existence is logically necessary, then what is at stake in the conversation is not tilting the probability scales in our favor, but rather providing a basis for epistemic humility as we discuss God's relationship with temporal evil. In other words, God's existence is not really in dispute when a classical theist engages with the POE, as there are no possible worlds in which God does not exist. It is logically impossible for anything to exist if existence as such isn't real. There are other concerns, of course, when a classical theist addresses the POE, concerns that are usually pastoral in nature. But this is undoubtedly different than God's existence itself being in dispute. As Tillich said, many "apologetic weaknesses" and confusions in metaphysics could be avoided if God were understood as the ground of all being, and as the reason why even the possibility of anything else can exist at all.[2]

As for God and science, classical theism turns those debates into a winning issue, as science and God are no longer occupying the same intellectual space. To inquire into God is to investigate the philosophical, particularly questions surrounding first principles. Scientific investigation concerns nature and physical realities. If classical theism becomes the paradigm through which these discussions take place, then people are free to go wherever science may lead, as it has nothing to do with God's existence. Should one deny God's existence, it must be done on metaphysical grounds, as observations of the physical universe do not pertain to the question of a Creator. Most notably, science and faith becomes a winning issue on classical theism precisely because the world becomes intelligible with God as its source. The existence of the immaterial, such as abstract objects, universals, and propositions are indispensable in scientific inquiry; these nonphysical entities are grounded in God. And only the classical theist can consistently hold to the PSR; it is God's existence that grounds the very concept of intelligibility. When framed in this manner, natural causations do not rival divine causation but are rather made possible by it. Consequently, science becomes dependent on God if science is presumed to be able to deliver intelligible answers to our questions about the physical universe.

Something similar can be said for moral arguments. If we were in a philosophical environment wherein brute facts were considered to be little different than magic, atheism would surely seem less intellectually attractive. The atheist would be left to choose between pure materialist accounts of morality, or to simply embrace nihilism as the alternative. Both are catastrophic disasters for atheism, and compelling issues for Christians. For Christians to allow atheists to conjure up moral propositions as brute facts is not only an error as it relates to our pursuit of truth, but also a massive strategic blunder. We should be on offense here! The atheist often wishes to portray Christianity as a kind of fairy tale, as something for the less educated masses to adopt. But we should be portraying atheism as essentially

---

2. Tillich, *Systematic Theology*, 235.

indistinguishable from belief in magic. We should be able to say that atheism makes existence unintelligible. Yes, most Christians want to say something like this, but it is classical theism that can enable Christians to consistently make this claim. There are no possible worlds where God does not exist. The existence of fundamental moral truth is logically impossible given naturalism. And the very concept on which scientific inquiry relies—the concept of intelligibility—finds its ultimate grounding in a God who is the ground of all being, a God who is infinite intelligibility.

Closing Remarks

MUCH MORE COULD BE SAID, but I believe I have said enough on the matter for now. To close, I should make a few clarifications that I have perhaps failed to make up to this point. First, I should say that the overt rejection of classical theism found in the modern alternative models of God is not solely responsible for the current state of Christian apologetics. Modernity arrived long before twentieth-century process theism or any other types of theistic personalism that were discussed in this book. As I briefly alluded to earlier, theistic personalism simply made more explicit a rejection of the classical logic of God's transcendence. But moves in this direction were already being made at the advent and arrival of modernity. Thus, while theistic personalism is somewhat responsible for, say, the tension between faith and modern science, I would not dare to claim these models of God are exclusively responsible.

Concerning my understanding of the relationship between science and faith, I am obviously aware that there are those who find so-called scientific arguments for God to be persuasive. My contention is that, on the whole, these arguments have proven to be deficient, for reasons I have already laid bare. And they have nothing to do with the question of God in the first place. They are a colossal diversion—and a losing one at that. Now, science may impact Christian faith in other ways. For example, though one must consider the literary genre and scholarship's findings on ancient Near Eastern literature, archeological and geographical evidence may also help to determine how one thinks about the historicity of the Adam and Eve story, the exodus, or the flood narrative(s) found in the Pentateuch. Those are fascinating questions, admittedly. But again, they do not concern the question of God, as he would be the ground of all being regardless of the historical status of such stories. I personally am not convinced that the historicity of these records should impact their theological or moral precepts, given my commitment to classical biblical interpretative methods. The point is, science can influence how we think about the sun standing still in the book of Joshua, but it cannot shed light on God. Therefore, when conversing with atheists, these exegetical questions about certain Old Testament annals should be left alone. If the atheist insists on speaking about them, a Christian apologist should simply be able to reiterate my prior point: these are interesting questions, but they have nothing to do with God's existence (or with the life, death, and resurrection of Christ, for that matter). In the same vein, I do not mean to propose a definitive view on human evolution. I am not a biologist, and I have not studied the topic adequately. I am not qualified to offer an opinion on the matter. One last time, I simply mean to say that the question is a scientific question and thus should have no bearing on the Christian's defense of God's existence.

Nor do I mean to disparage most of the apologists with whom I have had disagreements, whether they be theistic personalists or classical theists. I say most, because I'm happy to be rather hostile towards Calvinism. To be sure, there are undoubtedly Calvinists who have done great work in metaphysics and even in apologetics throughout the centuries. One modern Calvinist I am particularly fond of is Gavin Ortlund. I would also tend to agree with much of Calvin's work on the Eucharist, and some of Zwingli's comments on ecclesial authority. Nevertheless, a Calvinism explicitly preached is a moral calamity, and I have nothing positive to say about such a vision of God's relationship with the world. Moral mistakes are much less tolerable than metaphysical inaccuracies, though there can be overlap in those departments, as has been demonstrated. As for the non-Calvinist theistic personalists, many are doing their best to work within the parameters provided to them by our current intellectual environment. Those like Craig and Swinburne and Plantinga are clearly brilliant men, and have done much for the cause of Christ. Greg Boyd's work on the POE is, to my mind, some of the best in the modern era. Disagreements with his open theism aside, much of what he says is applicable for every Christian. He unmistakably has a passion for defending the goodness of God.

There has clearly been a paradigm shift in thinking about God over the centuries. What I hope is evident by now is that we are in need of another. There are theological reasons for this, which perhaps I will explore at another time in another book. If nothing else, I pray this book has made it apparent that there have been profound apologetic consequences that have resulted from shifts in metaphysics and theology. God as classically defined is the one in whom we live and move and have our being, to use the language of the New Testament. As Hart has concluded, it is the knowledge of God that makes all other experience possible.[1] We should not lose sight of that. And we should not define God in such a way so as to sacrifice that very fundamentality.

---

1. Hart, *Experience of God*, 332.

Bibliography

Bañez, Domingo. *Commentaria in Summa Theologiae Sanctis Thomae*. Part 1. Salamanca, 1584.
Barr, James. *Biblical Words for Time*. London: SCM, 1962.
Barth, Karl. *Church Dogmatics*. Vol. 2.1: *The Doctrine of God* Translated by T. H. L. Packer et al. Edinburgh: T&T Clark, 1957.
Basil. *Homily Against the Sabellians, Anomoians, and Pneumatomachians*. In *On Christian Doctrine and Practice*, translated by Mark DelCogliano, 290–303. Popular Patristics Series. Yonkers, NY: St. Vladimir's Seminary, 2013.
Bauder, Kevin, et al. *Four Views on the Spectrum of Evangelicalism*. Grand Rapids: Zondervan, 2011.
Bavinck, Herman. *Reformed Dogmatics*. Translated by John Vriend. Grand Rapids: Baker Academic, 2004.
Berkhof, Louis. *Systematic Theology*. Grand Rapids: Eerdmans, 1996.
Boyd, Gregory. *God at War: The Bible and Spiritual Conflict*. Downers Grove, IL: InterVarsity, 1997.
———. *God of the Possible: A Biblical Introduction to the Open View of God*. Grand Rapids: Baker, 2000.
———. *Satan and the Problem of Evil: Constructing a Trinitarian Warfare Theodicy*. Downers Grove, IL: InterVarsity, 2001.
Calvin, John. *Institutes of the Christian Religion*. 2 vols. Translated by Ford Lewis Battles. Louisville: Westminster John Knox, 2006.
Carson, D. A. *The Difficult Doctrine of the Love of God*. Wheaton, IL: Crossway, 2000.
Carter, Craig. *Contemplating God with the Great Tradition: Recovering Trinitarian Classical Theism*. Grand Rapids: Baker Academic, 2021.
Cobb, John. *God and the World*. Eugene, OR: Wipf & Stock, 2000.
———. *The Process Perspective: Frequently Asked Questions About Process Theology*. Eugene, OR: Wipf & Stock, 2003.
Craig, William Lane. *God Over All: Divine Aseity and the Challenge of Platonism*. Oxford: Oxford University Press, 2016.
———. *How Do We Know God Exists?* Bellingham, WA: Lexham, 2022.
———. "Timelessness and Omnitemporality." In *God and Time: Four Views*, edited by Gregory Ganssle, 129–60. Downers Grover, IL: InterVarsity, 2001.
Davies, Brian. *An Introduction to the Philosophy of Religion*. 3rd ed. Oxford: Oxford University Press, 2004.

———. *The Reality of God and the Problem of Evil*. New York: Continuum International, 2006.
Dawkins, Richard. *The God Delusion*. Boston: Houghton Mifflin, 2006.
———. *River Out of Eden: A Darwinian View of Life*. New York: Basic, 1996.
Devenish, Philip. "Theodicy and Cosmodicy: The Contribution of Neoclassical Theism." *Journal of Empirical Theology* 4:2 (1991) 5–23. https://doi.org/10.1163/157092591X00092.
Dolezal, James. *All That Is in God: Evangelical Theology and the Challenge of Classical Christian Theism*. Grand Rapids: Reformation Heritage, 2017.
———. *God Without Parts: Divine Simplicity and the Metaphysics of God's Absoluteness*. Eugene, OR: Pickwick, 2011.
———. Review of *Thomas Aquinas on Good and Evil*, by Brian Davies. *Theological Studies* 73:2 (2012) 491–93. https://www.proquest.com/scholarly-journals/thomas-aquinas-on-god-evil/docview/1018086924/se-2.
Erasmus. *The Free Will*. In *Desiderius Erasmus and Martin Luther: Discourse on Free Will*. Translated and edited by Ernst F. Winter, 11–99. New York: Bloomsbury Academic, 2013.
Feinberg, John. *No One Like Him: The Doctrine of God*. Wheaton, IL: Crossway, 2006.
Feser, Edward. *Five Proofs of the Existence of God*. San Francisco: Ignatius, 2017.
———. "The Thomistic Dissolution of the Logical Problem of Evil." *Religions* 12:4 (2021) 268. https://doi.org/10.3390/rel12040268.
Frame, John. *The Doctrine of God*. Phillipsburg, NJ: P&R, 2002.
Fretheim, T. E. *The Suffering of God: An Old Testament Perspective*. Minneapolis: Fortress, 1984.
Ganssle, Gregory. "Introduction: Thinking About God and Time." In *God and Time: Four Views*, edited by Gregory Ganssle, 1–15. Downers Grover, IL: InterVarsity, 2001.
Garrigou-Lagrange, Reginald. *God: His Existence and His Nature; A Thomistic Solution of Certain Agnostic Antinomies*. Vol. 1. Translated by Dom Bede Rose. St. Louis: B. Herder, 1939.
———. *Predestination: The Meaning of Predestination in Scripture and the Church*, Translated by Dom Bede Rose. St. Louis: B. Herder, 1939.
Gavrilyuk, Paul. *The Suffering of the Impassible God: The Dialectics of Patristic Thought*. New York: Oxford University Press, 2006.
Giles, Kevin. *The Eternal Generation of the Son: Maintaining Orthodoxy in Trinitarian Theology*. Downers Grove, IL: InterVarsity, 2012.
Goetz, Ronald. "The Suffering God: The Rise of a New Orthodoxy." *Christian Century*, April 16, 1986.
Gregory of Nyssa. *Homilies on the Song of Songs*. Translated by Richard A. Norris. Atlanta: SBL, 2013.
———. *The Life of Moses*. Translated by Abraham Malherbe and Everett Ferguson. Mahwah, NJ: Paulist Press, 1978.
Griffin, David Ray. *God, Power, and Evil: A Process Theodicy*. Louisville: Westminster John Knox, 2004.
———. "Process Philosophy of Religion." *International Journal for Philosophy of Religion* 50:1/3 (2001) 131–51. https://www.jstor.org/stable/40020987.

Gupta, Rajendra P. "JWST Early Universe Observations and ΛCDM Cosmology." *Monthly Notices of the Royal Astronomical Society* 534:3 (Sept. 2023) 3385–95. https://doi.org/10.1093/mnras/stad2032.

Hallman, Joseph. *The Descent of God: Divine Suffering in History and Theology*. Repr. Minneapolis: Fortress, 2007.

Ham, Ken. *The Lie: Evolution/Millions of Years*. Rev. ed. Green Forrest, AR: Master, 2012.

Hart, David Bentley. *The Beauty of the Infinite: The Aesthetics of Christian Truth*. Grand Rapids: Eerdmans, 2003.

———. "The Devil's March: Creatio ex Nihilo, the Problem of Evil, and a Few Dostoyevskian Meditations." In *Theological Territories: A David Bentley Hart Digest*, 77–97. Notre Dame: University of Notre Dame Press, 2020.

———. *The Doors of the Sea: Where Was God in the Tsunami?* Grand Rapids: Eerdmans, 2005.

———. *The Experience of God: Being, Consciousness, Bliss*. New Haven: Yale University Press, 2013.

———. *The Hidden and the Manifest: Essays in Theology and Metaphysics*. Grand Rapids: Eerdmans, 2017.

———. "Impassibility as Transcendence: On the Infinite Innocence of God." In *The Hidden and the Manifest: Essays in Theology and Metaphysics*, 167–90. Grand Rapids: Eerdmans, 2017.

———. "No Shadow of Turning: On Divine Impassibility." In *The Hidden and the Manifest: Essays in Theology and Metaphysics*, 45–69. Grand Rapids: Eerdmans, 2017.

———. *That All Shall Be Saved: Heaven, Hell, and Universal Salvation*. Repr. New Haven: Yale University Press, 2021.

———. *You Are Gods: On Nature and Supernature*. Notre Dame: University of Notre Dame Press, 2022.

Hartshorne, Charles. *Anselm's Discovery: A Re-Examination of the Ontological Proof for God's Existence*. La Salle, IL: Open Court, 1965.

———. *The Logic of Perfection*. La Salle, IL: Open Court, 1962.

———. *Omnipotence and Other Theological Mistakes*. New York: State University of New York Press, 1984.

Hasker, William. "'God's Only Begotten Son': A Reply to R. T. Mullins." *European Journal for Philosophy of Religion* 9:4 (2017) 217–37. https://doi.org/10.24204/ejpr.v9i4.1942.

———. *Metaphysics and the Tri-Personal God*. Oxford: Oxford University Press, 2013.

Helm, Paul. "Divine Timeless Eternity." In *God and Time: Four Views*, edited by Gregory Ganssle, 28–60. Downers Grover, IL: InterVarsity, 2001.

———, et al. *God and Time: Four Views*. Edited by Gregory Ganssle. Downers Grove, IL: InterVarsity, 2001.

Highfield, Ron. *Great Is the Lord: Theology for the Praise of God*. Grand Rapids: Eerdmans, 2008.

Hitchens, Christopher. *God Is Not Great: How Religion Poisons Everything*. New York: Twelve, 2009.

Hollingsworth, Andrew. "Mere Social Trinitarianism, the Eternal Relations of Origin, and Models of God." *Journal of Analytic Theology* 11 (2023) 23–40. https://doi.org/10.12978/jat.2023-11.001322071407.

Hughes, Christopher. *On a Complex Theory of a Simple God: An Investigation into Thomas Aquinas' Philosophical Theology*. Ithaca, NY: Cornell University Press, 1989.

International Council on Biblical Inerrancy. "The Chicago Statement on Biblical Inerrancy." https://library.dts.edu/Pages/TL/Special/ICBI_1.pdf.

Laing, John D. "Introduction to New Atheism: Apologetics and the Legacy of Alvin Plantinga." *Southwestern Journal of Theology* 54:1 (Fall 2011) 6–12.

Launonen, Lari, and R. T. Mullins. "Why Open Theism Is Natural and Classical Theism Is Not." *Religions* 12:11 (Nov. 2021) 1–16. https://doi.org/10.3390/rel12110956.

Lewis, C. S. *Mere Christianity: A Revised and Amplified Edition, with a New Introduction of the Three Books, Broadcast Talks, Christian Behavior, and Beyond Personality*. New York: HarperOne, 2009.

Lister, Rob. *God Is Impassible and Impassioned: Toward a Theology of Divine Emotion*. Wheaton, IL: Crossway, 2013.

Mackie, John. "Evil and Omnipotence." In *The Philosophy of Religion*, edited by Basil Mitchell, 92–104. London: Oxford University Press, 1971.

———. *The Miracle of Theism*. Oxford: Clarendon Press, 1982.

Mawson, T. J. "Cognitive Science of Religion and the Rationality of Classical Theism." In *The Roots of Religion: Exploring the Cognitive Science of Religion*, edited by Roger Trigg and Justin L. Barrett, 149–66. New York: Routledge, 2014.

Moltmann, Jurgen. *The Crucified God: The Cross of Christ as the Foundation and Criticism of Christian Theology*. Minneapolis: Fortress, 1974.

———. *The Trinity and the Kingdom: The Doctrine of God*. Minneapolis: Fortress, 1981.

Morris, Thomas. *Our Idea of God: An Introduction to Philosophical Theology*. Notre Dame: University of Notre Dame Press, 1991.

Mullins, R. T. *The End of the Timeless God*. Oxford: Oxford University Press, 2016.

———. "Episode 109: Reformed Thomism and Salvation: Southern Baptists and Aquinas with Owen Strachan." *The Reluctant Theologian Podcast*, Nov. 30, 2022. https://podcasts.apple.com/us/podcast/ep-109-reformed-thomism-and-salvation-southern/id1455521623?i=1000588069154.

———. *God and Emotion*. Cambridge: Cambridge University Press, 2020.

———. "Hasker on the Divine Processions of the Trinitarian Persons." *European Journal for Philosophy of Religion* 9:4 (2017) 181–216. https://doi.org/10.24204/ejpr.v9i3.1941.

———. "Simply Impossible: A Case Against Divine Simplicity." *Journal of Reformed Theology* 7:2 (2013) 181–203. https://doi.org/10.1163/15697312-12341294.

Nash, Ronald. *The Concept of God: An Exploration of Contemporary Difficulties with the Attributes of God*. Grand Rapids: Zondervan, 1983.

Nietzsche, Friedrich. *Thus Spake Zarathustra*. Translated by Thomas Common. New York: Random House, 1930.

O'Connor, Timothy. *Theism and Ultimate Explanation: The Necessary Shape of Contingency*. Chichester: Wiley-Blackwell, 2012.

Ogden, Schubert. "The Reality of God." In *The Reality of God and Other Essays*, 1–70. Dallas: Southern Methodist University Press, 1992.

O'Keefe, John, and R. R. Reno. *Sanctified Vision: An Introduction to Early Christian Interpretation of the Bible*. Baltimore: John Hopkins University Press, 2005.

Olson, Roger. "Postconservative Evangelicalism." In *Four Views on the Spectrum of Evangelicalism*, 161–87. Grand Rapids: Zondervan, 2011.

Oord, Thomas. *God Can't: How to Believe in God and Love After Tragedy, Abuse, and Other Evils.* Grasmere, ID: SacraSage, 2019.

———. *Open and Relational Theology: An Introduction to Life-Changing Ideas.* Grasmere, ID: SacraSage, 2021.

Orr, Brian J. *A Classical Response to Relational Theism: A Reformed Evangelical Critique of Thomas J. Oord's Evangelical Process Theology.* Eugene, OR: Pickwick, 2022.

Packer, J. I. *Concise Theology: A Guide to Historic Christian Beliefs.* Carol Stream, IL: Tyndale House, 1993.

Penelhum, Terence. *Survival and Disembodied Experience.* London: Routledge and Kegan Paul, 1970.

Pinnock, Clark. *Most Moved Mover: A Theology of God's Openness.* Grand Rapids: Baker Academic, 2001.

Pinnock, Clark, et al. *The Openness of God: A Biblical Challenge to the Traditional Understanding of God.* Downers Grove, IL: InterVarsity, 1994.

Plantinga, Alvin. *Does God Have a Nature?* Milwaukee: Marquette University Press, 1980.

———. *God, Freedom, and Evil.* Grand Rapids: Eerdmans, 1974.

———. *Warranted Christian Belief.* New York: Oxford University Press, 2000.

———. *Where the Conflict Really Lies: Science, Religion, and Naturalism.* Oxford: Oxford University Press, 2011.

Pollard, Evan. "The Impassibility of God." *Scottish Journal of Theology* 8:4 (Dec. 1955) 353–64. https://doi.org/10.1017/S0036930600020238.

Pruss, Alexander. "The Leibnizian Cosmological Argument." In *The Blackwell Companion to Natural Theology*, edited by William Lane Craig and J. P. Moreland, 24–100. Oxford: Wiley-Blackwell, 2009.

Rice, Richard. "Biblical Support for a New Perspective." In *The Openness of God: A Biblical Challenge to the Traditional Understanding of God*, 11–58. Downers Grove, IL: InterVarsity, 1994.

———. *The Future of Open Theism: From Antecedents to Opportunities.* Downers Grove, IL: InterVarsity, 2020.

Roberts, Alexander, et al., eds. *Ante-Nicene Fathers: The Writings of the Fathers Down to A.D. 325.* Peabody, MA: Hendrickson, 1994.

Rowe, William L. "The Problem of Evil and Some Varieties of Atheism." *American Philosophical Quarterly* 16:4 (1979) 335–41. http://www.jstor.org/stable/20009775.

"Sam Harris: Trump, Religion, Wokeness." Triggernometry, Aug. 17, 2022. https://www.youtube.com/watch?v=DDqtFS_Pvcs.

Sanders, John. "Historical Considerations." In *The Openness of God: A Biblical Challenge to the Traditional understanding of God*, 59–100. Downers Grove, IL: InterVarsity, 1994.

Schaff, Philip, and Henry Wace, eds. *Nicene and Post-Nicene Fathers: A Select Library of Writings.* 2 series. Peabody, MA: Hendrickson, 1994.

Sproul, R. C. *Chosen by God.* Wheaton, IL: Tyndale, 1986.

"Survey Results." PhilPapers Survey 2020. https://survey2020.philpeople.org/survey/results/all.

Stenger, Victor J. *God: The Failed Hypothesis; How Science Shows That God Does Not Exist.* Amherst, NY: Prometheus, 2007.

Sterba, James. *Is a Good God Logically Possible?* London: Palgrave Macmillan, 2019.

Swinburne, Richard. *The Coherence of Theism*. 2nd ed. New York: Oxford University Press, 1993.
———. *The Existence of God*. 2nd ed. Oxford: Oxford University Press, 2004.
———. *Is There a God?* Rev. ed. New York: Oxford University Press, 2010.
Temple, William. *Christus Veritas*. London: Macmillan, 1924.
Tillich, Paul. *Systematic Theology*. Vol. 1: *Reason and Revelation, Being and God*. Chicago: The University of Chicago Press, 1951.
Van Inwagen, Peter. *Metaphysics*. Boulder, CO: Westview, 1993.
Walton, John. *The Lost World of Genesis One: Ancient Cosmology and the Origins Debate*. Downers Grove, IL: InterVarsity, 2009.
Ware, Bruce. *God's Lesser Glory: The Diminished God of Open Theism*. Wheaton, IL: Crossway, 2000.
Whitehead, Alfred. *Process and Reality*. Corrected ed. Edited by David Ray Griffin and Donald W. Sherburne. New York: The Free Press, 1985.
Wolterstorff, Nicholas. "Unqualified Divine Temporality." In *God and Time: Four Views*, edited by Gregory Ganssle, 187–213. Downers Grover, IL: InterVarsity, 2001.
Wright, N. T. "Christianity Offers No Answers About the Coronavirus. It's Not Supposed To." *Time*, Mar. 29, 2020. https://time.com/5808495/coronavirus-christianity/.
———. *Evil and the Justice of God*. Downers Grove, IL: InterVarsity, 2006.

Index

A

a priori reasoning, 53, 61, 63, 66–67, 129
abstract objects, 71–74, 127–28, 149, 180
actus purus, 8, 21, 63, 94, 114, 131, 134
allegorical exegesis, 20
analogical predication, 71, 115, 119, 135, 148, 170–171
annihilationism, 142–43
Anselm of Canterbury, 25, 33–36, 61–64, 66–67, 129–132
apatheia, 3, 17
Aquinas, Thomas, 10, 21, 25, 31, 37, 49, 51, 53, 58, 60, 71, 76, 111, 114, 121, 129, 134, 137, 142
Aristotle, 3, 67–69, 156
aseity, 10, 21, 25, 28, 51, 126–28
Augustine, 12, 25, 50, 74, 80, 85, 88, 152–53, 160, 165, 170

B

Bañez, Domingo, 117
Barth, Karl, 8
Basil of Caesarea, 147, 153
Berkhof, Louis, 9
Big Bang theory, 68, 77, 104, 157
Boyd, Greg, 6–7, 13, 85, 92–97, 99, 120, 136, 142–44, 160, 165, 170–171, 174, 183
brute fact, 52–53, 84, 129–130, 149–150

C

Calvin, John, 40, 162–63, 183
Carson, D.A., 4–5, 7
Carter, Craig, 5, 18–19
Clarke, Samuel, 51, 77
classical theism, x–xi, 1–2, 4–5, 7, 9, 11, 14, 16, 19, 25, 39–42, 60, 82, 92, 113, 115, 129, 132, 138, 143, 145, 147–48, 150, 155, 157–59, 161–62, 165, 169–170, 172, 179–182
Clement of Alexandria, 17
Cobb, John, 8, 103–6, 139–140, 171
cognitive science of religion, 39–42
compatibilism, 47, 92, 163–65
cosmological argument for God, 30–31, 37, 52–53, 56, 124, 127
Craig, William Lane, 13–14, 18, 25–26, 29–34, 124, 127, 149–150, 183
creatio ex nihilo, 13, 104, 118–9, 121, 127, 135, 138–140, 144, 153, 161, 170

D

Darwin, Charles, 80, 154
Davies, Brian, 2, 110–114, 133–35, 165, 173
Dawkins, Richard, 30–32, 34, 79
determinism, 86, 91, 119, 121, 134–36, 163–65, 169–170

doctrine of divine simplicity, 9–12, 23–25, 58, 125–27, 146, 148–150, 170, 174
Dolezal, James, 2, 4–5, 8–9, 15–16, 21–25, 27–28, 65, 114, 134

E

Erasmus, Desiderius, 164–65
eternal conscious torment, 141–42, 144
Euthyphro Dilemma, 49, 116
evidential argument from evil, 173–74
existence question, 56, 58, 67, 125, 130, 149–150

F

Feinberg, John, 3, 8, 11, 38, 61, 85, 91–92, 104, 125, 128, 133–34, 140, 164
Feser, Edward, 67–78, 115–17, 127, 129, 134–35, 141, 150, 173–74,
fine-tuning argument for God, 32–33, 59, 61, 124, 177–79
foreknowledge of God, x, 2, 13, 39, 41, 47–48, 89, 94–95, 136–38, 170, 172
Frame, John, 6
free will, 12–13, 39, 41, 47–48, 88, 90–91, 95, 97, 100, 111, 116, 133–34, 136–37, 162–63, 165–66, 168–69, 171–72, 174
Freud, Sigmund, 83

G

Gagarin, Yuri, 154, 156
Garrigou-Lagrange, Reginald, 76, 117
Gavrilyuk, Paul, 3, 16–17
grammatical-historical exegesis, 5–6, 18
Greek philosophy, 4, 11, 16–17, 51, 62
Gregory of Nyssa, 20–21, 80, 152, 168
Griffin, David, 19, 106–9, 140–141

H

Ham, Ken, 152–3
Harris, Sam, ix, 149, 154–55

Hart, David Bentley, 2–3, 9, 16–17, 22–24, 27–28, 31, 33, 67, 78–82, 85, 87, 117–122, 126–27, 129–130, 135–38, 140, 142–44, 153–55, 157, 163, 170–171, 173–74, 177, 183
Hartshorne, Charles, 2, 36, 61–66, 100, 104, 130–132
Hasker, William, 41, 146
Hawking, Stephen, 81, 126, 156–57
Helm, Paul, 25–26, 146
Hick, John, 111–12
Highfield, Ron, 67, 82–84, 129
Hippolytus of Rome, 165–66
historical-critical scholarship, 18–19, 152
Hume, David, 77, 158

I

immutability, 2, 5, 15–16, 21, 23, 50–51, 60, 62, 136
impassibility, 2, 5, 7, 15–16, 21, 23, 94, 136
intellectualist model of freedom, 136, 163
Intelligent Design theory, 80–81, 126, 151–2, 157, 177, 179

J

John Chrysostom, 79
Justin Martyr, 96, 169

L

Launonen, Lari, 39–42, 123
Leibniz, Gottfried von, 51–53, 76–77, 128
Lewis, C.S., 120, 171, 178
libertarian model of freedom, 41, 47–48, 91, 111, 133–36, 163
Lister, Rob, 7–8
Luther, Martin, 164

M

Mackie, John, 86–87, 92, 111, 115, 133–34, 172–73
Marx, Karl, 82–83

Maximus the Confessor, 173
Moltmann, Jurgen, 22, 112
monism, 143–44, 161, 174
moral argument for God, 31, 38, 55, 128–29, 178
Mullins, Ryan, x, 2, 11, 13, 25–26, 39–42, 123, 146, 148

N

Nash, Ronald, 11
natural evil, 88, 96, 98–99, 104, 111, 137
natural theology, 59–60, 80
naturalism, 18–19, 56, 82–83, 150, 177
negative theology, 148, 170
neoclassical theism, 2, 29, 39, 140, 172
Newman, John Henry, 80, 153
Nietzsche, Friedrich, 82
nominalism, 11, 72, 174

O

O'Connor, Timothy, 56–60, 124–26, 149–150
O'Keefe, John, 19–20, 152–53
Ogden, Schubert, 3, 131, 155
Olson, Roger, 1
omnipotence, 33, 36, 45, 58, 86–87, 96, 100, 104, 106, 110, 119–120, 126, 130–131, 134, 137–39, 161, 172
omniscience, 33, 36, 41, 46–47, 58, 94, 123, 126, 130–131, 136–38
ontological argument for God, 33–38, 60–62, 125, 129–130, 132
Oord, Thomas, 2, 19, 27, 85, 100–104, 139
open theism, 1–2, 4–7, 27, 39, 41–42, 136, 142–43, 155, 172, 183
Origen, 20, 79, 96, 152–53, 166–69
Orr, Brian, 19

P

Packer, J.I., 7–8
Pinnock, Clark, 1, 7, 155
Plantinga, Alvin, 10–11, 24, 33–37, 40, 83, 86–89, 92, 124–25, 127–28, 130–131, 137–38, 148, 183
Plato, 63, 73
Plotinus, 71
principle of sufficient reason, 52–53, 76–78, 127–29, 149–150, 177, 180
problem of evil, 11, 14, 27, 39, 60, 66, 84–93, 97, 99–100, 103–4, 106–7, 110–115, 120–123, 128–29, 133, 135, 137–144, 160–162, 165, 171–74, 179–180, 183
process theism, 2, 8, 61, 107, 132, 138, 140, 161, 182
Pruss, Alexander, 76, 150

R

realism, 48, 72–3, 127, 149–150
  Aristotelian Realism, 73
  Platonic Realism, 73
  Scholastic Realism, 73
Reno, R.R., 19–20, 152–53
Rice, Richard, 1, 6
Rowe, William, 172–73
Russell, Bertrand, 158

S

Sanders, John, 4
Satan, 13, 88, 93–97, 120–121, 136, 142, 144, 171–72,
Spinoza, Baruch, 18, 58
Sproul, R.C., 93
Stenger, Victor, 79
Sterba, James, 115–16
Strachan, Owen, x
Swinburne, Richard, 13, 38, 41–56, 97–100, 111, 123–24, 127–29, 136, 138, 149–150, 164, 178–79, 183

T

The Chicago Statement on Biblical Inerrancy, 6, 152
theistic personalism, 1, 4, 8, 12, 15, 17–18, 27, 39, 60, 86, 115, 126, 133, 135–36, 148, 151, 155, 162, 172, 176, 179, 182

theory of evolution, 154, 156, 183
Tillich, Paul, 38, 125, 157, 180
timelessness, 2, 12–15, 25–26, 40, 51, 60, 94, 145–46
Trinity, 2, 9, 22–23, 26, 42, 145–47

U

universalism, 121–22, 143–44
universals, 71–73, 126, 128–29, 149, 180
univocal language, 6–7, 13, 115, 117, 135, 146, 151–55

W

Ware, Bruce, 1, 5, 8, 15, 27
Whitehead, Alfred, 3, 8, 60–61, 107–8, 128
Wright, N.T., 4, 27, 89–91, 136, 141

Y

Young Earth Creationism, 151–54

www.ingramcontent.com/pod-product-compliance
Lightning Source LLC
Chambersburg PA
CBHW062038220426
43662CB00010B/1558